THE PALESTINIAN UPRISING

A War by Other Means

THE PALESTINIAN UPRISING

A War by Other Means

F. ROBERT HUNTER

University of California Press
Berkeley   Los Angeles

University of California Press
Berkeley and Los Angeles, California
By arrangement with I.B.Tauris & Co. Ltd, London, UK

Copyright © 1991 by Frederick Robert Hunter

Library of Congress Cataloging-in-Publication Data
Hunter, F. Robert, 1940–
    The Palestinian uprising : a war by other means / F. Robert
Hunter.
        p. cm.
    Includes bibliographical references.
    ISBN 0–520–07489–0
    1. Intifada, 1987– I. Title.
DS119.75.H86 1991
956.95′3044—dc20   91–10136
                                                    CIP

Printed and Bound in Great Britain by
Hartnolls Limited, Bodmin, Cornwall.

Contents

To my wife Joan

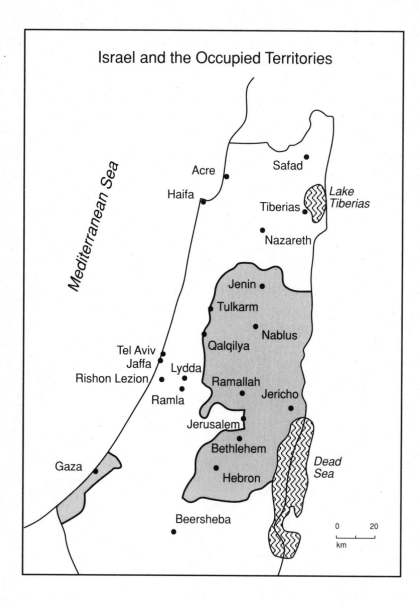

Israel and the Occupied Territories

Abbreviations

DFLP	Democratic Front for the Liberation of Palestine (PLO faction)
EEC	European Economic Community
FBIS	Foreign Broadcast Information Service, Daily Report, Near East and South Asia
IDF	Israeli Defence Forces (Israeli Army)
PCP	Palestine Communist Party
PFLP	Popular Front for the Liberation of Palestine (PLO faction)
PLO	Palestine Liberation Organization
PNC	Palestine National Council
UNL	Unified National Leadership (of Intifada)
UNRWA	United Nations Relief Works Agency

Foreword

This is a study of the Palestinian Revolt or Intifida (in Arabic, a 'shaking off') from a historical perspective. I have done this in two ways: (1) by relating it to the prior development of the problem of Palestine; and, more importantly, (2) by tracing the evolution of the revolt according to its own inner dynamic, showing how what began as a simple rejection of the Israeli occupation of the West Bank and Gaza developed a political programme and strategy which ultimately affected the policies of the PLO, the government of Israel and the US administration. I have endeavoured to explain its root causes, analyse its leadership, and examine and assess its achievements and setbacks during its first two years. I have also sought to capture the spirit of this revolt and bring it to life in a vivid and concrete way. Based upon traditional research techniques and oral history evidence, this book attests that a popular movement like the Intifada cannot be fully understood without going to the source itself: the Palestinian people. This is all the more important given the crippling shortage of primary documentary materials and the consequent dependence of researchers upon the print media. A historian's Intifada, mine is an attempt to view it, as it were, from the inside.

This book would not have been written had a chance opportunity not placed me in Jerusalem during the entire first year of the Intifada. When the Intifada erupted on 9 December 1987, I had recently taken up residence in West Jerusalem to begin a year as Visiting Research Scholar at the Hebrew University. I was on sabbatical leave from Tulane University, and had been invited to spend the year there to write a book on Egypt and Tunisia that I had been preparing. This would be my first extended stay in Israel.

A historian of North Africa, I have spent long periods in Egypt, especially in the Arab-language archives of Cairo, where I researched a doctoral dissertation that turned into a book on nineteenth-century Egyptian administration. In 1983–4, I was a Fulbright Research Fellow in Tunisia. Though I had taught university courses on the Arab–Israeli conflict, and was generally familiar with the literature on the subject, I had neither researched nor written about Israel or the Palestinians prior to my arrival in Jerusalem.

I am not the first American scholar to have gone to Israel and found himself caught up in a dramatic event that altered his professional plans. Professor Charles Smith of San Diego State University, likewise a historian of modern Egypt, was Visiting Scholar at the Hebrew University in 1982 when Israel invaded Lebanon. Professor Smith subsequently wrote a book on the Arab–Israeli dispute that is standard reading in US college and university courses on the subject. As I look back upon this project, although the final decision to write a book was not made until after my return to the US, I realize that it really began as an attempt to explain the Intifada to myself. From the outset, I was fascinated by this dramatic turn of events. Each day brought some new development, as the Intifada grew in intensity and spiralled out of Israel's control. Here was history in the making, something few historians have an opportunity to witness or record. I wanted an explanation for what I read about and saw happening around me, and I wanted to know more. I began having long conversations with Jewish colleagues and friends at the Harry S. Truman Institute and elsewhere at the Hebrew University. A sociologist returned from a stint of army reserve duty in the West Bank recounted his experiences. Menahem Milson, Professor of Arabic Literature and former civilian governor of the West Bank, discussed what he described as the failure of Israel's system of control. In my speaking engagements to fellow historians at Haifa and Tel Aviv universities, I found that our conversations invariably turned to the subject of the Intifada. I read more on the subject, not just in newspapers like the *Jerusalem Post* or the Palestinian weekly, *al-Fajr*, but also from entries in the Daily Reports of the Foreign Broadcast Information Service (Near East), which contain English translations of newspaper articles and news broadcasts from radio and television stations in the Middle East. These told me what the Hebrew-language press in Israel was saying about the Intifada, and they also contained the leaflets issued by the Intifada's clandestine leadership (broadcast as 'calls' over Arab radio stations) and other Palestinian groups. My interest waxed rather than waned. The Intifada had grabbed me by the throat and would not let go. Finally, I decided to meet people who could provide information not found in the newspapers. Most of all, I wanted to meet the people who were making this revolt: the Palestinians themselves.

In early September 1988, I met with Dr Azmi Bishara, an Israeli Arab who is Associate Professor at Birzeit University on the West Bank. Until then, I had spoken with few Palestinians, the most notable exception being an elderly gentleman whom I had employed to help improve my spoken Arabic. A well-informed and highly intelligent analyst of Israeli and Palestinian politics, Dr Bishara had given talks at the Hebrew University and had been interviewed in both the Hebrew and Arabic-language press. We met in the lobby of the National Palace Hotel in East Jerusalem, and for an hour Dr Bishara answered all questions I put to him across a wide range of subjects. Thus began my venture into oral history.

What Dr Bishara said aroused such interest that I decided to talk with other people – Palestinians and Israelis – who could provide information and offer a perspective upon what by then had become a major event of world importance. I subsequently met with other Palestinian intellectuals who held Ph.D.s and taught in universities. Most were good English-speakers accustomed to addressing Western audiences. Some were associated with political organizations. Dr Bishara, for example, was a member of the Communist Party in Israel. Most, however, were self-styled 'independents', not members of any political organization, but filling a role as scholars of the Palestinian movement and spokesmen for their people. (Some also provided ideas to the political leaders.) In their meetings with Western journalists and others, their aim was to influence opinion in Europe and the US. If a few (e.g. Sari Nuseibeh) were indeed politicians, the vast majority were serious scholars. Writing some English, these men published mostly in Arabic. Their scholarly works and findings, with some exceptions, were not well known in the West, however visible certain individual members of this group may have been (some came to Europe and even the US on speaking tours). The advantage of using these men was that they had well-considered analyses which differed from one another on particular points, and that with wide-ranging contacts in the occupied territories, they were the ones who were researching and writing about the Intifada. Through interviews and by reading some of their works, I became acquainted with their ideas and findings. One such person was Dr Ali al-Jarbawi. Author of an important book in Arabic on the Intifada, Dr al-Jarbawi was Assistant Professor of Political Science at Birzeit University. I visited him many times in his home, and we became friends. A privileged stratum in society, these men were a vital source of information and ideas about the Palestinians and their revolt.

I sought out Israeli journalists with specialist knowledge of the West Bank and Gaza – men like Danny Rubenstein, who writes for the Hebrew-language daily, *Davar*, and who for many years has covered events in the occupied territories. Possessing their own sources, these men provided me with ideas and perspectives that went beyond the daily news stories.

I took trips into the occupied territories, travelling with groups of US Congressional aides, with church organizations, by myself. I spoke with Palestinian children at an orphanage in Tulkarm, met the co-founder of the popular committee in the village of Taibeh, spent a morning with young activists in the village of Husan and visited a hospital in Nablus filled with young people who had been shot or beaten – a moving experience to say the least. I also accompanied an Israeli lawyer to attend a trial of Palestinian youths charged with stone-throwing and other offences. Many of my conversations were in English, some took place in Arabic.

At first, my questions were broad and general. What did the Intifada mean? What did the Palestinians really want? How was the revolt organized? Why had it occurred? How had the PLO acquired so much support among Gazans and West Bankers? How effective were Israeli measures to stop it, and how did Palestinians cope with them? What was the Intifada's impact upon Israel? Where would it lead? Could anything bring it to an end? As I learned more, my questions grew more sophisticated, and I became a bolder and more systematic interviewer. An idea gradually emerged of how I could organize the information I was gathering into a book. I also began to identify the kinds of people who could provide the information I was seeking and became more selective about whom I interviewed. I talked with officials of UNRWA, and with spokesmen of the International Red Cross in Jerusalem. I began meeting with people who could help me understand Israeli society and its reaction to the Intifada – among them, Tom Segev, a journalist for the Hebrew-language daily *Haaretz* and author of a best-selling book about Israel. My reading on the Palestinian–Israeli conflict became more focussed, and I 'discovered' the works of the West Bank Data Base Project, directed by Meron Benvenisti, Israel's unofficial statistician of the West Bank and Gaza. Authoritative and detailed, these studies are used by journalists, academics and people everywhere who are interested in the subject of Israel's occupation of these territories.

Meetings with Palestinians were relaxed, yet businesslike. People who are fighting a war have little 'recreational' time. Like other peoples who have been the victims of oppression, Palestinians tend to believe that their suffering is unique. Some equate the suffering they have experienced at the hands of Israelis with what the Jews themselves went through under the Nazis. 'Like Hitler, only in a different way', was a phrase I heard many times. At the beginning of an interview, I sometimes felt that the interviewee was more interested in having me write an exposé of violations of Palestinian human rights than in answering my own questions. However, once people realized that I was there to do serious research, they became quite willing to provide information and state their views. I came to admire the Palestinians for their tenacity, their willingness to sacrifice for the collective, and their capacity to endure in circumstances that most Westerners would find intolerable. Palestinians I talked with were utterly realistic. Confronting an Israeli society much larger than theirs, and backed by the financial and military might of the US, they were keenly aware of their vulnerability. 'Palestine' is not Vietnam or India. Hence the need to compromise. Hence, too, their realization that international support will be required if they are ever to succeed in attaining their goal of an independent state alongside Israel. Palestinians were absolutely determined, however, to achieve it, come what may.

I also found myself repelled by the harsh methods which Israel has used to deal with the Intifada, and I regretted the refusal of its political establishment to deal seriously with the political causes of the revolt. However, I came to understand the reasons for such behaviour and began to perceive the whole conflict as a great human tragedy for Israeli Jews and Palestinians alike. Many people in Israel want and long for a political settlement, and are willing to compromise on the question of Gaza and the West Bank. The policies of Yitzhak Shamir, the Likud and their hard-line supporters do not command anything like 100 per cent support. This conflict is tragic because Palestinians should understand the fears that Jews have for their own security, and Jews should understand the bitterness and determination to persevere that suffering can induce, and the counter-productiveness of relying upon force. This tragedy is all the greater because of the parallels that exist between these two peoples – the Palestinian, like the wandering Jew of old, living in exile, resisting assimilation, preserving his traditions, clinging to his identity. This has not been lost upon some Israelis. Author and journalist David Grossman wrote of visiting an elderly Palestinian refugee woman whose stories reminded him of his grandmother and the tales she told about Poland, from which she had been expelled. Israeli Jews do not have to look hard to see in the Palestinians' plight a reflection of themselves as they once were.

In all I conducted 57 formal interview sessions in the West Bank and Jerusalem (including one at Lod, near the Ben Gurion Airport), each lasting between one and three hours. I also made two trips to the Gaza Strip, visiting five refugee camps and an UNRWA clinic, meeting with UNRWA officials, and interviewing many Gazans. These interview sessions took place in the autumn and early winter of 1988, and during a two-and-half month return trip in the summer of 1989. Informal and unscheduled 'interviews' also occurred, owing to chance encounters in fortuitous circumstances. A three-hour wait to pay my electricity bill led to a lively discussion with a member of the Jewish settlement movement. During my stay in Jerusalem's Old City, a Palestinian employee from the town of Beit Sahour would come to my room to tell me what he had seen or what had happened to him and his family. Sometimes when I was conducting a formal interview, people (e.g. a relative or neighbour) would enter the room and spontaneously offer their views on a subject, or remain afterwards, keeping me longer than I had intended. All of this was part of my 'education'.

These interviews were important in several ways. They produced information about specific events or developments, sometimes providing eye-witness accounts of incidents which had received brief coverage in the newspapers. They told me about the manner in which things were done – for example, how communities organized themselves to survive Israeli-imposed curfews. They offered views and assessments that generated new ideas and avenues of exploration, as, for example, the value of the prison experience in producing leaders of the revolt. In short, they helped me to establish the relative significance of events and to discover for myself how to interpret the Intifada. By talking to the participants and getting to know something about their lives, I found it easier to avoid simplistic judgments and began to see the revolt through the eyes of the people who were conducting it. The printed sources then assumed a different meaning, and I was able to read between the lines, to penetrate behind the surface. In other words, a more accurate judgment and deeper under-standing of the Intifada became possible.

Despite the attention I have paid to the oral sources, the print media was also extremely important both for establishing the chronology of the revolt and for providing much hard information about it. The value of having available a public record of events should not be underestimated. When I began the research for my book on nineteenth-century Egypt, the very basic question of what happened when could not be answered, since no newspapers existed to chronicle the march of day-to-day life. On balance, the Israeli press has done a creditable job of reporting the Intifada, providing many Israelis with more knowledge than they found palatable. Some journalists – Joel Greenberg of the *Jerusalem Post*, for example – distinguished themselves by producing reports of the highest quality. The real problem, of course, is that journalists do not cite their sources. If a researcher does not know on whose evidence a particular account is based, he cannot know how much weight to assign it. This leads to distortion of all kinds, including the planting of information, not to mention factual errors honestly made – a common occurrence in the news media. Early in the Intifada, the *Jerusalem Post* reported that the

Islamic Jihad organization held seats in the UNL, the Intifada's clandestine PLO command body. A serious error, this has been repeated in at least one book written about the revolt. Excessive reliance upon the print media also places the researcher at the mercy of the press view or interpretation of events. Those developments, occurrences and personalities that receive the widest publicity may not be the 'facts' most needed by the researcher to understand the Intifada. For example, Israel's deportation in early 1988 of Mubarak Awad, the Palestinian Director of the Centre for Non-Violence and an American citizen, received far more publicity in the Israeli and foreign press than his salience in the Intifada actually warranted.

Naturally, difficulties also arose with respect to the oral documentary evidence. Occasionally, a Palestinian would request that I conceal his identity entirely; others would say, 'do not quote me here'. For most, the reason was fear of arrest or retaliation by the Israeli military authorities, something that surely would have occurred had I revealed the names of the popular committee members interviewed. (One Palestinian village activist was arrested shortly after the Israelis had seen him talking to me.) A few were anxious to avoid criticizing fellow Palestinians and Palestinian organizations in print, when all energies had to be directed against the occupation. This created a problem for me. I did not want to bring danger or harm to anyone; yet as a historian, I had an obligation to readers and to my profession to make everything available as part of the public record. I decided to assign pseudonyms (enclosed by quotation marks) to a few people, and to others I occasionally gave the protection of 'an anonymous Palestinian source'. To satisfy the public's right to know, I have placed my original interviews in a depository in the Howard-Tilton Memorial Library at Tulane University, with the stipulation that they be publicly released after thirty years. Until then, individual researchers may consult these documents with permission of the donor.

The other problem I faced was that of verification. One usually validates oral interviews by cross-checking them with data gathered from other interviews, or with material from documentary sources. Given the formidable obstacles of travelling and meeting people in Gaza and the West Bank, I considered myself fortunate just to be able to see some of my interviewees for a second or third time with follow-up questions. A number of these people, however, lived in or near Ramallah, a short distance from Jerusalem. As my work progressed, I would approach those who I felt were well-informed and with whom I had built a relationship of trust, and question them on various points or matters that other interviewees had brought up. I also tried to corroborate the information given to me with media accounts of events. Of course, this does not constitute anything like a proper verification of oral evidence; nor does it guard against mis-representation, distortion or being unduly influenced by my interviewees. I can only say that I sought to be as open-minded as possible, to exercise critical judgment, to interview people who held different views, and never to forget that I was there to get at the truth about the Intifada.

As for the documentary sources, these barely exist. For example, the brochures, pamphlets, working papers, leaflets, booklets and other materials printed (in limited copies) and issued locally by popular committees, PLO factions and Islamic groups have yet to be collected and analysed, and the context for each established. The official Israeli documents (e.g., Cabinet records; intelligence data, especially informants' reports; secret investigations and inquiries) will be kept from public scrutiny for years to come, as will the records of the meetings between US and PLO officials in Tunis, and the correspondence between the US and Israeli governments.

For this reason, an account of the Intifada deriving from direct observation of its immediate impact has especial value. One cannot fully grasp the spirit and determination which this revolt has aroused without meeting the youthful activists themselves; or understand the suffering and heavy price that Palestinian society has paid without seeing the wounded and maimed who lie in hospital beds. Nor can the profound popular disillusionment with the 'peace process' be appreciated without talking to the Palestinian rank and file. How Palestinians view things, what they think and feel, their motives, expectations, hopes and fears: all are as important for future scholars of this event as they are for our present understanding of it. The oral evidence contained here has thus added something to the historical record. Through interviews I have uncovered not only the views and attitudes of Palestinians, but also entirely new information – material that exists nowhere else and which might otherwise have been lost to posterity. And since only about 50 per cent of my collection was utilized in this study, the documentary material I have gathered will benefit future researchers as well. Historians need the vantage-point of time to comprehend the importance of events. As more materials become available in the years ahead, my interviews can be verified and checked against the documents, and thus help produce a more complete and accurate picture of the Intifada. Meanwhile, this preliminary study, carefully researched and documented, sympathetic to its subject but not uncritical of it, will bring to a Western audience a clearer and more direct understanding of this historical event.

The list of persons whose help made this work possible is necessarily a long one. I shall begin with Lesley Abukhater, an American from Kentucky, fluent in Arabic and married to a Palestinian, who provided my entrée into Palestinian society; Dr Ali al-Jarbawi, scholar of the highest standard, whose perspectives and assessments have found their way into nearly every chapter of this book; and Albert Hourani, teacher, adviser, and friend for more than two decades, whose belief that I was the one to write the history of the Intifada gave me confidence at the time I most needed it, and whose comments and criticisms contributed greatly to the outcome. Other people who helped in ways large and small, include the following: Hanan Ashrawi, Clair Grimes, Raymond Cohen, June Meeker, Kamal Abdulfattah, Maher Abukhater, Edy Kaufman, Fateh Azzem, André Rosenthal, Ibrahim Karaeen, Moshe Negbi, Nora Kort, Marty Rosenbluth, Chris George, Jad Issac, Ruth Scoralick, Danny Rubenstein, Meron Benvenisti, Patrick Maney, Dr Shye, Don Reid, Azmi Bishara, Clarence Mohr, Joshua Schoffman, Nadia Habash, Zuhayra Kamal, Mahdi Abd al-Hadi, Amnon Zichroni, Nasser Juber Taha Hamammreh, Roger Owen, Yehuda Litani, Menahem Milson, Rolf van Uye, Sari Nuseibeh, Laurent Corbaz, Tom Segev, Ziad Abu-Amr, Hashim Abu Sidu, Naomi Chazan, Rev Gordan Davies, Yifrah Siberman, Carl Brown, Abdelghani Assaf, John Damis. Of those persons whose names I have omitted, I ask your forgiveness. My thanks also go to Ms Maureen Kelleher, typist extraordinaire; the students in my Arab–Israeli Conflict course at Tulane, who criticized and commented upon the manuscript; and to my wife for her support during the two years that it took to research and write this book.

Introduction

The popular uprising in the West Bank and Gaza that began on 9 December 1987 was part of a struggle waged for almost a century between two peoples – Zionist Jews and Arab Palestinians – over the same piece of land. This long-standing conflict has been fought over every tree, hill and historic site. It has been accompanied by the development of stereotypes on both sides to dehumanize and de-legitimize the other. It has led to the death of thousands on the field of battle, and of others at the hands of organized terrorist groups, Jewish and Palestinian. Practically everything has become a weapon, even children. 'Babies are our atomic bomb,' confided one Palestinian shopkeeper in the Old City of Jerusalem. 'Well armed' ran the caption under a photograph on the cover of the *Jerusalem Post*'s Weekend Magazine, showing a pregnant Jewish woman – obviously a West Bank settler – pointing a handgun at some distant object. Demography has thus been added to the many other weapons used in this struggle.

One side, however, has prevailed. In the 1948 Arab–Israeli War, a state for the Jewish people was established in an area comprising roughly 80 per cent of historic Palestine. The greater part of its Palestinian population was displaced. Scattered all over the Middle East and throughout the world, Palestinians could be found as refugees in camps in Lebanon, Syria and Jordan, as well as the Gaza Strip and West Bank – areas controlled after 1948 by Egypt and Jordan, respectively. In June 1967, another war between Israel and the Arab states broke out. Israel took possession of Gaza and the West Bank, where it imposed a harsh military rule upon the Palestinian residents, many of them refugees from the original 1948 exodus. Thereafter, Israel began seizing land and other resources in these occupied territories, and establishing Jewish settlements in order to make the entire area a permanent part of the Jewish state. Resistance by the Palestinians, who saw their property being taken, was inevitable.

Resistance to Israel's occupation existed before 1987, but these eruptions were sporadic and localized and could be contained by Israeli troops. The 1987 uprising, a movement of the entire population of the West Bank and Gaza, was something quite different. At no other time under the occupation had Palestinians simultaneously carried out acts of political resistance in so many places, or joined together and sustained a revolt for so long. The Intifada was the beginning of a new stage of activism in the struggle of Gazans and West Bankers against the Israeli occupation. It marked the end of *sumud*, an Arab noun meaning 'steadfastness' or 'staying put'. The strategy of Gazans and West Bankers since 1967, *sumud* had connoted a determination by Palestinians to construct, build and cling to their lands. By 1987, Palestinians had decided to put an end to Israel's occupation of an area they considered their homeland. However, the Intifada was a struggle for the freedom and independence of Gaza and the West Bank only, and it was a war waged with limited means. Palestinians renounced the use of conventional weapons (e.g. firearms and explosive devices) and relied upon stones to symbolize their revolt. In the course of it, Palestinians also recognized the existence of the state of Israel for the first time and accepted the idea of partition – that is, two states, Israeli and Palestinian, living side by side.

The Intifada did not emerge full-blown in a day, week or month. Rather, it developed in stages. It began mostly as a revolt of youth, a 'children's crusade', consisting of large-scale demonstrations, also supported by commercial strikes. At the outset, the mass of society did not participate in it directly. However, the Israeli government's decision to employ collective force against the entire population brought virtually everyone, young and old, rich and poor, actively into the struggle. When this happened, the revolt moved rapidly from stone-throwing and commercial strikes to partial civil disobedience measures. Palestinians also began boycotting Israeli goods, manufacturing their own products, growing vegetable gardens, and building health-care and other institutions. The Intifada thus became a way of life for everyone.

Parallel to this was the emergence of a clandestine leadership, or central command, whose presence was manifested in the issuing of leaflets that stated the goals of the revolt and called for strikes and other activities. Its instructions were followed by Palestinians throughout the occupied territories. This central command became a new national authority whose presence could not be eradicated. A political programme also emerged. In the early days, the Intifada was merely a statement, expressed by stone-throwing youths, of rejection of the occupation. Later, Palestinian political objectives were defined as self-determination and independence for Gaza and the West Bank, to be achieved through negotiations at an international conference convened by the members of the UN Security Council, and attended by Israel and the PLO. In November 1988, an independent Palestinian state was proclaimed. The Intifada thus passed through a complex evolution, possessing a dynamic independent of what Israel or anyone did.

The Intifada was a political movement whose economic and other activities were designed to support the goal of ending the Israeli occupation. It was not a social revolution. Women, for example, did not acquire a new status or role (they had helped to organize, and participate in, resistance activities before), but only greater responsibilities – something true of every other social category. In the process of the revolt, however, some social changes did occur, but these were not massive. People with college degrees, rather than heads of clans, performed mediating functions, for example. The most striking social change was the reversion to old ways. Throughout the Intifada the Palestinian press featured articles on the return to customary law and emphasized through pictures traditional motifs like the shepherd guiding his flock.

The Palestinian Revolt also represented an important shift in the balance of Palestinian politics. During the 1960s and 70s, the focus of the PLO, the standard-bearer of Palestinian nationalism, was fixed more upon the Palestinians who lived in the Diaspora than upon those found within the bounds of historic Palestine – *viz.*, Israel, Gaza, and the West Bank. Until 1982, Beirut was more important than the West Bank town of Nablus for the PLO leadership abroad. After the Intifada, however, the Palestinian Diaspora carried less weight in the calculations of PLO leaders than did the people in the occupied territories, where the problem of Palestine had come to be centred. PLO Chairman Yasser Arafat had to take into account popular opinion in Gaza and the West Bank in ways that he had never had to previously. This change, however, was the result of a long and complex evolution.

To the surprise of some, the Intifada revealed the widespread support that existed for the PLO. Over the years, an organic relationship had been built up between Gazans and West Bankers, on one hand, and the PLO on the other. Thousands of people in the occupied territories were members or followers of one or another PLO faction, and thousands more supported the PLO in a general way, regarding it as the symbol of their desire for freedom and self-determination. The central command that emerged to lead the revolt was itself a PLO body, made up of local faction leaders and commanding a huge following in Gaza and the West Bank. For these reasons, and because the PLO's chain of authority was hierarchical – orders were sent from the leadership abroad to PLO faction members in Gaza and the West Bank – no true separation can be said to have existed between the PLO and the mass of Palestinians in the occupied territories. To be sure, differences did exist, among the factions and between PLO members and supporters inside Gaza and the West Bank and the leadership outside. Following the outbreak of the Intifada, groups and personalities in the occupied territories acquired more weight in the decisions and policies of the PLO leadership, and local PLO factions had more responsibility for planning activities on the ground, in coordination with the leadership abroad. However, more intense communication between the PLO leadership in exile and its factions inside the occupied territories strengthened, rather than weakened, the connection between the two.

The Intifada also unblocked a 'peace process' frozen for almost a decade, pushed the PLO leadership to moderate its positions, and brought the US government into a dialogue with it. The proclamation (on 15 November 1988) by the PNC, the PLO's parliament-in-exile, of an independent Palestinian state was accompanied by a peace offensive. The PLO officially recognized Israel, renounced the use of terrorism, and accepted UN Resolutions 338 and 242, which stated the principle of peace in exchange for the return of lands conquered by Israel in the June 1967 War.

The PLO, however, was not the only Palestinian leadership. Islamic political parties were also active in Gaza and the West Bank. The 'Islamic forces', as they were called, provided an alternative to the PLO. Composed of ideologically-motivated élites and benefiting from an institutional structure of mosques, charitable societies and religious schools, the Islamic political organizations had as their aim the establishment of an Islamic state governed by the holy law, or Sharia, in the whole of 'Palestine', including the area forming the state of Israel. The vast majority of Palestinians, as PLO supporters, subscribed to the goal of a secular, democratic state and supported an accommodation with Israel whose centrepiece was Palestinian statehood in the West Bank and Gaza. The Islamic organizations did not ask Palestinians to reject the PLO or to disobey instructions in the leaflets issued by the local PLO clandestine leadership. Representing a small minority of the population, these groups desired support from the wider society; and of course all Palestinians were struggling for an end to the occupation. From the start members of the Islamic political parties had participated in the Intifada alongside secular Palestinian nationalists. They followed the rules laid down by the national forces – for example, using stones and gasoline bombs rather than firearms or grenades. From time to time, factions from the Islamic and national 'camps' co-ordinated their activities. As time passed, the sacrifices made by the Islamic groups brought them greater respect and acceptance. The Islamic parties consequently increased their membership and following; but so did the PLO groups. No fundamental shift in the balance of power occurred between the Islamic and national forces.

During its first year, the Intifada was the dynamic producing all change. In the second year, the leaders of the revolt had to respond to initiatives coming from outside, especially from the US and Israel. This led to divisions within the movement that weakened it politically. Inside the occupied territories, Palestinians were having increased difficulty maintaining the earlier momentum. They were unable to develop their new institutions beyond a rudimentary level or to establish full local control. None the less, the revolt had become firmly embedded in the fabric of life in the occupied territories. Through economic boycotts and other measures, Palestinians destroyed the profits that Israel had derived from the occupation. For the first time, the Israeli public had been forced to confront the reality of Palestinian nationalism, and international sympathy for the movement remained high. If the future could not be predicted, the ability of the Palestinians to mount and maintain a revolt for two years in the face of superior Israeli military power was the most significant achievement of the Intifada.

* * * * * * * * * *

An outgrowth of a century-long struggle between two peoples, in a sense the Intifada had its antecedents in a decision by a small number of Jewish nationalists in late nineteenth-century Europe to found a movement whose aim was the conversion of Palestine into a state for Jews. During the second half of the nineteenth century, Jewish thinkers began writing about the need for the Jewish people, scattered all over Europe and indeed throughout the world, to become a nation in the modern sense. One spur to this was the invention of modern Hebrew, which could serve as a common language for all Jews, who until then were speaking either the native tongues of their resident countries, or mixed languages like Yiddish and Ladino. Influenced by Western ideas and European nationalist currents (e.g., socialism, Romanticism), and drawing upon elements in their own history and culture, these Jewish thinkers began to focus attention upon those epochs when Jews had been proud warriors and kings in ancient Palestine. The Jewish people, they began to argue, possessed all the prerequisites of nationhood save one: a place of their own. This incipient nationalism culminated in Zionism, whose core belief was that the Jewish people could revive and preserve their identity only by having a state of their own in Palestine.

The Zionist movement had its official beginning in two related developments: (1) the publication in 1896 of *The Jewish State*, a book by Theodore Herzl, who argued that a state of their own would save Jews from the evils of anti-Semitism, and who offered ideas about how such a state could be achieved; and (2) the convening of the first Zionist Congress under the presidency of Herzl in Basle, Switzerland in 1897. This Congress adopted a platform designating Palestine – the land where the early Israelite kingdoms had been centred – as the site of the homeland-to-be. In order to raise funds and gain support for the new movement, the World Zionist Organization was also created.

Palestine, however, was overwhelmingly Arab. At the end of the nineteenth century, almost half a million Arabs, most of them Muslims but some of them Christians, were living in this land. Many could trace their roots in Palestine over generations, even centuries. About 50,000 orthodox Jews also lived there, concentrated mostly in Jerusalem and its environs. At this time, Palestine was little more than a geographical expression, defining an area with no clear-cut boundaries. To the east lay the Jordan River, a boundary of sorts. In the north, it was impossible to know where Galilee, or northern Palestine, ended and southern Lebanon began. To the south, the land gradually blended into and became the Sinai Peninsula, and in the West lay the Mediterranean. Such was the Palestine known to the traveller, the Western merchant, the Christian pilgrim, and the European diplomat of the late nineteenth century. The entire region, including Beirut, Damascus and points beyond, was part of the vast Ottoman empire, ruled by Turkish-speaking Muslims from their capital in Istanbul. This empire, however, was coming under great pressure from an expanding and industrialized Europe, whose major powers had already conquered parts of it (e.g., Algeria and Tunisia, which were under French control; and Egypt, occupied by Britain) and were casting covetous eyes upon the rest.

The Arabs of Palestine were basically an agrarian people, divided along clan and family lines, and with traditional life styles and modes of production. An individual's loyalty went to the local unit – the village, for example – and beyond this, to his religion. A rural–urban cleavage also existed. Many country folk lived in the hilly and mountainous areas of central Palestine, which during much of the nineteenth century had been half autonomous, and whose people therefore had acquired a large measure of autonomy. The towns, by contrast, contained semi-modernized élites, exposed to influences from the West. Palestinians were not yet a nation.

For the Zionists to reach their goal of a Jewish state, two things were necessary: immigration, in order to create a Jewish majority; and the establishment of settlements, in order to gain control of the land. By the turn of the nineteenth century, considerable sums of money had been made available by Jewish bankers and other wealthy persons, and the number of European Jews arriving in Palestine began to increase. Almost from the start, however, disputes broke out between the newcomers and the local inhabitants. Jewish settlements and neighbouring Arab villages clashed over water and grazing rights, and over land purchases by the Jews. Some Arabs became aware of the political movement in Europe that lay behind the increased immigration. In 1901, illiterate Muslim peasants asked an official in Jerusalem if it was true that Jews wanted to take over the country. The obstacles to Zionist success were formidable indeed. On the eve of World War I, despite increased immigration, Jews still represented a small minority of the total population of Palestine. Presenting their movement as a humanitarian cause – something which the West owed the Jewish people – Zionist officials, including Theodore Herzl, had laboured unsuccessfully to persuade the European powers to back it. (In order to avoid upsetting the Ottomans and others, Zionists used the word 'homeland' rather than 'state' to define their ultimate goal.) No matter how much energy and money the Zionist movement possessed, and however artful its diplomacy, success could not possibly come without Big Power support.

The year 1917 marked a turning-point in the history of this dispute. Invading from Egypt, a British army wrested control of Palestine from the Ottomans, who had joined the side of Germany in the war, and established a rule that would last until 1948. At almost the same time, the British government issued the Balfour Declaration, by which it pledged to facilitate Jewish immigration into Palestine and work for the establishment of a Jewish homeland in it, providing that nothing be done to prejudice' the civil and religious rights of its existing non-Jewish communities. British rule and the Balfour Declaration had been imposed upon the Arabs of Palestine without their consent and against their will. In their view, Britain had broken a pledge made in 1915 to Sharif Husayn, guardian of Mecca, to support the establishment of an independent Arab Kingdom at the war's end in return for Arab military assistance against the Ottomans. Led by Faysal, son of Sharif Husayn, an Arab army had aided the British forces in 1917–18, and had been permitted to enter Damascus, where the Arab flag was raised and where in March 1920 an Arab Congress proclaimed Faysal King of Syria. Several months later, however, Faysal's government fell to invading French troops, acting in accordance with a secret war-time agreement with the British to divide up the former Ottoman domains. France took control of Syria and Lebanon, while Britain kept control of Palestine and Iraq (also conquered during the war). This action was legitimized by a mandate from the League of Nations in 1922 by which these areas were placed in a tutelary relationship with the two big powers.

British rule provided a spur to the development of a distinctly Palestinian nationalism. This was made possible by (1) the fall of Faysal's government, which dashed the hopes of many Palestinians for a Pan-Arab kingdom; (2) the establishment by Britain of a single governmental and administrative structure within the bounds of historic Palestine; (3) and a continuity of aims based upon the sentiment that Palestine was Arab and should be ruled by Arabs. Palestinians thus became united in their opposition to British rule, and to increased Jewish immigration and land settlement – a threat not faced by Arabs in Syria, Lebanon or Iraq. Of course, Palestinians sought the support of other Arabs and Muslims, but a basic perception existed that Palestinian problems were unique. A Palestinian national consciousness developed rapidly. In 1919, many people would have supported the inclusion of Palestine in an independent Syria, but by the mid-1920s this aspiration was dead. Throughout the years of British rule, Palestinian national demands, articulated first by the Arab Executive (1920–1934) and then by the Arab Higher Committee – the leadership organs of the Palestinian national movement – were remarkably consistent: a national government responsible to a parliament elected by the people; and an end to the establishment of Jewish colonies on Palestinian soil.

In the meantime, the Zionist Jews, armed with a document (the Balfour Declaration) recognizing their political rights, and supported by British power, worked to strengthen their position. The Jewish Agency was established to represent the Jewish community in Palestine officially. The Zionist labour movement, propelled by socialist ideals including the idea of work on the land, expanded its institutions and membership. The Zionists held many advantages over the Palestinians – among them, access to outside funds, superior organization, the ability to intervene with the British government in London, and, of course, the support of the British administration in Palestine. Yet in the 1920s and early 1930s, they were still a long way from attainment of their objectives. The ascendancy of Hitler in Germany and the beginning of the persecution of Jews turned the tide in their favour. New immigrants from Europe poured into Palestine. Between 1932 and 1937 the Jewish population in Palestine more than doubled, rising from 175,000 to 400,000. This influx brought with it new capital as well as growing support for the Zionist movement worldwide. Jewish land acquisitions multiplied, helping produce a landless Arab peasantry. Zionists were at last acquiring the power of numbers.

Palestinians soon realized that their demographic position was endangered. They knew that the Zionists intended to convert Palestine into a Jewish state when the introduction of immigrants gave them a majority. It was possible to project these figures to show how Jews could swamp the local inhabitants. The Arab sense of injustice was thus heightened, and panic and desperation hit the Palestinian community. A threat was posed to its very existence. In 1936, the Palestinian leadership called a general strike, repeating earlier demands for a national government. In 1937, a violent insurrection engulfed the country. Lasting for two years, it was finally extinguished by British troops, with heavy loss of Palestinian lives. With their leaders dead or in exile, Palestinian Arabs emerged from this experience thoroughly demoralized and in no mood to compromise. In 1939, they rejected a British offer – the May White Paper – that would have limited Jewish immigration into Palestine, increased the role in government for Palestinians, established a representative body after five years, and led to an independent Palestine in ten years.

A fundamental change of British policy, this offer infuriated the Zionist community, which was numerically too strong and politically too mobilized to be contained, even by Britain. Zionists increasingly turned militant, and some groups began carrying out terrorist attacks against British installations and personnel, and against Palestinians. The decline of Britain as a world power, the rise to prominence of the US, and an awakened conscience in the West as a result of Nazi genocide against the

Jews, all worked in the Zionists' favour after World War II. By 1947, British efforts to construct a joint Anglo-American policy for Palestine had failed, and Britain announced its intention to terminate its control, turning the whole problem over to the newly-created United Nations. A new period in the history of the conflict was about to begin.

Th Arab–Israeli War of 1948 was a turning-point in more ways than one. It gave birth to the modern state of Israel (proclaimed on 14 May 1948), but it also led to the large-scale displacement of Palestinians from their homes and the confiscation of their lands and other properties by the Israeli government. The mass exodus was triggered by fighting in populated areas and by fear of fighting, but it was also caused by psychological and terror tactics used against Palestinians by organized Jewish groups and by pressure from the Israeli armed forces, which emptied village communities of their inhabitants as they advanced. This created a burning sense of injustice among Palestinians, who felt that they had been forced to pay the price for Hitler's persecution of the Jews. While Jews and their supporters in the West were celebrating the establishment of Israel as the triumph of justice long denied, Palestinians could only feel outraged by a state built upon their own dispossession. Yet Palestinians had contributed to their own defeat. In 1947, they rejected a UN General Assembly plan (accepted by the Zionists) for the partition of Palestine, which would have given them a small state and international recognition as a nation. Be this as it may, Palestinians had not beaten themselves. They were defeated by stronger, more power-ful forces against which they had become relatively helpless.

After the 1948 War, Palestinians and Israelis were separated from each other – a very important fact. Little over 120,000 Arabs remained within the borders of the Jewish state. The rest of the Palestinian population was scattered, being subjected to Egyptian, Syrian, Lebanese and Jordanian rule. Separated from themselves, Palestinians could no longer work together in their struggle. Henceforward, they would have to develop their nationalism in an Arab context. As for Israel, the Zionist nation possessed sovereignty at last, and the Jewish people had a refuge from persecution; but Zionism had lost its European context. Israel was now located in a world implacably hostile to its existence.

As a result of the 1948 War the focus of this conflict shifted. It had begun as a civil war between Palestinians and Zionist Jews (later called Israelis). After six months, with the Palestinians defeated, the neighbouring Arab states (principally Egypt, Jordan and Syria) had entered the field of battle against Israel. Their overwhelming and embarrassing defeat by the Jewish armed forces, and their subsequent refusal to accept it by making definitive peace treaties with Israel, turned the conflict from a dispute between Palestinians and Zionists/Israelis into a confrontation between the Arab world and Israel.

In 1948 a new era began, one that would be marked by four major wars and many minor skirmishes, but also by long ceasefires, amounting to de facto peace. This may be broken down into two sub-periods: (1) the years between 1948 and June 1967, when the conflict was one between Israel and the Arab countries, or more especially Egypt, Syria and Jordan (the so-called confrontation states); (2) and from June 1967 to the present, when it moved back to the original core of Palestinian versus Israeli, and the first peace treaty was signed between an Arab state and Israel.

After 1948, the political environment was generally hostile to the settlement of this dispute. The 1948 War had undermined the authority of the established Arab regimes and facilitated the rise of a younger generation of leaders, mostly military officers. In the 1950s, ruling groups were overthrown in Egypt, Syria and Iraq. New governments came to power that professed adherence to socialist ideals, attacked Western influence in the Middle East, and called for the unification of the Arab-speaking peoples. The symbol of the new trend was Egyptian president Gamal Abdul Nasser, who came to power in a military *coup d'état* in 1952, but its most tangible political expression was the union between Egypt and Syria, achieved in 1958. The new tendency affected all Arab countries, including King Hussein's Jordan. During this period, all Arab states were hostile to Israel, but no real policy, collective or individual, existed for dealing with it. The Arab countries insisted upon the right of the Palestinian refugees to return to their homes. Egypt, Jordan and Syria demanded major revisions of the borders between them and Israel. Without them, there would be no Arab recognition or acceptance of the Jewish state. To isolate Israel in the region and mobilize support against it internationally, the Arab countries employed a variety of tactics, from economic boycotts to the passage of UN General Assembly resolutions critical of Israel, in alliance with Third World and Eastern bloc countries. At the same time, however, these states endeavoured to prevent a hostile situation from getting out of control. 'No war, no peace' was the preferred solution.

For its part, Israel insisted upon Arab recognition and acceptance. It refused to consider major border rectifications and demanded that the Arab governments absorb the Palestinian refugees, whose return it either rejected or tied to the conclusion of peace agreements. Israel was particularly concerned about the security of its borders. Across-border raids by Palestinian and other guerrilla groups elicited powerful Israeli counter-strikes against the countries from which the infiltrators had come. A major war broke out in 1956, during the Suez Canal Crisis, when Israel, with the connivance of Britain and France, launched a strike against Egypt by invading and taking the Sinai Peninsula. As a result of US opposition, Israel was later obliged to withdraw its forces from Sinai. However, this invasion brought about a ten-year truce on Israel's border with Egypt.

Palestinians too refused to accept defeat. In refugee camps and elsewhere, a dream of return was nourished, deriving from the conviction that a terrible injustice had been perpetrated and that 'right' would eventually triumph, and also from the sheer need to survive in a new and difficult environment. Parents transmitted to their children stories about houses left behind, the size of the fruit in their orchards, the beauty of their gardens and olive groves. Wherever they went, Palestinians founded institutions, from labour unions to student organizations and women's associations. Without realizing it, they were reconstructing their shattered society and laying the foundations for a new national movement, based upon the idea of self-determination and allegiance to their homeland.

Developing their nationalism in an Arab political context meant that Palestinians would differ from one another ideologically and organizationally. Palestinians became associated with a wide variety of groups in the Arab world, including Islamic parties. Some Palestinians formed opposing factions. Many were attracted to the idea of Arab unity. During the 1950s, it became almost axiomatic that the recovery of their former homeland could be achieved only by a union of Arab states which would defeat Israel in battle. However, the break-up of the union between Egypt and Syria in 1961 caused some Palestinians to realize that they could not depend upon Arab unity to achieve their goals. Long before this, Palestinian militants had formed guerrilla squads and led raids into Israel, attacking installations and developing terrorist tactics from bases in Arab countries. One of these new commando organizations was al-Fatah, whose belief that Palestinian military action should precede, rather than follow, Arab unity challenged the prevailing orthodoxy. The Arab states, of course, worked to prevent these organizations from drawing them into a war with Israel. In order to control the resistance groups, Egypt and the other Arab states created the PLO in 1964. Designed to represent Palestinians everywhere and to symbolize the Arab world's commitment to their cause, the PLO was led by an old guard of Palestinian notables who were militants in rhetoric only. Popular struggle was not really part of their programme. The creation of the PLO, however, was not without importance. An institutional framework had been erected that would give concrete expression to the Palestinian national objectives of freedom and self-determination. And the old guard of toothless tigers would soon give way to a new generation of Palestinian activists, many of them Christians, who were rising within the resistance organizations.

Arab hopes of isolating and weakening Israel failed. Quite the reverse, the fledgling state of 1948, helped by new immigration and massive infusions of aid (including reparations' payments from West Germany), became a great success story. A society of European Jews, many of them holocaust survivors, Israel was a vibrant socialist democracy firmly planted within the Western community of nations. It was also developing into a military powerhouse, although this was not so obvious in the 1950s and early 1960s. During this time, Israel learned how to limit and contain Palestinian raids and terrorist actions, which posed no serious danger to its survival. In June 1967, Israel's military superiority over the Arab states was clearly demonstrated. In only six days, Israel decisively defeated the armed forces of Egypt, Syria and Jordan, and conquered the Sinai Peninsula, the Golan Heights, East Jerusalem, the West Bank and the Gaza

Strip. Israel now had control over all of historic Palestine that had been ruled by Britain – and more.

In 1967, the conflict began moving back to its original centre: a dispute between Palestinians and Israeli Jews. This shift occurred slowly, almost imperceptibly, proceeding in fits and starts, but pushed by key developments, including a growing confrontation between Palestinians and Israeli occupation forces in the West Bank and Gaza. The Arab world as the main arena of confrontation thus began to fade, but not without another war. In October 1973, Egypt and Syria launched a military strike against Israel that took the Jewish state by surprise, but which ended in such a way that neither side could claim victory. This was a prelude not to intensified conflict, but to a peace settlement. In 1978, Egyptian President Sadat and Israeli Prime Minister Begin, meeting with US President Jimmy Carter at Camp David, agreed to sign a peace treaty between their two countries that entailed the end of economic boycotts, the establishment of full diplomatic relations, and the return of Egypt to the Sinai Peninsula. A second agreement was also reached which stipulated autonomy for Palestinians in Gaza and the West Bank, under continued Israeli rule. Less than a year later, a peace treaty was concluded between Egypt and Israel (the autonomy agreement, however, was never implemented). The removal of Egypt – the largest and most powerful confrontation state – from the field of countries hostile to Israel guaranteed that no other Arab state would be willing to risk another war against this regional superpower. Though unwilling to enter into formal peace accords with Israel, the Arab states none the less became reconciled to the changed situation. New priorities arose, and the Arab–Israeli confrontation receded from public view.

After 1967, Palestinian nationalism acquired new purpose, force and direction. Following the June War, Palestinians understood that the Arab states would never be able to destroy Israel in a conventional military conflict. This worked to the advantage of al-Fatah, which had argued all along that Palestinians must take charge of their national struggle. After the June War, organized commando groups, fuelled by the growing sentiment of Palestinian nationalism, proliferated. The resistance organizations began advancing claims to speak on behalf of the Palestinian people. Support for them grew. Eventually, al-Fatah succeeded in establishing its authority over the burgeoning resistance movement by winning control of the PLO in 1969 and bringing the diverse commando groups under the PLO's wing. The reconstituted PLO thus became the institutional manifestation of a popular guerrilla movement. Palestinian nationalism now had a structure to direct and represent it. Controlled by the commando groups, the reconstructed PLO did not, of course, command the automatic allegiance of Palestinians everywhere. It would have to compete for influence with many other groups, including traditional Palestinian notables, both in the Diaspora and in the West Bank and Gaza. Much work lay ahead.

Israel's conquest of Gaza and the West Bank also helped move the dispute back to its original core. Palestinians and Israelis were once again face to face. After 1967, close to half of the entire Palestinian population lived under Israeli control. Israel's victory had also brought a people previously separated together again. Arabs living in Galilee or other parts of the state of Israel entered into contact with the West Bank, shopping in the markets of Jenin, for example, while West Bankers became acquainted with Palestinians living in Gaza. A sense of unity and purpose could be forged, especially among Gazans and West Bankers who lived under Israeli military rule. Two nationalisms – Israeli and Palestinian – confronted each other. The conflict was becoming again a Palestinian–Israeli one.

Two processes were underway. Among Gazans and West Bankers, a rebuilding effort (called 'restructuring') began, similar to that which had earlier taken place in the Diaspora, and in a sense the continuation of it. The other process, initiated by the Israelis, was a gradual encroachment upon Palestinian resources, manifested in the seizure of land and the establishment of Jewish settlements in Gaza and the West Bank. In time, it became clear that Israel intended to annex these areas de facto, to make them part of the Jewish state. Palestinians began to perceive the Israeli occupation as a threat to their survival as a people. Something like this had happened before. Unlike 1948, however, Palestinians would not run, but stay and fight. It is to these two processes – of construction, on the one hand, and of creeping annexation, with the threat of dispossession, on the other – that we now turn.

1

The restructuring of Palestinian society in the West Bank and Gaza

On the eve of the Intifada in 1987, at least 1,701,435 Palestinians were living in the West Bank and Gaza Strip, exclusive of annexed Greater Jerusalem, which contained 136,000 Palestinians.[1] These two areas together comprised 5,875 square kilometres, or 20.7 per cent of the area of mandatory Palestine that had been ruled by the British. In the West Bank, a chain of mountains ran from north to south like an elongated spine. To the east of this mountainous bloc lay the area of the Syrian–African Rift, that is, the Jordan River Valley; and to the southeast, the Judean Desert and Dead Sea. To the west lay the coastal plain, containing the towns of Tulkarm and Qalqilya. The longitudial axis of this mountainous chain formed a north–south route along which were located the major population centres: Jenin, Nablus, Ramallah, al-Bireh, Bethlehem, Beit Sahour, Jerusalem and Hebron. Divided by numerous wide valleys, this long central region was the site of many of the West Bank's 403 villages (including smaller towns). The area also contained an underground system of water, which emerged in freshwater springs or was pumped from wells. (Water was not abundant, but a precious and limited resource.) Altogether, some 1,067,873 Palestinians lived in the villages, towns, cities and other localities of the West Bank.

The Gaza Strip, by contrast, was a sliver of land 45 kilometres long and between five and twelve kilometres wide from the northeast to the southwest.[2] An extension of the coastal plain, Gaza had a total area of only 300 square kilometres, of which more than 30 per cent was sand dunes. Crammed into this space were 633,562 Palestinians. Population density per square kilometre was 1,730 in Gaza, compared to 193 in the West Bank. Two-thirds of the Palestinians in Gaza were refugees (i.e.,

stateless persons), many of whom originated from that part of
pre-1948 mandatory Palestine which had become the state of
Israel. These people lived in eight camps (total population:
245,000), which were maintained by UNRWA, in towns (e.g.,
Gaza City, Khan Yunis, Rafah) and in a few villages. Large
numbers of Palestinian refugees also lived in the West Bank,
where 20 camps (including one within the muncipal boundaries of
Jerusalem) housed 95,000 persons. UNRWA provided refugee
aid of one type or another to about 25 per cent of the people in
the West Bank. Of these, 15 per cent lived in villages, the rest in
the camps.

Palestinian society was differentiated according to many
criteria. To a certain extent, it was hierarchical, based upon
family and clan, and therefore structured along lines of personal
dependency and obligation. The centuries-old distinction between
town and countryside, each giving rise to quite different lifestyles
and values, had by no means disappeared entirely. In recent
years, the spread of education has been an important leveller,
and growing opposition to the Israeli occupation has brought
together Palestinians of different backgrounds and income levels.
The activities of Palestinian self-help and voluntary organizations
covered the length and breadth of Gaza and the West Bank, thus
helping erode compartmentalization and the separation of town
from countryside. The emergence of a large wage-earning
proletariat as a result of employment opportunities in Israel – one
of the most important social changes that occurred under the
occupation (see chapter 2) – had siphoned people off the land
and contributed to the decline of the agricultural sector. (Many
Palestinians, however, remained in their villages as small,
peasant farmers.) Palestinian society also contained a rudimentary
upper and middle class, made up of landowners, businessmen,
merchants, white-collar workers, retailers, professionals, and
people who provided financial services, among others. Not a
large grouping, this was more of a social stratum than a class, at
least as understood in the West. The pull of family and other
loyalties was simply too strong for a class structure to exist.

Palestinians living in villages, towns and refugee camps had
their own local authorities.[3] In some villages, one or more
mayors (*mukhtar*, in the singular form), drawn from prominent
families, represented their communities to the Israeli governors,

who in turn appointed them. The powers of these village mayors, however, were limited mostly to the signing of documents. In other villages, local councils managed community affairs. Palestinian towns and cities were organized into municipalities, numbering 25 in all, which were headed by mayors or local councils. Refugee camps were administered by camp managers, under the jurisdiction of UNRWA, and by local councils. Indigenous courts too existed. Eight Islamic courts of first instance operated in the West Bank under the authority of an Islamic Appeals Court that sat in East Jerusalem. Religious courts were overseen by the Supreme Muslim Council, but subordinated to the Ministry of Pious Endowments in Amman, Jordan. (The salaries of the religious judges were paid by the Jordanian government.) Local secular courts were also in place. In 1985, these included magistrates' courts in nine cities, district courts in three other cities, and one court of appeal, with a total of 27 judges and prosecutors. However, the fact that Israel's Military Government could transfer cases out of their jurisdiction, or nullify cases by ruling them to be against the public interest, greatly reduced the scope and authority of these judicial bodies. Few means existed even for implementing their decisions.

From the time of Israel's occupation of the West Bank and Gaza in 1967, Palestinians had been ruled by a Military Government. The system was harsh and oppressive. Palestinians had no political rights, and no real administrative control over their own lives. In March 1981, a Civil Administration was set up to exercise many of the civil powers previously discharged by the Military Government, whose work became restricted to security matters and some other specified administrative duties.[4] The Civil Administration had charge of a large bureaucracy, employing 11,614 civil servants (most of them Palestinians) in 1985. It functioned through more than 30 staff officers, who were subordinated to, and received directives from, civilian ministries in Israel proper.

The services that existed to sustain this growing population (in Gaza, the rate of natural increase was 3.2 per cent annually) came from five sources: Israel, UNRWA, Jordan (and other Arab states), non-indigenous associations and voluntary societies (most from the US and other Western countries), and Palestinian organizations.[5] These funded and operated programmes in the areas of health (hospitalization and preventative medicine), education, and relief and welfare. The Israeli Civil Administration's budget for Gaza and the West Bank far exceeded that of UNRWA, Jordan, and all other contributing organizations. However, the expenditures allocated by Israel for services to the general population (as against expenditures budgeted for infrastructure) were actually quite low and did not meet its growth needs. UNRWA also played a vital support role, but its operations were confined to Palestinians who were officially registered as refugees. As for Jordan, its estimated 1987–8 annual budget for the West Bank and Gaza – $75 million – was equal to that of UNRWA. Non-indigenous associations were also very active. These included Save the Children, Catholic Relief Services, the International Committee of the Red Cross, the Mennonite Central Committee, and the Near East Council of Churches, to name just a few. As for local Palestinian societies, their programmes supported clinics and hospitals, schools and vocational institutes, and provided relief for the disabled and needy.

The Israelis permitted only two region-wide Palestinian institutions to operate: the Supreme Muslim Council, which managed religious endowments and supervised the Islamic courts; and the Palestinian press, located in East Jerusalem, which was active in spite of Israeli harassment and censorship.[6] Something akin to a region-wide Palestinian association was the Council of Higher Education, which co-ordinated the activities of universities in the West Bank and Gaza Strip, established criteria for academic accreditation, and so on.[7] Every Palestinian university was represented on this Council. Israel provided no funds for Palestinian higher education, which relied upon outside sources of financial assistance.

Education in Gaza and the West Bank operated at four levels. Through the elementary (six years), preparatory (three years) and high school (three years) levels, education was compulsory. If they qualified, and if money was available, students could pass to a fourth level of vocational or technical training, or go to a college or university. By the mid-1980s, five accredited, degree-granting universities existed in the West Bank, and one – the Islamic University (enrolment: 500) – was operating in Gaza.[8] The total university and college student population in the West

Bank stood at 15,000 in 1985.[9]

Education at the first three levels was provided by Israel, UNRWA, and foreign organizations. In the West Bank, where education was tied to the Jordanian system, 75 per cent of the 1,076 schools were government schools, run, that is, by the Israelis.[10] In Gaza, on the other hand, UNRWA operated 145 schools containing 90,000 students, as against 98 government schools, with a student population of 76,500.[11] Youngsters were educated in UNRWA schools through the preparatory level, then went to government high schools. UNRWA also operated vocational and teacher training programmes.

As for health care, according to official Israeli sources, there were eight general government hospitals (654 beds), one hospital for the mentally ill (320 beds), and eight private hospitals (391 beds) in the West Bank in 1984.[12] In Gaza, al-Shifa was the government-supported hospital, while al-Ahli was Arab-run. (al-Nasser was a third Gaza hospital.) The total number of hospital beds in Gaza was 935. Palestinian organizations provided ambulance services, a blood bank, help for the handicapped, rehabilitation, and much more. The Red Crescent Society of Gaza made a wide range of services available through its clinics and first-aid centres.

With respect to relief and general welfare, UNRWA provided food rations, distributed clothes and blankets, improved shelters in the camps, and gave limited financial aid to those in dire need.[13] In Gaza, the Near East Council of Churches' Committee for Refugee Work also dispensed clothing, food, and made cash grants to the needy, as did other church-sponsored groups. Palestinian charitable organizations like the Family Rejuvenation Society (*Jamiyat in'ash al-usrah*) helped poor families improve their situation and made many other contributions. Some of these Palestinian groups had been established before the Israeli occupation, but a very rapid Palestinian institutional development took place after 1967. In 1983, for example, Palestinian charitable organizations in the West Bank numbered 166, as against 89 on the eve of the Israeli occupation in 1967.[14] Their budget, financed by contributions from the Arab world and from secular and religious organizations abroad, was five times greater than the total welfare budget of Israel's Civil Administration.

In the mid-1970s, Palestinians began forming organizations of all kinds. Institution-building was regarded as the best way of responding to the occupation and blocking the advance of Israel's annexationist measures. Of course, Palestinians also had to find ways of overcoming the obstacles placed in the path of their development. College and university administrations, for example, had to deal with everything from the entry of troops onto their campuses to the payment of heavy duties on educational equipment. Birzeit, a college before 1967, became a university in the early 1970s. Israel licensed its establishment, but provided no money. 'Israel tried to stop the university from developing by closing it down and refusing to grant an import licence,' Dr Bishara observed. 'Birzeit had to pay taxes on laboratory instruments, books, and many other necessities, which all had to be imported.'[15] (The Israeli strategy was to grant permits but to restrict Palestinian development so as to contain the intellectuals, students, and others.) Taking advantage of every opening, Palestinians pressed ahead. They availed themselves of the possibilities inherent in Israel's annexation of East Jerusalem by locating their press institutions there, where the application of Israeli law would presumably provide some protection against arbitrary and high-handed governmental action.

Palestinians poured a great deal of money into the development of their institutions. Schools that had existed before the occupation were expanded, and technical institutes, colleges and universities founded. Bethlehem and al-Najah universities were started, and a college established at Hebron. Such institutions were developed by Palestinians themselves, and evolved on their own, with a third and then fourth year being added to their curricula. Medical organizations, social clubs, professional associations (for lawyers, doctors, engineers), and workers' unions arose. In Gaza, for example, the six trade unions that had been in existence in 1967 were re-established in 1979 (subject to severe restrictions).[16] Charitable societies and women's committees also appeared, contributing to the improvement of health, learning and culture.

Charitable associations supported hospitals, clinics, vocational institutes, adult literacy and education programmes, libraries and kindergartens. They organized aid to the needy, to orphans, and to children and mothers whose fathers and husbands were in prison. In 1977, West Bank charitable societies, formed into three large regional groupings, spent almost $4.5 million on their activities.[17]

In 1978, the first women's work committee was founded, in Ramallah. Its purpose was to provide training and assistance to women in order to make them more useful to themselves and to society. The membership of this committee eventually rose to 8,500 women, distributed among 225 villages and refugee camps. 'Our committee,' commented its founder, Ms Zuhayra Kamal,

has training courses of a traditional kind – sewing, needlework, food production. This is connected with a health programme, preventative care, to reduce reliance upon physicians. Women are trained in basic nutrition and first aid, how to stop bleeding, for example, or, if a bone is broken, what to do or not to do. In Gaza and the West Bank, we also have 46 literacy classes. If a village woman is doing accounting work and needs special training, we send her to take a course for one year. We train women to be leaders, to run local kindergartens, for example. Instead of bringing an outsider with a university degree into a village, we train women – mothers – who come from the village, and who have had between seven and nine years of secondary education only. They do a very good job.[18]

Three other women's committees were founded in the 1980s. They organized women in the rural areas, created their own local branches, and so on. By 1987, according to Ms Kamal, over 25,000 women were active members in these four work committees.

Such organizations had a basic, grass-roots character. Involving people from towns, villages and camps, they helped break down the barriers which had hitherto separated communities, but by not bringing in outsiders they also preserved the independence of those communities. Decisions were often made locally, and by elected committees rather than one 'leader'. This ensured continuity and survival when individual members were arrested or detained. Palestinians were increasingly feeling the satisfaction of helping themselves.

Mutual aid, self-help and other groups acquired a national focus by affiliation with the political organizations. Founded in 1973, the Palestine National Front and its successor, the National Guidance Committee (created in 1978), called for Palestinian self-determination and the formation of an independent state, achieved through negotiations, in the West Bank and Gaza. These were umbrella organizations, mobilizers of public opinion in the occupied territories. Led by local nationalist leaders, men drawn from what Sahliyeh has called the new urban élite of professional people oriented toward modern achievement norms, the political organizations helped foster the development of a Palestinian national identity and led campaigns of passive resistance by organizing strikes and demonstrations against the occupation.[19] They brought under their wing trade unions, charitable societies and a myriad of other groups. Their chief contribution was to promote greater awareness of the political situation. 'As women became more aware of politics,' recounted Ms Nadia Habash, a Palestinian women's activist,

they become more active in unions, and would meet with men to discuss national issues. Lectures and discussions were held in public libraries and clubs. The Palestine theatre was started. Women began to participate more and more in mass-based work, and to connect their lives to the national liberation movement.[20]

The political organs themselves did not survive. The National Guidance Council was outlawed by the Israeli authorities in 1982, accused of being a front for the PLO. The new urban élite, or 'patriotic bourgeoisie', as the leadership was called, did sympathize with the PLO. Those among them who were chosen as mayors in the municipal election of 1976 came to power because they were supporters of the PLO. 'The feeling of the people was with the PLO, so that when they became mayors they reflected the PLO,' explained Dr al-Jarbawi, Assistant Professor at Birzeit University. 'They were a copy of the support the PLO enjoyed.'[21] The waning and disappearance of the political organizations, then, did not spell the end of politics. For PLO influence was growing, manifested increasingly in the activities of its mainline factions.

'From the beginning of the occupation,' Dr Bishara noted,

the national movement meant two things: the political organizations on one side, and the resistance organizations, on the other. The resistance organizations like Fatah, the Popular Front for the Liberation of Palestine [PFLP] and the Democratic Front for the Liberation of Palestine [DFLP], were directed by the PLO.[22]

The PFLP, headed by George Habash, was a self-proclaimed Marxist organization which believed that the liberation of Palestine, including the part 'occupied' by Israel, could only come through Arab unity and the struggle of the Arab peoples against Israel. The DFLP, led by Nayef Hawatmeh, and formed in consequence of a split within the PFLP, was also Marxist–Leninist, but much less extreme and more willing to accept compromise. Under the leadership of Yasser Arafat, al-Fatah, formed in 1959, was pragmatic and non-doctrinaire. al-Fatah welcomed and embraced all shades of opinion, including Islamic tendencies, so long as the nationalist struggle received priority. The unity of the Arab world should not take precedence over the Palestinian national struggle against Israel.

Possessing their own central commands, these three major guerrilla organizations (which were not the only PLO resistance groups) enjoyed a large measure of independence from one another, even though all came under the umbrella of the PLO. Occasionally, a group would break away from the PLO leadership. (In 1968, the Popular Front for the Liberation of Palestine – General Command, founded by Ahmad Jibril, seceded from its parent organization.) As was true of the headquarters and offices of the PLO, the leadership, supply sources and fighters of these three main groups were all located outside the occupied territories. Inside the West Bank and Gaza, each faction had its organizational extension, comprising active members and a body of supporters, some of whom had contacts with the activists. In refugee camps, villages, towns and cities, these PLO factions competed with each other for influence. Lively discussions ensued. Entire camps became affiliated with a particular ideology or 'tendency'. The three women's committees founded in the 1980s were groups that broke away from the original women's work committee as a result of ideological differences stimulated by support for or opposition to one or another of these PLO factions.[23] Hot debates and discussions gave Palestinians an understanding of the basics of politics. And the factionalism stirred up by arguments and disagreements only deepened and broadened the national movement as a whole. Society was at last beginning to come together. In Gaza, political alliances based upon national politics were being forged that brought together social classes which before 1967 had been isolated from one another.[24]

One place where society came together and where the
resistance organizations found opportunities for recruitment was
the prisons. 'Always, at a minimum,' observed Dr Bishara, 'there
were several thousand persons in prison each year from both the
resistance organizations and the political ones. In time, there was
a mixture.'[25] Members of PLO factions mingled not only with
men from the nationalist organizations, but also with thousands
of young Palestinians who had never before been exposed to
politics. 'My son was 13½ years old when he first went to prison,'
said 'Ali', a resident of Jenin:

Someone from his class threw a stone at a passing Israeli car, so troops
came, gathered together a group of ten-year-olds, and asked them to
state the names of their friends. My son's name was on the 'list'. His
second arrest came four years later . . . he was elected by the prisoners
to be head of the committee that distributed meals and cigarettes.
Imagine it! My son; in charge of 25 people. One of them was president
of the teachers' union; another was an employee at Birzeit University
. . . When he came out, he was more calm, more deep in thought. He
had lost some of his bad habits. He used to be careless. Now he is
responsible. He came out more active than before. He became
politicized.[26]

Prisons were places of learning and training, where men
toughened by beatings and other humiliating experiences developed tactics of collective resistance to the Israeli authorities.
How many Palestinians received this kind of 'education'? The
true figure cannot be known. André Rosenthal, an Israeli lawyer
who has defended Palestinians in the military courts, estimated
that about 25 per cent of the Palestinian population passed
through the military court system, directly or indirectly.[27]
'In the mid-1970s,' commented 'Aziz', a former political
prisoner,

Palestinian political prisoners began learning how to counter Israeli
tactics of divide and rule, of treating with each prisoner individually.
Conditions in the prisons were terrible. Political prisoners were treated
far worse than the criminals. Anyone who did the slightest thing was
beaten. Tear gas was put into entire rooms of prisoners if one person
broke the rules. We realized that the Israeli government and the military
administration were one, so why shouldn't we be? There was a need to

unify all our factions into one opinion. Big strikes, hunger strikes, occurred. If the jail contained 200 persons, everyone did it. Our demands? To have books, medical treatment, better food, family visits, and the like. Prisoners wrote letters that were smuggled out to the United Nations, to human rights groups, even to the Pope. Demonstrations also took place in Jerusalem and Gaza in support of us. Some of us died but a Palestinian personality was being built up. Under pressure, Israel made concessions, and our conditions improved. We learned how to pass information and intelligence on to the people in other prisons, and eventually, to connect all prisons together. In Nafha [in the Negev desert] and other places, libraries were built. If a problem arose with some prisoner, the Israeli authorities had to speak with the leader of the committee of his block, not with him individually. This was a protection for us. We could deal with collaborators more effectively. Prison became like an education.[28]

For 'Ahmad', an al-Fatah supporter from a village in the central West Bank, this certainly was true.

Between 1979 and 1981, I was in prison four times. From morning until night we had meetings and courses, organized at different levels. Some dealt with the origins of the Palestinian people, and their rights to their land. Older prisoners taught courses on Vietnam, the Cuban revolution, imperialism, and the Islamic movement. Questions were asked about the material to make sure that we all understood. We also read books about Israel, the Zionist movement, and the PLO and its factions. We had good discussions. When I was released, I visited Bethlehem University and had political discussions with the students. They could not believe that I had only a secondary school degree. I told them that I had attended a university: prison.[29]

When Palestinians left prisons, many had already become affiliated with one or another of the resistance organizations, or at least had adopted one of their ideologies. Some returned to their villages and camps to become leaders there. Others enrolled in the universities where, in the late 1970s, they rose to positions of influence in the youth movement, using their PLO connections to advance the interests of their student groups.[30] Fertile ground had been created for the spread of PLO influence in the territories.

In the early years of its existence, the PLO had paid much less attention to the Palestinians in the West Bank and Gaza than to those living outside the occupied territories. Two reasons accounted for this. First, the PLO's support base (for the recruitment of new members, etc.) lay outside the occupied territories, in refugee camps in Jordan (until 1970, when King Hussein expelled the PLO from his country), and in Lebanon. Second, its programme, at least until the mid-1970s, called for the recovery of all of 'Palestine' (including the area taken up by Israel) through armed struggle. The PLO rejected all proposals for a Palestinian state in any part of historic Palestine, just as it opposed negotiations with Israel and a political solution to the conflict.

Not surprisingly, Palestinians in the occupied territories tended to be more moderate in their politics and tactics than the PLO leadership abroad. As political awareness developed among them, many began to regard a separate Palestinian state in the West Bank and Gaza as the only practicable solution to the conflict. 'The position of the Communist Party, whose leadership and hierarchy is here, inside, has almost always been a two-state solution,' observed Dr al-Jarbawi.[31] The main reason for this sentiment was that West Bankers and Gazans were living under occupation. They wanted their independence, but they were not inclined to support solutions they considered unrealistic, such as the replacement of Israel by a 'secular, democratic state' – the proclaimed goal of the PLO leadership.

From the outset, however, the PLO enjoyed great popularity among Palestinians in the occupied territories.

In the years between 1967 and 1973, the PLO was carrying out an armed struggle first from Jordan, then from Lebanon [explained Dr al-Jarbawi]. The resistance movement had a high status among Palestinians after the defeat of the Arab armies in June 1967. Here were Palestinians fighting and inflicting casualties upon the enemy. Because the PLO was champion of armed resistance, the loyalty of Palestinians in the occupied territories was de facto. The PLO did not have to try to get the support of the people. You cannot deny support to the PLO when everyday it is carrying out armed resistance. Only after 1973, when the PLO began its diplomatic moves, did it have to compete with groups in the West Bank and Gaza.[32]

In 1973, the PLO began paying more attention to the occupied territories. The cause was the October 1973 Arab–Israeli war, which restored Arab pride and opened possibilities for a negotiated solution to the dispute. The UN Security Council passed Resolution 338, which urged all parties to begin negotiations for a settlement based upon UN Resolution 242, issued six months after the June 1967 Arab–Israeli war. This Resolution had stated the principle of Arab recognition of Israel in exchange for Israel's release of territories occupied in 1967. An international conference met briefly in Geneva, and the Arab states ended the oil embargo which they had imposed upon the West. It now appeared that if a Palestinian state were to be formed at all, it would have to be in the West Bank and Gaza. These developments led to changes in PLO political thinking and modifications of its policy. Certain groups within it began to speak of the need to build a 'national authority' in 'any liberated part of Palestinian territory'. Henceforth, the PLO would focus more and more upon the West Bank and Gaza. A shift had occurred in the relative political weight assigned the population of the occupied territories vis-à-vis the Diaspora.

The development of Palestinian nationalism in the territories was also a reason for the PLO leadership to become more interested in events there. The PLO leaders needed people inside to represent their organization. But according to a well-informed Palestinian analyst who requested anonymity, they also

feared that if a credible leadership – a national leadership – was established inside, it might be dangerous for the future. For a struggle might start between the inside and the outside. The PLO did not want a strong independent leadership to emerge, independent of the PLO that is. So it decided to have a hierarchy here, an elaborate organization.

The PLO was thus galvanized into striking even deeper roots in Gaza and the West Bank. The PLO created institutions to parallel the nationalist ones, and burrowed deep down into existing local structures. The West Bank General Federation of Labour Unions, once a stronghold of Communist influence, had by the mid-1970s allied itself with the PLO.[33]

The PLO created public organizations [remarked 'Aziz', the former political prisoner] with many committees, for health, education, and so on. A PLO hand inside made Palestinians feel better. For example, many villages had no clinics, public services, or medical centres. So Fatah followers built clinics in Salfit or in a camp like Deheishe. Fatah would pay to send someone from inside Deheishe to a university abroad to be a physician. In return the man would promise to open a clinic inside Deheishe. PLO organizations had lawyers, doctors – all kinds of skilled people.[34]

The PLO performed many services, not least of which was mediation. The Council for Higher Education in the West Bank received most of the financial aid needed for universities and other institutions via the PLO, through the mediation of Yasser Arafat in Kuwait and elsewhere.[35]

Local Palestinian groups also sought out PLO support, and not just for material reasons. As Lesch has observed, '. . . identification with the political structure that represented the entire Palestinian community helped to strengthen the morale and reduced the sense of isolation among those living under occupation.'[36] This was particularly true of the urban élite or patriotic bourgeoisie that emerged in the mid-1970s, whose members had proclaimed their support for the PLO.[37] 'If you are a local leader and want to be legitimate,' observed Dr al-Jarbawi, 'you must tie yourself to the PLO in some way.'[38]

If the PLO and the people in the occupied territories sought each other out and co-operated, competition between them also grew. Indigenous groups willingly accepted PLO support, worked to spread PLO influence, and permitted it to speak for and represent them internationally; but they insisted upon making their own decisions locally. As time passed, people began to urge the PLO leadership to moderate its political stands.[39] Local nationalist leaders linked their calls for international recognition of the PLO as the representative of the Palestinian people with demands for an independent state in the West Bank and Gaza only. In the mid-1970s, they urged the PLO leadership to attend an international peace conference, if invited, and pressed it to spell out clearly its aims and adopt a more realistic policy.

The PLO responded in turn. It entered into intense competition with both the Palestine National Front and the Palestine Communist Organization, whose secession from the Jordanian Communist Party in the mid-1970s signalled its nationalist orientation and commitment to a separate Palestinian state in the

West Bank and Gaza. The PLO leadership also set up a group of political brokers, men drawn from the national bourgeoisie, who, it assumed, would follow its orders and act in its interests.[40] It sought to prevent prominent national leaders becoming too strong lest influential leadership independent of the external PLO emerge.

When you look at the people who were deported in the period before the Intifada, [our Palestinian political analyst said] they are people who can command a student body, or a trade union, or Birzeit [University], but Birzeit only, a trade union only. They cannot move the West Bank and Gaza. The PLO outside did not want to have any prominent leaders at the top of the hierarchy.

The Palestine National Front, the Palestine Communist Organization, and other local groups were not challenging the PLO for leadership of the Palestinian national movement. As Sahliyeh has shown, they were committed to the PLO as their representative. They desired only that the PLO grant more influence to local groups. Thus, despite the friction and occasional violence, the competition between the PLO groups and local nationalist organizations must be regarded as a kind of politics. Ultimately, there was a marriage, not a divorce. The PLO became willing to grant Palestinians in the occupied territories greater freedom to make decisions on matters affecting them. And it gave more political weight to Palestinians from the West Bank and Gaza. In the mid-1970s, the PNC assigned 100 of its seats to representatives from the occupied territories. Palestinians who had been deported from the West Bank and Gaza occasionally received appointments to the PLO's Executive Committee.[41]

At the same time, the PLO was able to strengthen its hand. By 1987, al-Fatah had moved into control of all six trade unions in Gaza, and had acquired influence in many mosques. On the West Bank, it commanded a vast infrastructure comprising voluntary societies, youth groups, research institutes, press agencies, and most of the Palestinian press.[42] In 1987, the PCP (the old organization had been officially formed as a party in 1982), which had long sought inclusion, received membership on the PLO's Executive Committee. An organic relationship between the PLO

outside and the Palestinians inside the occupied territories had
been achieved.

By the late 1970s and early 1980s, one important arena in the
competition between the local political organizations and the
PLO groups was Palestinian youth, who were fast becoming an
important part of the emerging nationalist movement. These
were the very people, of course, who would later ignite the
Intifada. How were Palestinian youths brought into politics? How
did they become part of the movement of opposition to Israeli
rule? Owing to a high birthrate and a diminished infant mortality
rate, Palestinians were becoming a young society. In 1984, almost
half of the population of the West Bank and Gaza was fourteen
years of age or younger.[43] Expanding education, especially in the
West Bank, drew youths from all levels of society. Working-class
parents, many from refugee camps and villages, found it possible
to send their sons and daughters to one of the technical institutes,
teacher training centres, junior colleges and universities that had
sprung up. (Tuition was low and scholarships numerous in the
late 1970s and early 1980s.) There, unrestrained by family
responsibilities, young people engaged in open political debate
and learned how to organize themselves.[44] The PCP, the political
organizations, PLO groups, and Islamic parties all competed for
influence among campus youth. The National Guidance Committee, for example, created a seat for a student member. Providing
both money and an organizational framework for student
activities, PLO groups made big inroads. University students
formed themselves into four large blocs, each representing the
viewpoint of one of the three main PLO factions or that of the
PCP. An Islamic student bloc was also formed and became
active. On the West Bank, Shabiba (the pro-Fatah bloc) became
the largest and most powerful student organization. This was due
partly to the fact that large numbers of former political prisoners
had joined it, but also because al-Fatah scholarships were highly
valued. As Sahliyeh has shown, the established political groups
not only helped transform Palestinian youth into a political force,
but also brought to it a greater awareness of Palestinian national
goals.

Campus organizations provided young people with a basic
training in politics. Student congresses formulated platforms for
elections to student councils, submitted lists of candidates, and

established the operating procedures. All kinds of skills – bargaining, persuasion, political manipulation – were required for success in student elections. Control of a student council enabled the winning group to organize rallies and demonstrations, mobilize other students, issue statements and make political demands. Higher education also brought experience in confronting the Israeli occupation. In 1980, student councils organized committees to mobilize students against Israeli rule. Students developed and perfected tactics of civil disobedience. They organized strikes and barricaded streets with heaps of stone, burning tyres, and so on. When these actions caused the Israeli authorities to close down schools, students learned how to arrange and co-ordinate political protests in ways that would not lead to the entry of troops onto the campuses. As Sahliyeh has also observed, students became adept at propaganda techniques, inviting foreign journalists to make visits, organizing lecture tours abroad for Palestinian academics, convening press conferences, and holding summer camps for foreign students.

Young Palestinians took care to maintain solidarity with the wider society. College and university students engaged in community work programmes. They harvested olives, paved roads, planted trees, and visited families of those who had suffered from harsh Israeli treatment. Such voluntary or 'outreach' work, a mandatory part of education at many universities, reinforced the bonds that tied students to their society, and gave the budding youth movement a certain credibility. (Students also worked to preserve Palestinian culture by organizing music and other kinds of clubs.) In the early 1980s, university students began recruiting support from among the high schools – a very important development. Committees were organized inside the secondary schools. In 1983, the General Federation of High School Students was established. The youth movement, a product of the growth of Palestinian nationalism, was broadening and developing a mass base.

Islamic groups also brought young people into political activity and provided a focus for their frustration. As early as the mid-1970s, Islamic organizations began making inroads and gaining recruits.[45] Their aim was the establishment of an Islamic state, one based upon Islamic law. Their adherents argued that the secular nationalist solution had failed and that the situation demanded a more comprehensive approach. Of these groups, the largest and most important was the Muslim Brotherhood. 'This organization started in Palestine in the 1930s,' explained Dr Abu-Amr, who has written a book on the subject:

In their view, they preceded al-Fatah and the PLO. They see themselves as the movement that has the history, the tradition. The Muslim Brotherhood perceives itself as a world movement. 'We won't obscure ourselves by working under the wings of the nationalist movement,' they say.[46]

In the 1970s and early 1980s, the Muslim Brotherhood gained social influence in lower-class sections of the towns and in refugee camps, and found fertile ground among young Gazans working in Israel, who were subjected to humiliating treatment, horrible work conditions and unprotected by any labour laws.[47] The Muslim Brotherhood then tried to infiltrate the educational institutions. Its three strongholds in the West Bank were al-Najah and Hebron Universities, and al-da'wa wa usul al-din, a religious seminary near Jerusalem; and in Gaza, the Islamic University. The Muslim Brotherhood and other Islamic groups captured control of student councils in various places and generally grew in strength (they gained influence at Birzeit University, for example). This competition naturally aroused the concern of the PLO leadership, which intensified its activities and mobilized its secular youth blocs against the Muslims.

These Muslim groups, however, did not make a great impact upon the secular national movement, because their approach was conservative, not radical. They emphasized reform of the individual as the first step towards changing society. They were basically apolitical. 'The Islamic Jihad was the only [Islamic] group calling for armed struggle against Israel in the months before the Intifada,' observed Dr al-Jarbawi.[48] The Muslim Brotherhood was not a movement to counter the occupation, but a movement encouraged by the occupation. How did the Israeli authorities help this movement? 'They did not give them money but moral support,' commented Yehuda Litani, correspondent for the *Jerusalem Post*.[49] 'Their men were not arrested or, when they were arrested, they would be released first.' The purpose behind this, of course, was to create trouble for the nationalists, and especially the PLO.

In the early 1980s, then, most Palestinians did not feel themselves threatened by the Islamic movement. Secular nationalism was too strong and deeply rooted. Society was coming together, not breaking apart. The influence of modern education, bringing together Christian and Muslim Palestinians and reducing the influence of the family and clan, and the effects of the occupation itself, were unifying factors. Palestinian youths, be they nationalists or members of Islamic groups, engaged in many common activities, working in villages and refugee camps, and organizing opposition to the occupation. Muslim youth groups found that they could work and cooperate with al-Fatah's Shabiba.

In the early 1980s, Palestinian youths of all persuasions began to turn more militant. There were three reasons for this. The downturn in the economy and rising inflation hit Palestinian incomes hard. 'The stagnation of the economy and true negative growth was a very important factor in the daily misery of the people,' noted Dr Bishara.[50] 'People who lost jobs in the [Persian] Gulf region could not find jobs here.' The grinding harshness of the occupation was another factor. More and more Palestinians were stopped, searched, detained, arrested, harassed and humiliated.

The third reason was a growing dissatisfaction and even disgust with the entire older generation for having failed to do anything to improve the situation. This disillusionment was fostered in part by a split that occurred within the PLO after the destruction of its political–administrative apparatus in Beirut, and the scattering of its fighting units in nine Arab countries, as a result of Israel's 1982 invasion of Lebanon.[51] This not only cut off the PLO leadership from its supporters in the refugee camps of Lebanon, but it also dealt a death blow to the PLO doctrine of armed struggle. How could the PLO carry out armed struggle when it no longer had a base of operations against Israel? After this, Yasser Arafat accelerated efforts, begun earlier, toward negotiation and compromise, aiming at a dialogue with the US. As a consequence, the PFLP and the DFLP broke with him (they were re-united in 1987). In February 1985, Arafat struck a deal with King Hussein (later cancelled), which called for a confederation between a future Palestinian state and Jordan. 'For twenty years we have been saying that we don't want Hussein,' exclaimed one frustrated West Banker, whose words probably expressed the sentiments felt by many Palestinians when they received the news of the Arafat–Hussein agreement. Their discouragement must have been compounded when certain senior Palestinian person- alities – men with no mass base or any real constituency – began speaking about unification with Jordan as the only way to end the occupation. Despair was causing some members of the old bourgeoisie to lower their expectations.[52] And with it, they were losing what little standing they had in the wider society, especially among young people.

Secular Palestinian youths had never been subordinated to the PLO leadership. al-Fatah and other PLO youth blocs were pro- PLO by choice. Supported by the PLO, they were none the less independent of it. Shabiba, for example, could take a position far more militant than that of al-Fatah. With the split in the PLO and the acceleration of Israeli efforts to annex the occupied territories (see chapter 2), many young Palestinians felt that they had to take matters into their own hands. These young people, as we have seen, were not divorced from their society. On the contrary, they were in close touch with the trade unions, women's committees and other groups which had grown up during the occupation and which formed the backbone of the nationalist movement. Yet time seemed to be running out. Action was needed.

In 1981, a cycle of violence began. Confrontations between the soldiers and Palestinians became more intense and occurred with greater frequency. High school youths became more involved in strikes and demonstrations. Palestinians from the working-class created by wage labour in Israel also began to defy Israeli troops, especially in Gaza. Rock-throwing incidents and demonstrations now sprung from local initiatives rather than externally planned or organized activity. This brought Meron Benvenisti to declare the inauguration of a new phase in Palestinian resistance. 'Violence,' he wrote in his 1987 Report, 'is largely carried out in broad daylight by individuals and groups who spontaneously express their feelings, undeterred by the consequences of their actions.'[53] The time had come for Palestinians to bring themselves out of their situation.

2

From acquiescence to resistance

In examining the reasons for the outbreak of the Intifada, one is forced to ask not only why this revolt occurred when it did, but why it took Palestinians twenty years to stage an uprising. Since the beginning of the Intifada, Palestinian youths have also asked this question of their fathers, who have had to explain to their sons why their generation did not rise up against the occupation. It is not true, of course, that no resistance occurred in two decades of Israeli rule. Gazans put up fierce resistance after the Israelis occupied the Strip in 1967. Revolts broke out in various localities in 1979, 1980 and 1982.[1] However, it took twenty years for a general uprising to materialize, and many West Bankers and Gazans would privately acknowledge that for a good part of that time Palestinians acquiesced in, rather than resisted, Israeli rule. Why? The answer to this question is a complex one.

My father was in his 20s in 1967 [commented one Palestinian youth]. 'People benefited from the occupation, at least at first,' he told us. 'The Jordanians had put a lot of pressure on us, and wouldn't let anything happen. Then the Israelis came in and let us work in Israel. Suddenly there was more money. No one wanted to revolt. This didn't mean that we liked Israel. Things did get worse in the 1980s. When the Likud came to power, pressure built up, so the younger generation didn't see things the same way that the fathers did.'[2]

The first cause of Palestinian acquiescence in the early years, then, was economic. In the late 1960s, the Israeli government, facing labour shortages, opened its market up to Palestinian workers. With wage scales higher in Israel than in the occupied territories, thousands of Palestinians began crossing the Green Line each day to perform unskilled or semi-skilled work in

agriculture, the construction industry and municipal services.
Higher income earnings meant greater purchasing power, and
this was reflected in increases in per capita food consumption, per
capita GNP, and other areas.[3] In the early 1970s, the Israelis also
began investing selectively in branches of Palestinian production.
The aim was to increase commercial farming without transforming
the rural infrastructure itself.[4] New technology was introduced,
credit advanced to farmers, and joint projects sponsored.
Between 1967 and the end of the 1970s, the gross domestic
product of the West Bank and Gaza grew at an average annual
rate of 10 per cent and 8 per cent respectively.[5] The peak years of
economic growth came between 1970–6, when an expanding
Israeli economy made additional capital available and increased
the demand for labour.[6] By 1977, the percentage of persons from
the West Bank and Gaza Strip employed in Israel had reached
27.8 and 35 per cent respectively.[7]

Higher Palestinian incomes led to consumerism and further
integration into the Israeli economy. 'In 1970–1972, Israel put
electricity into Gaza,' recounted Danny Rubenstein, correspondent for the Hebrew-language daily *Davar*.[8] 'People started buying
refrigerators, television sets, radios so the standard of living went
up dramatically.' Israeli state monopolies like Tnuva, which
manufactured dairy products, began marketing their goods in the
occupied territories. Israeli companies sent threads to the West
Bank where Palestinian women worked them up into nearly-
finished fabrics that were returned to Israel, completed and then
re-exported to the occupied territories where they were purchased
by Palestinians. West Bankers and Gazans became accustomed to
buying old refrigerators, television sets and used cars from
Israelis, thus helping maintain the cycle of production. 'You
would be astonished at the consumer habits of the upper and
middle classes,' said Dr al-Jarbawi.[9] 'People used to buy a lot.
You would see very expensive new cars. Every year you would
change a car.' To supply the population with foodstuffs and
provisions from Israel, distributors and other middle-men –
brokers, importers–exporters, businessmen – arose. 'We used to
call these people the "war rich",' said Dr Jad Issac of Beit
Sahour.[10]

If increased incomes and consumer spending prevented many
Palestinians from apprehending the dangers posed to them by the

occupation more quickly, the safety valve of work in the Arab world also helped produce acquiescence. During the 1970s, owing to increased oil production and higher prices, many Palestinians found lucrative employment in the Persian Gulf. Transfer payments from Palestinians outside to their families inside the occupied territories were a very important source of exchange. This additional income contributed to consumerism, but it also made possible higher education for Palestinian children (which raised political awareness) and the building of all kinds of social organizations that later became a base for opposition to the occupation.

By the mid-1970s, the West Bank and Gaza had become economically dependent upon Israel in ways that disadvantaged Palestinians. Israeli agricultural produce, for example, could enter the territories without restrictions, but Palestinian farmers were not free to send their goods to Israel.[11] Quotas placed upon West Bank produce were lifted only in times of shortages or excessive demand. Israeli investments in the occupied territories were directed toward crops that would not compete with its own. In Gaza, the Israelis emphasized vegetable production rather than citrus – the mainstay of Gaza's economy.[12] In the West Bank, it was olives and mutton – produced in limited supplies in Israel – that received the most attention.[13] The Palestinian economy itself was left unprotected against the price fluctuations and slowdowns of the Israeli economy, which benefited from direct and indirect supports.

Palestinian workers in Israel subsidized a system that discriminated against them.[14] Wages paid to registered Palestinian workers were considerably lower than those given their Israeli counterparts, who also paid lower effective tax rates. One per cent of registered Palestinian workers' wages was automatically deducted for the Histadrut (Israel's General Federation of Labour), even though it refused to provide them with services or permit them to become members. A much larger amount was deducted from their wages for pension, health and social services, although they received scarcely any of these benefits. 'The Palestinian workers came to realize,' said Danny Rubenstein, 'that though some Israelis might make the same amount in salary as they do, their real earnings are only one-half of what Israelis receive because they obtain no benefits.'[15] Whilst Palestinians had welcomed their increased salaries and enhanced purchasing power, the passage of time brought growing awareness of the disadvantages of economic dependence.

Another reason for Palestinian acquiescence was that in the early years, the occupation did not greatly interfere in the daily lives of most people. Minimum intervention was the policy of the Labour government, which believed that if it could enable the population to lead a 'normal' life, Palestinians would be brought to accept the status quo and weaned away from their own national aspirations.[16] Improving the lives of the people was the major justification for Israel's establishment and maintenance of elementary schools, hospitals and clinics in the occupied territories. In keeping with this policy, the military government – master and absolute ruler of the territories – endeavoured to confine the use of its coercive powers to particular cases, rather than applying them indiscriminately to large segments of the civilian population. Localized rather than collective punishment was the rule. Not until the mid-1970s, for example, did curfews begin to be widely used as a means of collective punishment in order to curb demonstrations and other disturbances.[17] Even though they could have restricted Palestinian physical planning much more, Israeli authorities limited their intervention to preventing construction in military areas.[18] They were also disposed to grant permits and licences. 'During the early years, very few requests to open a newspaper were refused,' commented Ibrahim Karaeen, a Palestinian journalist in East Jerusalem.[19] 'There was harassment, but the policy was to interfere in as few aspects [of life] as possible. To a large extent, there was freedom of movement, all within the context of the occupation.' 'The special case of being a Palestinian under Israeli occupation became clear only in the mid-1970s,' observed Dr Azmi Bishara, Associate Professor of Philosophy at Birzeit University.[20]

Palestinians realized that Israel would give them certain things, let them do certain things, that they had a choice to build or not build universities, make trade unions. Saying 'yes' to this put Palestinians on the road to mass political struggle. There was no democracy under the occupation, but they [Israelis] would let you print papers. Trade unions were allowed to operate with harassments, but they still functioned.

By permitting a measure of free action, the occupation authorities hoped to control and contain developments in the Palestinian sector.

Israel, of course, had had to provide some outlet for the pent-up energies of a people who had long since become a nation and who possessed a strong sense of their own identity as Palestinians. Otherwise, something like an Intifada might have occurred then and there. Enjoying higher wages and improved living standards, people thus attempted to lead 'normal' lives with the occupation on their backs. This did not mean that they accepted Israeli rule, only that in the early years at least, most Palestinians did not regard the occupation as a direct threat to their survival.

As time passed, some Palestinians began to perceive such a threat. Shortly after its conquest of the West Bank and Gaza, Israel began confiscating land and settling its own Jewish nationals on it. In doing so, the occupation authorities relied upon interpretations of old Ottoman and Jordanian laws, which were kept in force; when precedents could not be found, they issued orders and regulations themselves. The most common early means of acquiring land was to requisition it for military purposes. A piece of land would be declared necessary for security needs, seized, and a Jewish settlement established. This action was accepted by Israel's High Court of Justice, which had agreed to rule on petitions from area residents against the occupation authorities. Jewish settlements, the Court declared, were part of the territorial defence system and thus fulfilled a security need.[21] The second method of confiscating land was to declare it to be 'state property'. When Israel conquered the West Bank and Gaza, it took over all land registered in the name of the Jordanian government, and subsequently added to this properties which could be considered state land on the basis of old government documents.[22] Under the Labour government (1967–77), 40 settlements were established in the West Bank.[23] These contained a Jewish population of 5,023 in 1977. Most of these settlements were located in the Jordan Valley region or the Etzion Bloc (southwest of Jerusalem, north of Hebron).

Such concentration was based upon a geopolitical strategy for peace first presented by Labour minister Yigal Allon in July 1967 and revised four times.[24] This 'Allon Plan' called for permanent annexation by Israel of the Jordan Valley and the south Mount Hebron area, and administration by Jordan of the highland areas, where the bulk of the Palestinian population lived. These areas, along with a portion of the Gaza Strip, would eventually form part of a Jordanian–Palestinian state. The argument advanced was that Israel's security required defensible borders, and that these should be the Jordan Valley and the Judaean desert, with a line of Jewish settlements as a guarantee. Areas containing large Palestinian populations should not be annexed to Israel. (East Jerusalem, annexed by Israel in 1967, was the exception to this rule.) Jewish settlements established by the Labour Party thus tended to be located in areas far from Palestinian population centres. To avoid the incorporation of the West Bank into Israel proper, the Labour government also made no changes in the road system, built by the Jordanians, which ran on a north–south axis.[25] During the first decade, the average absolute annual settlement growth was 770 settlers – not a large number.[26] Nevertheless, this was a very important beginning.

The settlements unite two factors [observed Dr Bishara]. The economic factor is confiscation of the land, stretching for a long period, so there is less possibility [for Palestinians] to develop agriculture, to invest. The other side is political, and emphasizes that you are not in control, that you are under the sovereignty of Israel. This causes frustration and political resentment against the occupation.[27]

By the mid-1970s, more and more Palestinians were becoming aware of what it meant to be occupied by Israel.

From the beginning of the occupation, Palestinians enjoyed neither political rights nor administrative control over their lives. Direct Israeli rule was imposed through the medium of a military government which was free of all checks and balances. The area commander was both the chief executive and a supreme legislative authority. He also appointed local officials, including court judges. The only Palestinian part of the Israeli control system was the large network of agents and informants, recruited and paid by Israeli intelligence, who reported everything that occurred in their localities to the military authorities. By requiring Palestinians to obtain licences for nearly every activity, the Israelis enhanced their control and created greater dependence. Family reunification permits, for example, were widely sought by Gazans and West Bankers for relatives who had been residing outside the areas at the time of the June 1967 War or who had emigrated shortly thereafter. A very sensitive issue among Palestinians, family reunification was used by the Israelis as a device to reward those who co-operated with the military government.[28] The withholding of permits was a way of punishing malcontents and others. This method – the 'carrot and the stick', as it was called – became a characteristic feature of Israeli rule.

In the occupied territories, the military government was the law. Juridically, its power derived from both Jordanian legislation and the harsh provisions of the British Defence Emergency Regulations. Military orders also had legal force and enjoyed the status of primary legislation, which could not be overturned by the Israeli High Court of Justice. A law could therefore be found or manufactured to justify practically anything, and it was this that enabled the Israeli government to claim legality for its actions in the West Bank and Gaza.

There was, of course, another body of law that could be applied to the Palestinians. In the view of the world community, including private relief and other organizations, the West Bank and Gaza were 'occupied territories', areas temporarily under Israeli control pending a final settlement. This meant that the Palestinian population was subject to international law – specifically, the provisions of the Hague Regulations (1907) and the Fourth Geneva Convention (1949), which dealt with the treatment of civilians in areas occupied by military forces.[29] Among other things, these rules forbade deportation, the transfer of civilians to areas outside the occupied territories, and the destruction of real or personal property.[30] Israel's attitude toward these regulations was equivocal. In 1971, its Attorney General stated that Israel took upon itself to follow the humanitarian provisions of international law as it applied to the West Bank and Gaza.[31] With the passage of time, however, this position was eroded. Israel's military government cancelled the precedence of the Geneva Convention over the orders issued by the West Bank military commander; and the Israeli government itself subsequently argued that international law did not apply to Gaza and the West Bank. These areas, it maintained, had not been under the sovereignty of Egypt and Jordan at the time they were occupied by Israel, and thus were not 'occupied territories', strictly speaking. Israel's government opposed efforts to bring its actions under the provisions of international law, arguing before the High Court of Justice that the Geneva Convention was binding only between governments, and that Palestinian residents had no right to take legal action to secure its implementation. In a sense, this debate was moot, since international law gave an occupying power wide latitude to act in matters relating to its own security. 'The High Court of Justice has its hands tied in the territories,' observed Moshe Negbi, an Israeli journalist and legal commentator for the Hebrew-language newspaper *Hadashot*.

In the appeals process, a military commander can always claim security as justification for an action. Once he gives an affidavit to the [High] Court [of Justice] that something is needed for security, it [the Court] has to have evidence that the army is lying and this is difficult. It would be his word against that of the Arab. In twenty years of occupation, only twice has the High Court of Justice ruled for an Arab and against the military in cases where the military claimed security as reason.[32]

The role of the High Court of Justice was thus a secondary one, and international law was no guarantor of Palestinian rights.

In the occupied territories, political expression by Palestinians was considered subversive and punishable by law.[33] Palestinians who openly criticized Israeli policies could be placed under house arrest, that is, confined to their places of residence for six months, with the requirement not to leave the house at night and to report regularly (sometimes twice daily) to the police. People could be punished for holding certain opinions, or for refusing to inform on their friends.

To enforce its writ, Israel's military administration had available a wide range of powers. Censorship could be enforced against Palestinian publications and public performances.[34] Israeli military authorities had the power to confiscate, seal, and destroy houses.[35] A home might be demolished if a bomb had been thrown or shots fired from it; if it lay on a road near, or was located in an area, where a security offence had been committed; or if it belonged to the family of a person who was suspected of having committed a security offence. The commander did not have to make a report on his action, nor had the owner of the house to be charged with any offence. The blowing up of a house was carried out prior to the opening of legal proceedings against a suspect, and only hours after the family occupants had been notified of it. Entire extended families were thus put out into the streets. (They were not entitled to receive any compensation from the government.) Israeli military authorities could also close off areas and impose curfews.[36] Curfews might be precautionary, declared in anticipation of trouble (as, for example, following a house demolition); or punitive, imposed upon areas where an incident or rioting had taken place. In many cases, people were not allowed to leave their homes. Food supplies and services were disrupted, and wage-earners deprived of work. Administrative detention was also permitted. Palestinians could be apprehended without a warrant, and held for a period of three or six months without charges ever being brought against them.[37] Such actions, however, had to be reported within 96 hours to the counsel of the regional commander, and an appeals committee automatically reviewed each case. Palestinian administrative detainees could see lawyers, but the evidence against them remained secret. In addition to this, the military government could avail itself of town and house arrest; arrest with trial (for the commission of a crime), held in military courts; and the deportation of Palestinians from the occupied territories. This last measure, expressly forbidden by the Geneva Convention, was none the less accepted by Israel's High Court of Justice on the grounds that this provision of the Geneva Convention had been aimed at preventing large-scale population transfers, rather than the expulsion of individual persons (as with deportations from the West Bank and Gaza).[38]

Palestinians thus possessed no rights that could be defended against the authorities of an occupation which was by no means benign. By the end of 1968, forcible exile and other pressures had caused between 60,000 and 100,000 Gazans to emigrate to Arab countries. Between 1967–78, 1,224 Palestinian houses were sealed or demolished.[39] In large part, this was the result of Israeli efforts to eliminate resistance and eradicate PLO structures and membership. Such actions were applied in particular cases, but were not the general rule.

After 1977, the situation began to change. This was the result of the triumph of the right-wing Likud bloc, led by Menahem Begin, whose victory in the 1977 election spelled the end of the domination of government by the Labour Party. Under Labour, Israel's presence in the West Bank and Gaza had been justified by reference to its security needs, and the occupation not regarded as permanent. Under the Likud, an all-out effort was made to render the occupation permanent by tying the areas irreversibly to Israel. By taking control of land and other resources, the Likud hoped to confront the international community with a fait accompli and prejudice the outcome of any final settlement on the disposition of the occupied territories.

The dividing line of 1977 should not be regarded too schematically, however, since the process of annexation had begun earlier. It was Labour that had introduced changes proscribed by international law.

The idea of territories being occupied is that you [the occupying power] are to hold onto the area without changing it [observed André Rosenthal, an Israeli lawyer]. You are not to impose new taxes, you can't build new roads and settlements. You can't do anything in the occupied territories that will have an effect after the occupation [has ended]. But the military government did impose new taxes, did bring civilians in, and the High Court of Justice let them get away with it, saying that there never has been an occupation that lasted this long, so it is unique.[40]

The Labour government had also made the occupied territories into a market for Israeli-manufactured products and a source of cheap labour, not to mention its inauguration of the land confiscation and settlement programmes. Military orders issued during Labour rule would also serve as precedents for the Likud to advance its own policies. Labour thus helped start a process that became known as creeping annexation – the gradual imposition of Israeli control and jurisdiction at all levels without a formal act of annexation.[41]

Labour leaders possessed an ideological commitment to the land of Israel, and this had made it difficult for them to resist temptations and pressures arising from Israel's victory in the June 1967 War. This victory had had an intoxicating effect upon many Israelis, who began referring to the West Bank by the names of Judaea and Samaria, drawn from the history of ancient Israel. Calls arose for Jews to take possession of these lands. Gush Emunim, a religious Zionist movement advocating the establishment of Israeli sovereignty over the West Bank and Gaza, founded settlements outside the areas of the Allon Plan, but with the full backing of Shimon Peres and other Labour leaders.[42] The

Labour Party itself even 'fudged', authorizing the establishment of settlements in the highlands beyond the areas permitted by the Allon Plan.[43] Labour leaders too, it seems, could not resist the temptation to 'reclaim the ancestral heritage'.

It was under the Likud, however, that the status of the West Bank and Gaza was fundamentally altered and the ground prepared for the Intifada. The Palestinians had long since become a nation with a strong political consciousness and the capacity to sustain itself. The Likud's attempt to vest more and more control in its own hands, and to assert Israeli sovereignty over the whole of the West Bank and Gaza, was bound to meet with resistance, especially as Palestinians had never accepted the legitimacy of the occupation. In the early years (before 1977), Palestinians had mollified themselves with the thought that the occupation was temporary. By the mid- and late 1970s, many realized that Israel had come to stay, and they were beginning to understand what this meant for them. 'The denial of natural rights and more harsh treatment caused eventually an awareness that "we are occupied,"' commented Dr Abu-Amr, a political analyst and lecturer in cultural studies at Birzeit University. 'Everyone felt threatened. Your national existence was targeted. This realization finally sunk into the consciousness of Palestinians, so the occupation was rejected.'[44]

Likud policy had three purposes: to acquire control of land and its resources; to establish a massive Jewish presence through settlements, and to construct an infrastructure of legal and support services for them; and to restrict Palestinian development. Official Israeli blueprints spoke of the need to fragment Palestinian population areas, but to connect those areas of Jewish settlement.[45] Soon after the Likud took power, Israeli authorities began studying the land situation and learned that most Palestinian properties in the West Bank were not registered.[46] Land registration had occurred during the British mandate, and this was continued by the Jordanians, but had proceeded slowly. In the rural areas, land located near villages was customarily designated for use of the villagers, or for communal pasture, or for future village use. Villagers knew which lands were held in common tenure and who owned what, so most people felt no need to register land. Once it had learned of this situation, the Likud government established a new definition of state lands, based upon its own interpretation of the Ottoman land law of 1858, which was in fact the application to the occupied territories of criteria prevailing in Israel.[47] All uncultivated and unregistered lands were automatically declared state property unless Palestinians could prove ownership. Had Palestinians been able to continue registering their lands, the Israelis would undoubtedly have been unable to take control of properties on so massive a scale, but this option was denied Palestinians after a 1968 Military Order interrupted the process of land registration that had been continued from the period of Jordanian rule.[48]

By adopting this new definition of state land based upon the double criteria of non-cultivation and non-registration, Likud planners made it clear that Israeli control was no longer provisional. (Requisition of land for military purposes – the chief means of confiscation under Labour – had emphasized the temporary nature of the occupation.) By 1984, the total amount of land taken by Israel under this category had reached 1,800,000 dunams (one dunam = 0.25 acres). Lands were also seized through various other mechanisms, as, for example, expropriation for public use (50,000 dunams were so taken, with 100,000 being designated for future expropriation).[49] Military orders were also used. According to Order 393 (1970), a military commander could prohibit construction in an area. By the mid-1980s, 580,000 dunams had been placed under such restrictions.[50] Other lands were declared combat zones (Military Order 271, 1968), and thus rendered virtually inaccessible to Palestinian property-owners. By the mid-1980s, 250,000 dunams had been declared to be 'nature reserves', another way of restricting Palestinian land use and construction. While purportedly aimed at protecting the environment, nature reserve declarations were regarded by the military authorities as part of Israel's effort to gain control of land.

The main object of the Likud's land seizure programme was to acquire sufficient space for Jewish settlements, which became greatly expanded, quantitatively and qualitatively. The magnitude of the change can be grasped by a comparison with settlements under the Labour Party. Between 1978 and 1987, the average growth was 5,960 Jewish settlers a year, as against 770 during the years of Labour rule. Under Labour, $750 million of public money were invested, compared with $1.67 billion spent by the Likud.[51] Labour settlements tended to be agricultural in nature, and were located in areas far from Palestinian population centres. Under the Likud, settlers tended to be white-collar, upper-middle-class Israelis who were placed in areas close to Palestinian population concentrations. Likud concentrated particularly upon locating settlers within easy commuting distance of Tel Aviv and Jerusalem. To the Likud's ideological criterion of redeeming the land, a new one – 'quality of life' – was thus added. By providing housing subsidies and other services at cut-rate prices, the Likud was able to attract non-ideological Jews to settlements in the West Bank for material reasons. The underlying purpose was to create a domestic lobby that would support the retention of the occupied territories by Israel.[52]

A master plan, drawn up in 1983 by the Ministry of Agriculture and the Settlement Department of the World Zionist Organization, called for the settling of 100,000 Jews in the occupied territories by 1986, the establishment of non-agricultural West Bank settlements in the Jerusalem and Tel Aviv metropolitan areas, the provision of infrastructure for them, and the creation of a maximum spread of Jewish settlement areas all over the West Bank (in order to surround and fragment Palestinian communities).[53] While the target figure of 100,000 settlers was not met, this plan achieved considerable success. A whole range of services was extended to Jewish settlers, who enjoyed full rights of Israeli citizenship, the protection of Israeli law, and control of their own local and regional councils. An integral part of the Israeli army, settlers were virtually independent of the military government, possessing their own weapons and serving under their own commanders.[54] The settlements not only constituted a privileged sector, but they also facilitated the physical absorption of the West Bank and Gaza into the Israeli system. Bypassing Palestinian population centres, roads were built from settlements to the metropolitan areas of Jerusalem and Tel Aviv. And in order to provide greater accessibility to the settlements, the old north–south road system was supplanted by one running on an east–west axis.[55] Physical planning was thus used to help link the occupied territories to Israel proper.

Since Israeli-controlled lands were to a great extent properties seized from Palestinians, the indigenous population naturally grew concerned. So much land had been transferred that the area of arable and grazing land available to Palestinians was reduced.[56] This growing apprehension was compounded by a feeling of helplessness, as Palestinians saw control over decisions about landed property taken out of the hands of indigenous bodies. When local West Bank courts, where land disputes had originally been litigated, began issuing injunctions against some land acquisitions, the Israelis removed authority from them and gave it to a military review board.[57] For a Palestinian, land, and the stone house that usually sat on it, was not just a piece of property. It was the place where one's father and grandfather had lived, where one had been born, and where one would die. It was an important source of identity and of family values. Its worth could not be measured in material terms, and the loss of even a part of it hurt.

The Israeli soldiers came in the early morning hours and put up a fence around part of our property [recounted 'Muhammad', a West Bank villager who lost 2.5 dunams of land under a requisition for military use order]. When we awoke, we saw the fence and a soldier sitting there. He said that the land belonged to the government. After a week, the people of our village tore down the fence, but the soldiers returned and put it up again. The entire village lost between 80–100 dunams. People had documents from the municipality proving it was their land, but the military said 'no'. A settlement was erected, and there is still a military camp there.[58]

Israel's land seizure and settlement programme placed Palestinians in active competition with Jewish settlers for scarce water and other resources. In Gaza, most Jewish settlements were located along the southern coast near the aquifers so that they could draw water easily from the underground springs.[59] Jewish settlers had more water allocated to them proportionately and had to pay less for it than Palestinians. Electricity usage for a Palestinian family was fixed by the Israeli authorities at less than half that for a Jewish family, and was even lower given that Palestinian families were on average 50 per cent larger than their Jewish counterparts.[60]

It did not take people long to apprehend that they were facing a collective, rather than personal or individual, threat. 'We want you out of Palestine,' was the message given the people, all of them,' observed Dr al-Jarbawi. 'And it was not only the uprooting, but that this was accompanied by a process of humiliating the Palestinians.'[61] Palestinian men who married women from East Bloc or Arab countries were prohibited from bringing their wives into the occupied territories to live with them. Wives could come for visits, but they could not stay.[62] Palestinian males between the ages of 16 and 60 resident abroad were not allowed to return to the West Bank and Gaza. Two years after the Likud came to power, the number of unprocessed family reunification permits had reached 150,000. Palestinians saw this as an attempt to induce them to leave, or at least to prevent their population growing. With the passage of time, increasing numbers of Palestinians had little doubt of Israel's intent to establish permanent control over the West Bank and Gaza.

After 1981, pressure really built up. Not only did the Likud intensify its restrictions and resort to harsh repressive measures, but economic hardships also arose that brought an end to the individual prosperity of earlier years. This painful development helped people perceive the dangers of dependence upon Israel, which by 1984 was providing 90 per cent of all West Bank's imports and taking 55 per cent of its exports.[63] Palestinian economic growth in the early years had been artificial. It had relied almost entirely upon externally generated sources of income, rather than an enhanced productive capacity in the economy. The Israeli authorities had discouraged the development of a strong Palestinian economic sector. Thus, when Israel's economy entered into its recession (beginning in the late 1970s), Palestinians lacked an infrastructure that could mitigate the difficulties. The effects were felt much more severely in the West Bank and Gaza than in Israel, where a system of direct and indirect supports existed.[64] (Israelis, for example, enjoyed automatic salary adjustments geared to cost-of-living increases.) Between 1981 and 1985, the Palestinian economy showed real stagnation.[65] In Gaza, citrus yields decreased, as did labour productivity and per capita income.[66] Dependence underscored the bitter truth that Palestinians had no real economic control over their lives.

Nearly everyone suffered. Those who worked in Israel (in 1984, 32.5 and 46 per cent of West Bankers and Gazans, respectively)[67] saw the earlier benefits of increased incomes destroyed by Israel's currency devaluations and inflation. Palestinian farmers in the Jordan Valley were hurt by the imposition of quotas upon the production of eggplants, tomatoes and other vegetables – a measure designed to protect Israeli farmers.[68] And Palestinian consumers in the West Bank suffered from price rises of close on 500 per cent.[69]

To be sure, other factors contributed to producing economic misery. Falling oil prices, the 1984 economic recession in the Arab countries, and the Iran–Iraq war spelt the end of good employment opportunities for Palestinian college graduates, who were forced into unskilled and semi-skilled work in Israel and the occupied territories, or into unemployment. 'Thousands of academics were unemployed,' commented Dr Bishara. 'Graduates of Birzeit [University] worked in restaurants.'[70] The slowdown in the Jordanian economy (which in 1984 took 45 per cent of Palestinian exports) decreased the demand for Palestinian agricultural products.[71] 1984 was also a bad agricultural year owing to drought, and a warm winter.[72] The root cause of these difficulties, however, was the occupation.

A case in point is the decline of Palestinian agriculture, until 1981 the most healthy area of the economy.[73] In the 1970s, as a result of mechanization, technological innovation, investment in expertise and capital, and new methods of cultivation, agricultural production had risen. But this had come about without any alteration in its resource base. No increase in available area or land under irrigation had occurred; marketing and credits remained undeveloped; and so on. As explained by Benvenisti, Palestinian agriculture had been permitted to develop, but only in ways that would not affect Israeli agriculture or involve a fiscal drain on the Israeli economy. It had been made to fit into the Israeli system, and in the process had become totally dependent upon it. Fluctuations in the Israeli sector had an immediate impact upon the Palestinian farming growth rate. After 1981, with Israel's economy in deep recession and Israel's inflation running in three-digit figures, Palestinian agriculture could no longer function within the limits imposed by Israel. Accordingly, productivity declined. The Palestinian economy had been kept in a permanent state of underdevelopment. The occupation had lost the single most important factor in concealing its true nature and thus in winning acquiescence. The money had dried up.

Coinciding with this was the intensification of Israeli pressure and the imposition of restrictions on the Palestinian population. 'The dividing line was [Ariel] Sharon,' said journalist Ibrahim Karaeen.[74]

After he became Defence Minister [in 1981] it took a long time to get permission to open a newspaper. After Sharon, you needed three types of approval, all disconnected. You applied for permission from the Commissioner of Jerusalem, who got permission from the Ministry of Interior. You applied to military headquarters, West Bank, for permission to publish and distribute the paper in the West Bank. And you did the same for Gaza. All three were separate. Once you got the permit there were limitations concerning the distribution of papers in the West Bank and Gaza. The Commissioner of Jerusalem had the power to suspend or withdraw your licence even after you got it, and you must submit all to the censor. What made it impossible for journalists to work was that censorship became unbearable, supported by new laws introduced by the Knesset. These laws made it a crime to express support in any way for the PLO. Even if you wrote an article in which it could be inferred that you supported the PLO, this was the basis for trial. I was interrogated six times.

Restrictions increased. Some newspapers and magazines were closed or banned. Journalists were arrested, and denied permission to travel abroad. Some photographers were even prohibited from taking pictures under threat of the confiscation of their cameras.[75]

Israel also began subjecting Palestinians to check lists.[76] People applying for permits and licences had to pass a security checklist, that is, a search into their background to ascertain where they stood politically, if they had ever been in prison, or if any of their family members had a record or a question mark in their history. On this basis, a licence was granted or withheld. Soldiers at check points also carried lists of names and could turn pedestrians or car drivers back as a result. 'Checklists symbolized the occupation,' observed Dr Bishara. '[They showed] that political considerations were the most important thing.'[77]

After 1981, the military also began applying its broad coercive powers to Palestinian civilians in an ever-widening arc. These measures were collectively known as the 'iron fist' or 'strong arm', a policy first implemented in 1982 under the command of Chief of Staff Rafael Eitan. After August 1985, they were reintroduced by Defence Minister Rabin.[78] Benvenisti is correct when he states that Rabin's 'strong arm' methods came in response to an increase in demonstrations and protest activities by Palestinians.[79] After 1982, Palestinian opposition to the occupation intensified, violence was committed, and stone-throwing attacks increased. The principal beneficiary of this, of course, was the PLO, which constantly managed to organize itself and find expression. In the 1980s, then, the Palestinian–Israeli confrontation was slowly moving into a more dangerous phase.

In 1985 – the year of the 'strong arm' – the Israelis installed a large troop presence.[80] Special army units were stationed in Palestinian towns; roadblocks were set up; random searches carried out; and arrests made. Israeli troops raided Palestinian book and art fairs. Universities were shut down, and students detained. The issuing of family reunification permits was sharply cut back. Curfews were also used as a method of collective punishment. While the standing orders to soldiers regarding the use of live ammunition remained unaltered (troops were to fire only if their lives were endangered and after warning had been given), they received special instructions which permitted them to open fire if they found difficulty in apprehending runaway suspects. Palestinian casualties increased – as did complaints of humiliating treatment at the hands of Israeli soldiers.

Israel's resort to repressive methods can be demonstrated statistically.[81] Between 1980 and 1985, no deportations were carried out. By February, 1986, however, 35 Palestinians had been deported to Jordan. Administrative detention, suspended in 1980 owing to international and local protest, was re-established in 1985. By the end of that year, 131 Palestinians were being held without trial, as against 62 for the entire period 1980–5. Israeli authorities also made wider use of house demolitions and sealings. Between 1982 and 1984, very few houses had been demolished for security reasons. In 1985, 55 were destroyed, followed by 48 in 1986.

The particular way in which people were arrested and detained upset many Palestinians. People were often arrested by soldiers in the middle of the night. 'Soldiers march into houses and scare the living daylights out of everyone, including children,' commented Israeli lawyer André Rosenthal, who for three years prior to the Intifada defended Palestinians in Israeli military courts.

The accused is not allowed to take with him a change of clothes. No family visits are permitted for a period of time. The whole thing is designed to scare people. If you are arrested, the general rule is: after you confess you can see a lawyer. Everyone is beaten either when they are arrested or to get a confession out of them. You must be very tough not to break in these circumstances.[82]

Rosenthal's observations are borne out by the findings of the 1987 Landau Commission, whose report revealed that for sixteen years officers of the Israeli intelligence had routinely beaten and tortured Palestinian prisoners, extracting confessions from them and offering perjured testimony, as a matter of policy, in the courts.[83] In 1984–5, military courts in the West Bank tried almost 3,000 cases (a considerable increase over 1983), practically all of which resulted in prison sentences.[84]

The cumulative pressures generated by Israel's annexationist policy built up to the point where people could live with the occupation no longer. Restrictions and the monitoring of people's daily activities became the most repugnant feature of the Israeli's control system. In 1987, a computerized Data Bank was set up for the occupied territories. This 'ultimate instrument of population control' was designed to provide the authorities with a wide range of information on individuals and their families, including the names of 'friendlies' and 'hostiles', that could be used to determine which Palestinian applicants to grant or deny permits on everything from driving licences to water quotas and travel documents.[85] Palestinians were finding it ever more difficult to move around.

A group of us Christians from Beit Sahour [said one Palestinian resident] wanted to take a vacation to [the port of] Eilat. A tour was organized by our priest. We paid him the money, everything. Then the [area] military commander said 'no', that we could not leave our area. He did not give us any reason. Is this not our land too? Don't we have rights?[86]

'I do not want to go to Eilat,' commented Dr Hanan Ashrawi, Professor of English Literature at Birzeit University.

But in just everyday life I was blocked. A checkpoint prevented me from going to my work – Birzeit University. It was a question of not being secure in my own home and having no rights. The army could besiege the campus and shoot students. I could not think of anything without taking into account that Israel interfered in everything. Before us, Israel stood naked, stripped of its propaganda – a hostile presence constantly interfering in the details.[87]

Israel thus lost advantage of the other factor which had induced Palestinians to acquiesce in the occupation: non-intervention in their daily lives.

Israel's settlement movement continued its forward march. Between 1983 and 1986, the number of Jewish settlers increased by 118 per cent, housing units for them by 45 per cent, and public investments by 56 per cent.[88] Almost half of all West Bank lands and 40 per cent of the Gaza Strip had been brought under direct Israeli control.[89] If Palestinians had never liked or accepted the occupation, and had needed time to realize that it would not be temporary, there could no longer be any doubt as to the threat it posed to their survival as a people in a place they considered their homeland. By the mid-1980s, many were beginning to believe that it might not be long before the Israelis took all of the West Bank and Gaza – the remaining 20.7 per cent of mandatory Palestine that had been ruled by Britain. Palestinians were being pushed, shoved and set aside. Some complained of not being able to 'breathe'. They also knew that no help would come from the Arab states, preoccupied with the Iran–Iraq war and relatively indifferent to their plight in any case. The PLO had also been gravely weakened as a result of Israel's 1982 invasion of Lebanon. By the mid-1980s, all Palestinians had been affected in some way, even the upper class – the landowning class – which had been hard hit by Israeli land confiscations and restrictions. Israel's annexationist policy had turned the status quo into a war. Because of the increased number of settlers, incidents between Palestinians and Jews grew. Palestinian youths threw stones at settlers' cars. Groups of settlers raided Palestinian communities, roughing up passers-by, breaking the windows of Palestinian cars, slashing tyres and firing their guns.[90] (The authorities' reluctance to punish such vigilante activities made the settlers bolder still.) Palestinians called Israeli soldiers 'wild beasts', 'animals' and 'murderers'. For Israelis, Palestinians were 'defectives', 'barbarians', 'primitives'. Hatred became mixed with fear. In these circumstances, it was only a matter of time before a spark would set off a wider conflagration.

3

A war, not a revolt

The Intifada began on 9 December 1987 after four Gazans had been killed and seven others injured by an Israeli vehicle in a road accident on the previous day. This seemingly innocuous incident, coming at a time of heightened tensions between the Israeli occupation forces and Palestinians, triggered a march by thousands of people from Jabalya camp, who were fired upon by Israeli soldiers, resulting in more Palestinian deaths. Large-scale demonstrations then erupted throughout the Gaza Strip. Catching the Israelis by surprise and acting before the government could bring in large numbers of reinforcements, Palestinians by the thousands moved onto the streets of Gaza's teeming refugee camps to battle Israeli soldiers for control of their areas. From the outset, it was a contest of will over who was in charge, who could impose his rules upon the other. As one reporter observed, it was a war, not a revolt, but one not played by conventional rules, with machine guns, tanks, planes and missiles. The Israeli army was unable to use its massive arsenal because it was fighting civilians armed only with slingshots, gasoline bombs and stones – a 'shepherd's war', Meron Benvenisti, former deputy mayor of Jerusalem, called it.[1]

Despite the limits imposed upon Israeli firepower, Palestinians, it seemed, would be no match for soldiers armed with M–16 rifles, smoke grenades, rubber bullets and tear gas. Surprisingly, in the days that followed the fatal road accident, Palestinians achieved considerable success. The key, one Gaza leader told a reporter, was control of the streets.

We don't have a timetable, but we already have a custom, waves of people going out, at 3 a.m., in the morning, at midday, early evening.

From the evening until 3 a.m., we sleep and organize. Sometimes, if the situation demands it, we even go out at 10 p.m., because during the night, the army doesn't effectively control the streets and doesn't know the local topgraphy, so we are in control. For instance, yesterday in Jabalya refugee camp, there were demonstrations all night and there was not a single soldier, even though there was a curfew. The soldiers simply fled, because thousands of persons formed a sort of moving human wall, and nothing will work against something like that, neither an iron fist nor bullets.[2]

'Yesterday,' he continued,

I made a few trips, from Khan Yunis to Rafah and from Rafah to al-Burayj. There were tens of thousands, and until 3 a.m. the army could not break in. The distance between the Gaza sentries and the army was fifty metres, and the army simply didn't dare to come in.[3]

This was how it began, in Gaza, perpetually on the verge of an uprising, where people are packed so closely together that the mere raising of a PLO flag or the throwing of a stone is enough to start a demonstration. Within the first few days of the fatal road accident, demonstrations also erupted in the refugee camps, towns and cities of the West Bank. On 10 December, youths from Qalandia refugee camp, north of Jerusalem, barricaded themselves in a local school, hoisted Palestinian flags on the roof and hurled stones and bottles at passers-by on the Jerusalem–Ramallah road.[4] Petrol bombs were thrown at Israeli vehicles in Ramallah, al-Bireh, and near Tulkarm. In Nablus, an IDF patrol was attacked by dozens of youths. Demonstrations also broke out in East Jerusalem. Surging crowds; PLO flags flying from rooftops and telephone lines; marches and demonstrations; hospitals filled to overflowing: these scenes were repeated in many places. According to the Israeli military, 1,200 confrontations occurred in the weeks following the fatal road accident.[5]

While some demonstrations were responses to Israeli provocations – for example, the riot at Balata refugee camp following shootings, beatings and the smashing of furniture there by Israeli troops[6] – the vast majority were efforts by Palestinians to gain control of their camps and neighbourhoods, to push the Israelis out and keep them away. Alleys, roads and streets were blocked by burning tyres or stone barricades, or both; cars driven by

Jewish settlers trying to pass through to their homes were stoned.[7]

Commercial strikes also figured prominently in the first days and weeks of the revolt. These occurred not just in Gaza but all over the West Bank, in Jenin, Ramallah, al-Bireh, Nablus, Tulkarm, Bethlehem and East Jerusalem. All means were sought to keep the uprising going, to maintain its momentum. The shooting dead of a youth could bring a wave of protest, as could the funerals of 'martyred' demonstrators. In Gaza,

we snatch the body from the hospital and bury it and turn this into a sort of spontaneous demonstration [the leader said]. We also forbade the doctors to give the bodies to the military authorities, and anyway the doctors are not in control of this, for we have no difficulty in snatching the bodies. For instance, in the past few days we have snatched four bodies and organized night funerals which have turned into demonstrations. Then the whole area, like Khan Yunis yesterday, is out on the streets. Not a single person stayed at home. Thirty-five thousand took part in that funeral.[8]

This tactic the leader attributed to 'new thinking' among Palestinians, but he could just as well have said a new strategy. Perfected during twenty years of occupation, mass political protest had brought gains for Palestinian political prisoners and had proven its worth in confrontations between Palestinian youths and Israeli troops that dated back at least to the mid-1970s. In theory, it was the perfect weapon for a people living directly under the guns of an occupying power. And in December 1987, this was given a new twist. Palestinians had decided not to use firearms (possessed by some people, but in small quantitites) or explosive devices. Stones would symbolize the revolt. Mass political struggle without conventional arms reflected an understanding of how to confront a military power like Israel, so heavily dependent upon outside aid and touted in the West as the only democracy in the Middle East, hence, presumably, a respecter of human rights. The aim, of course, was to draw the attention and sympathy of world opinion to the plight of the Palestinians, but also to avoid a bloodbath that would smother the Intifada and bring it to a quick end.[9]

Mass political protest required the tightest of discipline and great collective effort. Could the Palestinians, a people who historically had been weakened and undermined by their own factionalism, do it? In Gaza, and in the towns and refugee camps of the West Bank, the answer was given. Facing the hot steel of M–16 bullets and choking under the stifling effects of tear gas dropped from helicopters or fired by soldiers, the demonstrators fought Israeli soldiers with brickbats, clubs, stones and petrol bombs. Youths with slingshots hurled marbles at low-flying helicopters.[10] Protesters threw tear gas and smoke grenades back at the soldiers, then returned to the fray, carrying onions to counteract the effects of the gas.[11] 'For each casualty,' Makhul wrote from a hospital in Gaza, 'twenty people rushed to give blood . . . In the operating theatre, tens of doctors were working without a break, like a conveyor belt.'[12] For the first time, observed Yehuda Litani, veteran correspondent of the occupied territories for the *Jerusalem Post*, 'those in the West Bank and Gaza showed themselves as an independent entity that could prove themselves against the Israelis.'[13]

In the words of Mahdi Abdul-Hadi, Director of the Palestinian Academic Society for the Study of International Affairs, the Intifada was also the 'end of fear'.[14] This, of course, contains much exaggeration. Palestinian youths did not seek martyrdom as a passport to heaven; no one desired to be shot, maimed, or injured. Youths in demonstrations carefully planned their escape routes and conducted themselves in ways designed to avoid fatalities. By such exaggeration, Palestinians romanticize their revolt. However, Abdul-Hadi's words underscore the boldness of the 'new' Palestinian and the pride that came with it. 'Before the Intifada,' he explained, 'a Palestinian would avoid Israeli soldiers even if he had to cross a street to do it; now he stands up and looks them straight in the eyes and says "Why are you here? What do you want?"' Palestinians no longer backed down in confronting Israelis. Defiant and even fearless behaviour could be observed: the youth who made photocopies of a protest leaflet from the machine in the office of the Israeli Interior Ministry and then distributed them to passers-by in nearby Nablus road;[15] the young men who refused to move from their exposed positions even though Israeli security forces were firing shots at them;[16] the Gaza youth who, trapped by a soldier in the grounds of a hospital, '. . . opened his shirt, bared his chest and said "Shoot."'[17] (The soldier did, from a distance of 15 metres.) Little wonder that a cult of hero-worship and, when deaths occurred, even martyrdom (a way to cope with the loss and also continue the revolt) grew up around the youthful protesters.

In the beginning, the Intifada was a simple rejection of the occupation. 'Down with the occupation,' read the Arabic graffiti scribbled on the walls of the Christian quarter of Jerusalem's Old City. 'The message of the people was we cannot endure the occupation anymore,' commented Dr Bishara.[18] This observation is borne out by interviews with several dozen Gaza Strip youths who were arrested while in action during the first days and weeks of the revolt. The primary motive for their participation, they said, was hatred of the Israeli occupation and the restrictions which the authorities had imposed upon the residents of the territories. They stressed the humiliating treatment of local residents by soldiers at road blocks. Almost all of them claimed to have been gravely wronged at least once by the conduct of Israeli authorities, soldiers or employers.[19] The real message of the revolt, however, went beyond a mere rejection of Israeli control. 'It was a response,' continued Dr Bishara, 'to Palestinian leaders whose approach was to solve things by political manoeuvres, by talking with the Likud, or by having municipal elections.'[20] Rejection of Israel implied self-determination and Palestinian statehood.

The Intifada began as a movement mostly of the poor elements of the population. This in part helps explain why it started in Gaza. 'The West Bank is almost paradise compared to the Gaza Strip,' the Palestinian leader told Makhul. 'Even such a thing as a simple passport is denied to them. The only thing that most of them have is a refugee card.'[21] The youthful Gaza protesters interviewed came from the refugee camps, had received little education and had worked, or were working, in Israel. In the West Bank, too, demonstrations were concentrated in the poorest neighbourhoods, and in the refugee camps, although some wealthy people in Nablus and Jerusalem also participated.[22] 'People in the refugee camps are not necessarily the poorest segments of society,' cautioned Dr al-Jarbawi. 'People living in villages could be poorer. A refugee camp family often might have five members working in Israel, each bringing in 150 [Israeli] shekels a day.'[23] Many youthful West Bank protesters were students, some coming from upper- and middle-class families.

At first, and in the absence of central direction, demonstrations were often arranged at the local level by youths who belonged to many different organized groups. Formal organizations could mobilize large numbers of people and impose tight discipline on camps like Balata, whose residents were split between supporters of the revolt and those who remained uncommitted.[24] Organized groups, though, were not essential: 'leaders' existed everywhere.

Every quarter has its own leader, who is usually some major personality [commented the Gazan interviewed by Makhul]. He will be known for his high political consciousness, for his charisma, and he will not have to do that much persuasion, for the situation helps him, and he will just have to give the signal. Every one of these leaders has already become a symbol. In a large quarter, there will be two or three leaders . . . The leader creates around himself an organized mass which at any time can go and do whatever is necessary.[25]

Such 'organization' was very efficient. 'Yesterday,' he noted, 'five hundred women went to Bayt Hanun, and they only knew of the planned trip five minutes before they left.'[26] Was there any danger of being discovered by the Israelis? 'We have seen to it that the army does not know who the inciters are,' he replied. 'The authorities will not see another inciter. There is an instruction, and everyone goes out, quite spontaneously.'

If this was the first time that mass political protest had occurred on this scale in twenty years of occupation, the revolt still could not have lasted long without co-ordination and overall direction. Very quickly, a leadership began to emerge at both the local and national levels. Popular committees (*lijan shaabiya*) appeared in the neighbourhoods and quarters of many towns and refugee camps. These grass-roots structures, initially based upon the younger elements of the population, may have arisen out of the need to provide aid to camp residents being starved into submission by curfews.[27] Committees formed outside the curfewed areas collected food donations, while their counterparts inside the camps distributed them. Medical committees were also organized to go door-to-door in the camps to maintain the health of the inhabitants. Calls for aid elicited such a huge response that committees had large surpluses left over once the curfews ended. Lists of other needy people were compiled, and the committees remained in existence.

The committees, formed spontaneously, provided a loose and diffused local leadership. A group of neighbours, for example, would just meet and decide to help out in some way. If some members were arrested, other people would emerge to take their places. Popular committees were not entirely composed of youths. Many former political prisoners participated,[28] as did other older people of all kinds. The function of these committees was to keep the Intifada going in their localities at a time when the Israeli authorities were predicting the end of the uprising. By organizing strikes and demonstrations in the face of widespread arrests, curfews and an increased troop presence, they were able to maintain the original intensity of the revolt.

On 8 January, practically one month after the Intifada began, the UNL (in Arabic, *al-Qiyada al-Wataniya al-Muwahhada*) made its existence known through the issuance of an unnumbered leaflet. Two days later, a second leaflet appeared under its name, bearing the number two (all subsequent leaflets were serialized).[29] The Unified National Leadership (UNL) quickly made its presence felt. Palestinian support for its call for a three-day strike was so widespread that some merchants remained on strike long after the indicated period of time had elapsed.[30] Like the popular committees, the UNL was an underground leadership, but the similarity went no further. Popular committees dealt with social organization and the survival of local communities. The UNL was a political organization whose function was to provide central direction for the revolt. Popular committees could organize their own local strike days, for example, but they also followed the instructions issued by the UNL. The UNL thus stood above the popular committees, co-ordinating the activities of the Palestinian nation.

What did it mean to lead the uprising? About every ten days, the UNL drew up a leaflet that provided detailed instructions as to what Palestinians should do, and when.[31] The main types of protest activities were the general strike – one of these was usually called each week – the partial strike (lasting three to four hours each), and street demonstrations. Exhortations and appeals of all kinds were made to the Palestinian population. Congratulations were offered to groups and segments of society which had performed special services or displayed particular valour. Demands were also made – for example, that the Israelis end certain repressive measures. The leaflet was an explicit plan of action that could be routinely followed by Palestinians throughout the West Bank and Gaza.

The new unified command was an unmistakably PLO leadership. Its members – four men, with others who could replace them in a kind of rotation – came from the local leadership of the four principal PLO resistance organizations. These were: al-Fatah, the largest group and the one with the widest following in Gaza and the West Bank; the DFLP; the PFLP; and the PCP. The UNL made its PLO affiliation explicit by adding this organization's name, along with its own, to its third leaflet, which appeared on 18 January 1988. This and subsequent leaflets read 'Issued by the PLO/UNL of the Uprising'.[32] Dr Sari Nuseibeh, Professor at Birzeit University, shed further light upon the unified leadership's origins.

The first leaflet was probably issued by Fatah and the Democratic Front, or, at most, by co-ordinators of these two factions. They cannot be called representatives because they were not even doing it with the support and knowledge of all the people in these factions. The persons who issued the first [unnumbered] leaflet had no idea that there would be a second one. The second leaflet was probably issued by one faction – someone within the Democratic Front – and done because the one who wrote it felt that he had enough of a good relationship with the Fatah person he was in touch with to do it even in the absence of that person.[33]

The emergence of the UNL and the willingness of West Bankers and Gazans to follow it reflected the vast support which the PLO enjoyed in the occupied territories. The PLO had become a household word, and its presence was constant and concrete. Youthful protesters who went off to jail thought of themselves as PLO even though they were not members or followers of one of its factions. As we have seen, the PLO was an extra-territorial organization that represented the interests of Palestinians throughout the world. It ran hospitals and clinics, owned businesses, and had a social welfare programme, providing health care, free schooling and pensions. An idea as much as a formal structure, the PLO expressed the hopes and aspirations of Palestinians everywhere for national self-determination and freedom. It was the embodiment of Palestinian consciousness. By

1987, many West Bankers and Gazans belonged to one of its factions. The PLO, however, comprised much more than this. A quasi-governmental body, it had a parliament-in-exile, the PNC, and an Executive Committee, elected by the Council. The Executive Committee, headed by Yasser Arafat, its elected chairman, made decisions for the organization and implemented the policies of the Palestine National Council. Seats on the Executive Committee were allocated to affiliated resistance organizations, but also to 'independents', Palestinian trade unions, for example, which were not affiliated to the guerrilla factions. Some Palestinians who had been deported by Israel from the occupied territories held seats on the Executive Committee and occupied positions in other PLO bodies and offices. Despite many differences among its groups, the PLO was one organization, both inside and outside the occupied territories.

The cohesion of the four local PLO groups into one unified leadership was itself an important accomplishment. Even though more unity existed among PLO factions in the West Bank and Gaza than among these same groups outside the occupied territories, never before had they formed themselves into a united leadership. As the Palestinian scholar Dr Abu-Amr has observed, the UNL of the uprising surpassed all previous forms of co-operation among them.[34] Its establishment represented a victory over the factionalism endemic in the Palestinian national movement and matched the unity being displayed by the demonstrators and strikers in the camps, towns and cities. The credibility and standing it achieved was due not only to the centralization of command and the pressing need for unity, but also to the skill displayed by its members. The UNL was clever in finding different forms for the protests to take. It varied the location of the disturbances so as to give Palestinians a chance to rest. Palestinian demonstrators had at last found a leadership whose sentiments paralleled theirs, a leadership that was, to quote Dr Bishara, 'opposed to autonomy, opposed to Camp David, opposed to the so-called Jordanian option'.[35]

If the UNL provided direction for the mass of Palestinians in the West Bank and Gaza, it was not the only source of political leadership. The Intifada also revealed the power of Islamic groups that were not part of the secular national camp, as represented by the UNL. In Gaza, the way had been paved for the revolt by the activities of the Islamic Jihad, a small, secretive religious organization which had also provided leadership for the street demonstrations and other confrontational activities that began in December.[36] So important was its role that the UNL (in Leaflet 2) indirectly congratulated it for having helped ignite the revolt in Gaza. Unrelated to the other organization of the same name in Lebanon, the Islamic Jihad, in a communiqué issued 3 February, defined itself as part of the Islamic movement in the occupied territories, which included the Muslim Brotherhood, the largest of the Islamic groups. Like other Muslim organizations, the Islamic Jihad reflected the reawakening of an Islamic consciousness or identity among some Palestinians. Their common goal was the establishment of an Islamic rather than secular Palestinian state – the aim of the PLO and the vast majority of Palestinians. Prior to December 1987, the Islamic Jihad had called for armed struggle against the Israeli occupation forces. However, once the Intifada had begun, it foreswore the use of guns, grenades and explosive devices and limited its activity to the consensual tactic of confronting Israeli soldiers in the streets with stones and petrol bombs. The Islamic Jihad was not a large group. 'Its members numbered in the hundreds, not in the thousands,' observed Dr al-Jarbawi. 'But it had lots of followers. The Islamic Jihad issued leaflets only once in a while. On the operational level, it just followed the strikes called by the UNL.'[37] The presence and activity of Islamic Jihad was not regarded by Palestinians as injurious to the unity of the Intifada, but rather as adding something to it.

* * * * * * * * *

The Intifada began, then, as a revolt of youth. Its initial spontaneity had concealed a sophisticated 'organization' with deep roots that went back to the restructuring carried out during the occupation. This youth movement had then been harnessed, so to speak, by a somewhat older and more experienced group of PLO faction leaders, drawn mostly from the professions (but also comprising some students), who made up the UNL.[38] At the same time, local popular committees were being formed, largely out of practical necessity, but also in accordance with instructions from the UNL. The people who sat on these committees were members or supporters of local factions, or 'independents', people unaffiliated to any political organization. The UNL and the popular committees (barely underway) formed the organizational leadership of the uprising.

In January 1988 another group of leaders appeared. These were the 'brokers' or public personalities, several dozen men of middle age who issued a statement known as the Fourteen Points, a kind of political manifesto. The subsequent acceptance of the Fourteen Points by the organizational leadership made it a consensus document of the Intifada and brought these men into the movement, not as equal partners with the members of the UNL and the popular committees, but as important participants.

The political brokers were supporters of the PLO.[39] Mostly professionals by training, these men had no grass-roots constituency or mass base. 'Ask Sari Nuseibeh or Hanna Siniora when they last visited a village in the northern or southern part of the West Bank,' quipped one Palestinian. 'They know more about what is going on with the PLO outside than what is taking place here.' The public personalities were PLO followers, not members, but they were used by the PLO because they possessed a certain standing locally. Most, like Hanna Siniora, editor of the newspaper *al-Fajr*, and Fayez Abu Rahme, a lawyer and President of the Gaza Bar Association, were affiliated exclusively with al-Fatah and were of value to the PLO as spokesmen. 'Siniora and Abu Rahme were created as leaders by al-Fatah,' one Palestinian political analyst observed. 'They have an open line to the PLO, which is a kind of power, but the PLO can close it at any time.' Another informed Palestinian insider disagreed. 'Hanna Siniora was not set up by the PLO; he forced himself upon the PLO. Siniora does things on his own and says that it is PLO or lets people think it is.'[40] Men like Siniora and Abu Rahme had no traditional influence, but some of the other 'personalities' did. Sari Nuseibeh, Faisal Husseini and others came from families of landed or commercial wealth that continued to possess influence in a society still based, to a considerable degree, upon personal ties. Until the Intifada began, a few of these men (e.g., Elias Freij, mayor of

Bethlehem; Rashad al-Shawwa, mayor of Gaza) had had strong sympathies with Jordan.

During the 1970s, the public personalities had been able to develop a base by associating themselves with a national institution (e.g., the Palestinian press, a university), but it was not until after 1982, when the National Guidance Committee was banned and the mayors elected in 1976 removed or deported, that they emerged as influential figures. In the early 1980s, these politicians acquired a high profile. With the PLO having lost its 'outside' base in Lebanon and its 'inside' support after the departure of the nationalist mayors, Arafat had little choice but to rely upon Siniora and the others. Speaking the major Western languages, having contacts in Europe and the US, and living mostly in the accessible Jerusalem–Ramallah area, those men were highly visible and became well known to the foreign media, a position which afforded them some protection. Naturally, they had a conservative approach to the question of how to deal with the Israeli occupation. They objected to the use of violence by Palestinians, advocated negotiation and compromise, and believed in the value of appealing to 'progressive' forces in Israel. They would talk with anyone, even the Likud. Yet they were nationalists, sincerely believing in the right of Palestinians to self-determination.

In the summer of 1987, with violence increasing and the situation deteriorating, some began making proposals of their own. Sari Nuseibeh asked Israel either to give Palestinians rights equal to those enjoyed by Israelis or to set the occupied territories free.[41] 'Marry us or divorce us' was his proposal. That summer, he and Faisal Husseini, Director of the Arab Studies Centre in East Jerusalem, met secretly with Moshe Amirav, a Likud politician, to discuss ways of resolving the conflict.[42] In June, Hanna Siniora proposed to run in the Israeli-controlled municipal elections in Jerusalem.[43]

The mass of Palestinian society, of course, was moving toward rejection of, and separation from, Israel. (Nuseibeh was attacked and beaten by masked men shortly after he met with Amirav.) Most Palestinians had come to believe that stronger action was needed. With the outbreak of the Intifada, the public personalities were bypassed completely. 'Rashad al-Shawwa [patriarch of the traditional leadership in Gaza] . . . no longer has any influence

. . .,' the popular leader in Gaza told Makhul.[44] Surprised and appalled at the intensity of the confrontation between Palestinian youths and Israeli soldiers, the political brokers had little choice but to watch events from the sidelines. Some of them, like Siniora, were not even in the country when the storm broke.

Siniora's public call on 7 January for Palestinians to boycott the purchase of Israeli cigarettes and soft drinks thus took many people by surprise.[45] On the surface, it seemed out of place, hardly worth a comment. Intended as the beginning of a civil disobedience campaign, Siniora's initiative, apparently launched by him alone, was received with scepticism by other Palestinians. Elias Freij denounced it; but Siniora pressed ahead. His detention in Jerusalem's Russian compound prison (where he was fingerprinted and interrogated) showed that the Israelis at least took him seriously. His brief incarceration lent a certain legitimacy to his campaign. The Israeli press began to pay more attention to him.

It was then announced that Palestinians would meet on 14 January at the National Palace Hotel in East Jerusalem. Perhaps believing that this meeting would produce a renewed call for the boycott of Israeli products, Israeli authorities tried to stop the Palestinians from attending. According to the *Jerusalem Post*, they picked up Siniora and prevented three Palestinians, including the chairman of the Gaza Medical Association, from leaving the Gaza Strip. Two others, Ibrahim Karaeen, head of the Palestinian Press Service, and Bassam Ayyub were detained upon their arrival at the hotel.[46] Despite this, the conference took place, but Siniora's call was not renewed. Instead, Sari Nuseibeh, acting on behalf of the approximately two dozen Palestinian figures in attendance, presented a document consisting of two parts. One was a list of fourteen demands; the other was a proposal for the settlement of the Palestinian problem.[47]

The 'Fourteen Points', or 'Jerusalem Programme', as it has been called, was an attempt by the political brokers to attach themselves to the revolt, to gain acceptance by the Intifada leadership, to become part of the movement. Something more than this may also have been involved. The PLO leadership-in-exile did not start this uprising. Yasser Arafat himself admitted that he and his people had been taken by surprise.[48] For twenty years, the PLO had fought to prevent the emergence of an independent local leadership in the occupied territories. At the start of the revolt, the PLO must have been concerned about its ability to control events on the ground. For a month, until the appearance of the UNL, it could be sure of little. And not until 18 January did the PLO's name appear in the leaflets alongside that of the UNL. 'Until the Intifada occurred,' an informed but anonymous Palestinian analyst observed, 'the PLO leadership was not 100 per cent sure that it represented the Palestinians under the occupation.' What better way to enhance its influence and augment its control than through the local following which it had created. According to one report, the Fourteen Points were submitted to the PLO's Executive Committee, which recommended changes that were accepted by the local Palestinians.[49]

The Fourteen Points were designed to have the broadest possible appeal. 'Those who drew it up put down everything that was being talked about across a wide spectrum covering all major demands being mentioned by everyone,' noted Sari Nuseibeh. 'Its genesis was the second leaflet [of the UNL] which contained the rudiments of the Fourteen Points. It was a synthesis of the stated demands and potential areas of demands.' Some of these demands referred to grievances that predated the uprising. Israel was asked to cease settlement activities and land confiscations; return lands already confiscated; cancel VAT and various direct taxes bearing upon Palestinians; release monies deducted from the wages of Palestinian workers in Israel; remove restrictions upon building permits and licences for industrial projects and wells; rescind measures that deprived people of their water resources; abide by the Fourth Geneva Convention; and accept applications for family reunions. Other demands made of Israel followed directly from the revolt. Among these were the release of all persons arrested in the uprising, especially children; the release of administrative detainees; the lifting of the sieges of the refugee camps; and withdrawal of the Israeli army from population centres. Free municipal elections under the supervision of a neutral authority were also requested.

The political programme enunciated in the other part of this document could hardly have been clearer: recognition of the Palestinian right to self-determination, and the establishment of an independent Palestinian state under the leadership of the PLO, 'our sole legitimate representative'. This was to be achieved through the convening of an international conference, supervised by the US and the USSR, with the participation of the five permanent members of the Security Council and all other concerned parties, including the PLO as equal partner. Israel was asked to comply with the demands in order to prepare the atmosphere for the peace conference. This was the very programme articulated at the April 1987 meeting of the PNC in Algiers, and restated by Arafat in an interview on 13 January in words almost identical to those used in the Fourteen Points, issued one day later.[50]

Equally important were the motives which lay behind the publication of this document. The Intifada had given the message that the time for talking was over. Many Palestinians believed that appeals to Israel's 'conscience' or to the Israeli political left would lead to demands that would moderate and dilute the drive for sovereignty. In launching the Fourteen Points, these political brokers may have desired to give the Intifada a somewhat different direction. This desire may also have underlain Siniora's civil disobedience campaign, which was being supported by the same men who had issued the Fourteen Points.[51] According to Siniora, the Fourteen Points were intended to be a local palliative. A positive Israeli response would produce goodwill and help clear the air.[52] This view was echoed by Sari Nuseibeh. 'If Israel had responded to this document,' he said, 'the Intifada might have come to an end, because the idea was to present these as negotiable and hope that Israel would respond positively.'[53]

Siniora's civil disobedience campaign, gaining momentum by mid-January, had as one of its goals the 'conversion' of a portion of the Israeli public. By boycotting Israeli products, Palestinians could show the political left in Israel that its interest was to sit down and talk. Militant confrontation, he implied, would only hand victory to the right-wing parties.[54] Siniora, Nuseibeh and others who thought like them could only go so far, however, since their main goal was to link up with the uprising and be incorporated into it. Civil disobedience, Siniora argued, would promote Palestinian self-reliance in the struggle with Israel. 'The time has come,' he said in reply to criticisms of Freij, 'for our leaders to listen to the voices of the younger generation in the territories.'[55]

Siniora was shrewder than many people realized. At the time

that he launched his campaign, he knew that Palestinians had begun discussing the idea of a boycott of Israeli products. Mubarak Awad, Director of the Palestinian Centre for Non-Violence, reported a growing interest among people from refugee camps in the idea of civil disobedience.[56] During the weekend of 9–10 January, a pamphlet signed by a popular committee had in fact advocated a 17-point plan of civil disobedience.[57] Graffiti signed by al-Fatah also endorsed the boycott idea.[58] By being one of the first to call publicly for a campaign of civil disobedience, Siniora put himself at the forefront of this movement, and contributed something positive to it.

Not surprisingly, the Fourteen Points were first rejected by elements within the Intifada leadership. Sari Nuseibeh explained the opposition as follows. 'When the document became associated with specific people,' he said, 'when it was brought out by Siniora, Nuseibeh and others, then certain people began criticizing it, asking "what right have they to speak on our behalf; they are right-wingers." The Communist Party and other groups began attacking it. "Who are these right-wingers to do this?" they asked.'[59] There was, of course, more to the opposition than this. Many people felt that Palestinians would have to make more gains before they could enter into talks with an enemy as powerful as Israel. 'In the beginning,' explained Dr Bishara, 'the Fourteen Points were rejected by the real Intifada leadership because [people felt] it was not time for the Fourteen Points.'[60]

According to Nuseibeh, this document had been drafted with the approval of the various factions. Despite this, 'subsequent leaflets [by the UNL] dropped all calls for these demands,' he said. 'But eventually they [the leaflets] came back at some point to restating them.' And when this happened, journalists began discussing them. 'The whole Intifada is based upon this document,' Nuseibeh concluded, with some exaggeration. Dr Bishara disagreed. 'The Intifada is not the Fourteen Points,' he cautioned, 'but a movement of the disenfranchised sectors. Still, in the process of the uprising a form of unity has occurred between [these] two types of leadership.' The Fourteen Points were an attempt to capitalize politically upon the uprising, to use it to move the stagnant 'peace process' forward. With its subsequent acceptance by the Intifada leaders, the Fourteen Points' document became the manifesto of the revolt. And with it, a new social stratum had been added to the movement. While the brokers or public personalities were located at the margins, rather than the centre, of Intifada leadership, their incorporation made the structure complete.

The new nationalist leadership thus embraced differing approaches and orientations. In general, the organizational hierarchy, as represented by the UNL and the popular committees, regarded the Intifada itself as the vehicle for the achievement of Palestinian national goals. Emphasis was placed upon upgrading the struggle, which should not be compromised by premature political concessions. The public figures, on the other hand, believed that diplomatic manoeuvres should receive priority, and hence urged compromise, restraint and moderation.[61] This led to debates within the movement – for example, over the organization of the poorer segments of society by the popular committees. Some people felt that the development of a negotiating strategy was far more important, while others said that the time was not ripe for the discussion of diplomatic moves.

Differences also existed within and among the main PLO groups. Although al-Fatah commanded a voting majority in the PLO's decision-making bodies and was the most moderate of its factions, it contained three different trends or tendencies.[62] The PFLP, second to al-Fatah in numerical strength among secular Palestinian nationalists in the West Bank and Gaza, was more militant than al-Fatah and contained ideologically-motivated cadres. Ideologically closer to the PFLP than to al-Fatah, the DFLP was numerically weak and did not have a strong presence in the occupied territories. The 18th session of the PNC, in April 1987, had helped unify these groups after the PFLP and the DFLP had split with al-Fatah over the negotiating tactics of Yasser Arafat. At this session too, the PCP, small in numbers but well-organized (especially in the central West Bank), had attained full membership in the PLO by being given a seat on the Executive Committee. (Unlike the other three PLO factions, the leadership of the PCP was located inside the West Bank and Gaza.) Unity between the factions was thus re-established and the PLO structure solidified.

Differences among the nationalist forces were minor by comparison with the unity which the Intifada inspired. All were in agreement upon the uprising's main goals: Palestinian self-determination, and the establishment of an independent Palestinian state under the leadership of the PLO.[63] General agreement also existed as to basic tactics, both on the ground (e.g., the use of stones and petrol bombs rather than firearms and grenades) and in the political arena, as, for example, the convening of an international conference, with the PLO represented as equal partner. Opposition was universal to the Camp David Accords and to the idea of autonomy. If, prior to the Intifada, some of the public personalities had supported the notion of a union with Jordan, the uprising quickly put an end to such a thought.

This consensus among the secular nationalist groups was in the main supported by the Islamic Jihad – the only Muslim organization to have participated in the revolt from the outset.[64] Possessing a leadership of educated people from the poorer and middle classes, the Islamic Jihad was, as we have seen, a militant and clandestine group. Each person joining it received a six-digit number and an alias, and was assigned to the head of a unit who was responsible for him and who would be his only contact. Prior to the Intifada, its policy of not separating the religious from the national question had won the support and approval of many Palestinians from the national camp. From the start of the revolt, the Islamic Jihad avoided conflict with the secular groups by playing down its differences with them, and by emphasizing points and areas of common agreement. It did not object to being excluded from a seat in the UNL because, it said, leadership of the uprising was less important than the unity of the Palestinian people. It defined its goals as political, not military objectives. It avoided attacking the idea of an international conference. It did not explicitly reject calls for the establishment of a Palestinian state, even though it made clear its desire for a holy war to 'liberate' all of Palestine. Like the nationalist groups, the Islamic Jihad wanted an end to the Jewish settlements, an end to the occupation, and so forth. It also possessed long-standing ties with al-Fatah. Prior to the Intifada, these two groups had co-ordinated the activities of their youth organizations. al-Fatah had even provided the Islamic Jihad with funds, supplies and weapons. In its 3 February 1988 communiqué, the Islamic Jihad referred to its good relations with its 'brothers' in al-Fatah. Little wonder that its leadership joined that of the local PLO groups in directing the Intifada.

How did the new nationalist leadership structure actually function?

A Fatah person is a representative in the UNL [Dr al-Jarbawi explained]. He sits with three others – from the Palestine Communist Party, the Popular Front for the Liberation of Palestine, and the Democratic Front for the Liberation of Palestine – and decides with them on issuing a leaflet. Then he checks with his group on the points, and they accept. Then his group and all the other groups have to filter that to the base. There exist three or four copies of a leaflet, and each is sent to a different place, Jenin, for example, and copies are made. It is very clever.[65]

What made possible compliance with the leaflets' instructions?

The UNL is four people, representing the four groups [Dr al-Jarbawi continued]. If they have committees in [refugee] camps composed of these groups, you cannot deny the relationship between the UNL and these local groups. The UNL sits on top of a hierarchy of all the groups. If you are a Fatah supporter in Jenin, you have a representative in the UNL, and this is why you obey the leaflets. The UNL infiltrates every place in the West Bank and Gaza because you are talking about the leadership of the four groups.

The fact that many people who served on popular committees were members or followers of one of the four main factions greatly facilitated compliance with UNL directives. Popular committees were often the only source of of Intifada leadership in their areas. (Co-ordination between the UNL and the popular committees was extremely difficult, owing to the disruption of communications by the Israelis.) In addition, the success of the individual PLO factions in co-ordinating their activities – a development that led to the formation of the UNL itself – enhanced the high standing which these groups already enjoyed among the general public. And the presence of faction leaders in the midst of the fighting lent even more authority to their groups. All of this helps explain why the UNL could so quickly establish itself as a national authority, demonstrated by the willingness of large numbers of Palestinians to follow its instructions rather than the orders of the Israeli authorities.[66] A new popular authority had come into existence to challenge that of the occupation.

What place did the brokers have in the new arrangement? Because the UNL and the popular committees were underground, the public personalities served the Intifada in a managerial role. When a press conference had to be held or some other public task performed, the brokers made the arrangements or carried it out. Consequently, these figures were sometimes thought to have more power than they really possessed. By giving interviews and issuing statements, the brokers helped shape and mould public opinion in Israel and abroad. As many lived or had offices in East Jerusalem, they also served to highlight its Palestinian character and demonstrate that it was part of the West Bank rather than Israel proper. These men could also function as useful mediators in any talks that might arise, provided, of course, that they remained faithful to the instructions of the PLO leadership and did not depart from the PLO's basic programme.

What was the nature of the relationship between the local leadership and the PLO leaders abroad? The relationship between the 'inside' and the 'outside' was very complex, since the PLO leaders-in-exile had many links with the inside, not just one channel of communication. The UNL itself had a direct line to the PLO leadership, but not as an institutional body. Contact and co-ordination took place between the two through factional channels. 'Each faction sends reports to its leaders outside,' commented Dr al-Jarbawi. '[George] Habash gets reports from his people, [Nayef] Hawatmeh from his, and Fatah from its people. And Arafat reads them all.'[67] Instructions were passed down to the base by the UNL factions. If it wished, the UNL could bypass the political brokers, with whom it had no organizational link. The political brokers, however, had their own direct line to the PLO leadership outside.

If the Intifada pushed the PLO into prominence once again, it also brought pressure upon the leadership abroad to mobilize support for the Palestinian cause and to achieve political gains for the movement – things requiring special leadership skills. The revolt had caught the external leaders at a bad moment. Their spirits at a low ebb, they were eager to put an end to the stalemated situation in which they found themselves.[68] Surprised by the scope and intensity of the Intifada, the PLO leaders felt the need to assert themselves in some way. They began seeking advice from Palestinians inside the occupied territories. Preoccupied with its own concerns, the UNL did not as a rule give advice to PLO leaders on matters of politics, but the brokers did. Closely tied to al-Fatah, they took messages to and from Arafat and the leaders outside, and explained and interpreted the Intifada to them.[69] From time to time, they had the freedom to advance positions of their own. 'The PLO [leadership] uses the brokers because it does not want the genuine leadership to become too big and it can control the brokers,' observed one Palestinian political analyst, speaking anonymously.

Without doubt, the interests of Gazans and West Bankers were henceforth going to have much greater weight in PLO decisions and policies. While an organic relationship had been established between the PLO and the people of the occupied territories that was reciprocal and mutually reinforcing, the relationship between the outside and inside, as we have suggested, also contained elements of tension arising from differing perspectives and interests. One of the Fourteen Points called upon Israel to remove

the restrictions on political contacts between inhabitants of the occupied territories and the PLO, in such a way as to allow for the participation of Palestinians from the territories in the proceedings of the Palestine National Council, in order to ensure a direct input into the decision-making processes of the Palestinian nation by the Palestinians under occupation.[70]

This did not mean that the nature of the relations between the factions inside and outside the occupied territories had changed. A local leadership distinct from, or parallel to, the PLO had not emerged.[71] The commitment of organizational members to the decisions of their commanders outside was simply too strong. 'The ones who call the shots are outside,' commented Dr Abu-Amr.[72] 'Habash dictates to his people here. This is the point.' The Intifada had, if anything, strengthened the links between the PLO internally and externally. What had changed was the role of the organizational leaders. No longer merely the tools for implementing decisions made abroad, they had, as Dr al-Jarbawi has written, become much more independent in planning the plan of struggle. Inside the occupied territories, it was the UNL – the field command of the PLO – that would plot the strategy on the ground, in co-ordination, of course, with the PLO leadership abroad.

* * * * * * * * * *

The Palestinian Intifada has parallels with national liberation movements in various parts of the Third World, but also with the Black Civil Rights movement in the southern United States. Palestinians themselves realized this. Siniora spoke of his civil disobedience campaign doing what 'the Gandhi movement did in India and the black civil rights movement did in the US'.[73] Although different in nature, the Palestinian and civil rights movements had one basic similarity. While Palestinians and southern blacks were at the mercy of numerically and politically dominant societies alien to them in culture and antagonistic to their advancement, these societies were, in quite different ways, extremely vulnerable to external pressure. Consequently, Palestinians and southern blacks both sought to exploit this vulnerability by provoking outside intervention in order to ameliorate their condition. They adopted similar methods. Boycott techniques were combined with confrontation tactics in the streets. The manipulative dimension was very important. Demonstrations were designed to provoke violence by the authorities against a civilian population in hopes of grabbing headlines and arousing, shocking and angering an outside population. For Martin Luther King Jr., this was the northern US, where the passage of new civil rights legislation in Congress and active federal intervention would force the south to submit. For the Palestinians, the focus was upon Western Europe and especially the US, where public opinion, it was hoped, would lead governments to put pressure upon Israel. While both movements developed civil disobedience tactics, economic dependence upon the dominant society meant that civil disobedience could not be 100 per cent. Those most vulnerable economically were not expected to participate in the same way that others were. In the southern US, black maids continued to perform 'faithful' service to their white employers by day while participating in boycotts at night. Palestinians dependent upon jobs in Israel went to work most days, but stayed home on strike days.

Palestinians, of course, were not citizens of a federal republic with constitutional rights that had only to be enforced and strengthened by new or supportive legislation. They were a people under occupation. Nor were they seeking an equality of rights. They wanted separation, not integration. In this important respect, the Intifada was more akin to Gandhi's mass civil disobedience movement in India, which used similar tactics and also aimed at national statehood. Palestinians like Mubarak Awad borrowed many of their ideas from the Indian experience. Mahatma Gandhi, Siniora once stated, also began simply, by asking people to boycott salt, yet his movement succeeded in forcing a British withdrawal from India.[74] India, however, was a vast geographical space with a huge population located far away from the colonizing country. By comparison, Palestinian society was tiny and existed cheek by jowl with the occupier. Palestinians thus had much less room for manoeuvre than did their counterparts in India. While Palestinians were making a giant effort to get rid of the occupation, they also understood the crucial importance of obtaining outside support and external political intervention in order to achieve their goals.

The UNL followed a two-track policy. On the one hand, it began issuing calls for non-co-operation and civil disobedience. The acts to be undertaken, specified in the leaflets, reflected a wider strategy.

The leaflets are the surface or public literature of the Intifada [observed Sari Nuseibeh]. Leaflets contain the steps needed to achieve certain goals. They express a deeper thinking, ideas that are formulated and circulated clandestinely. How to disengage from Israeli control, for example. Working papers on this are circulated in secret. They are outlines of strategy presented by the different groups to each other for discussion in preparation for issuing the leaflets. A leaflet will say: the police are to resign; but this reflects a deeper strategy.[75]

Leaflets issued in January 1988 called for a boycott of Israeli products for which Palestinian alternatives existed. Palestinian merchants were asked not to pay the 15 per cent VAT.[76] Boycotting Israeli goods would provide an impetus for Palestinians to develop themselves. 'For example, we have five major pharmaceutical concerns in the occupied territories,' wrote Siniora.[77] 'Today they are operating at only 20 per cent capacity. In January, the production of Palestinian cigarette factories actually increased by 25 per cent,' as a result of the boycott he helped start. For success, much greater co-operation and sacrifice would have to occur among Palestinians. In January, civil disobedience had not yet taken hold among the population. Would the wider society respond to these calls?

Far more success was gained from street demonstrations – the other 'track' pursued by the UNL, without which the revolt would have gone unnoticed by the world community. Israeli troops unprepared and untrained for riot control acted as might be expected of eighteen- and nineteen-year-old soldiers faced with taunting, jeering, stone-throwing Palestinian youths. They began shooting, first with rubber bullets, then with live M–16 ammunition, in the air, in the ground, at the legs of demonstrators, and sometimes (more often than the IDF has admitted) directly into the crowds. Such high velocity ammunition was designed for use against other soldiers in wartime, not against a civilian population. 'Most of the damage we saw,' said a spokesman at Maqassed hospital in Jerusalem, 'came from live bullets.'

The bullet makes a small point of entry, but if it hits something hard, like a bone, the bone will fragment and so will the bullet. It causes heavy damage. These bullets are usually used in combat operations. Their use against unarmed civilians for this long is unique.[78]

Not all shooting deaths and injuries came as a result of confrontations between Palestinians and Israeli soldiers. One Palestinian woman was shot dead while hanging out laundry on her roof.[79] Others died in similarly innocent circumstances. By 28 December 1987, at least 21 Palestinians had been killed and 180 injured.[80] Roughly two weeks later, the toll of Palestinians had risen to 33 dead and 257 wounded.[81] Almost 2,000 Palestinians had been arrested.[82] By contrast, the Israelis had suffered no deaths. Sixty Israeli soldiers and 40 citizens had been injured.[83] (The first serious Israeli casualty – a settler – was recorded on 31 January.)

The reason for this disparity is that Palestinians were not using lethal weapons against the soldiers. Mines, bombs and firearms had been proscribed. It was important for the success of the revolt that the demonstrators be unarmed civilians facing a modern army. 'In no case have shots been fired at the army from among the demonstrators,' Makhul reported from Gaza, 'which would have been likely to lead to a bloodbath. The local leaders are responsible for this discipline.'[84] The PLO leadership abroad also issued instructions to Palestinians to refrain from the use of weapons, though it need not have.[85] Even when Palestinians had the opportunity, they refrained from taking Israeli lives – a remarkable fact given the deep bitterness most felt toward their occupiers and the atmosphere of violence that had arisen in the years preceding the outbreak of the Intifada. A border policeman who had been dragged into Jerusalem's al-Aqsa mosque during a skirmish was saved from a mob by a Palestinian.[86] Palestinians considered the humiliation of an Israeli soldier (the symbol of the occupation) to be more of a victory than the taking of his life. In Gaza, a soldier trapped by Palestinian youths was stripped of all his clothes, except his trousers, then allowed to go free.[87]

On the other hand, Palestinians seized every opportunity to expose their suffering. They understood the media, and took full advantage of its presence to show the Palestinian 'David' bravely battling the Israeli 'Goliath' – all before the eyes of the rolling cameras. This sudden and dramatic reversal of images constituted the first and most dramatic gain of the Intifada. Television pictures showed soldiers kicking Palestinians on hospital grounds, shooting around the corners of bazaars, and firing directly at fleeing youths. A plain-clothes Israeli security officer was photographed blasting away with a Uzi submachine gun at protesters after his vehicle had encountered several burning tyres placed part of the way across the road. Nothing had been thrown at his vehicle. He just opened fire, at body level.

The use of lethal force, and the heavy casualties that this inflicted upon people often no more than children, aroused condemnation in the West. Israeli Defence Minister Yitzhak Rabin was in Washington, DC, for meetings with American officials when the fighting broke out. At first, the issue was not brought up. Then came the evening news. 'From then on,' wrote Hirsh Goodman, correspondent for the *Jerusalem Post*, 'the issue was discussed at almost every meeting Rabin was to have, be it with the press, his advisers or American officials, both in Congress and the administration.'[88] Even President Reagan was said to be concerned about the disturbances. 'They are listening to us for the first time,' remarked an elated Palestinian.[89] The

Palestinians had finally succeeded in publicizing their message: Israel was violating the human rights of a defenceless civilian population living under its control and protection. Virtually overnight, the Palestinian issue had replaced the Iran–Iraq War and other conflicts on the international global crisis agenda.

Israel was criticized internationally more than at any other time since its 1982 invasion of Lebanon. Egypt, eager to regain its Arab position and embarrassed by the Israeli actions, fired off four strongly worded protests in ten days.[90] In the US, Israel was suffering a public relations débâcle that had its Jewish community worried.[91] Morris Abram, Chairman of the Conference of Presidents of Major American Jewish Organizations, issued a statement supporting the Israeli government's actions, but other prominent Jewish leaders were openly critical. Rabbi Alexander Schindler, President of the Union of American Hebrew Congregations, urged Israel to end the status quo rather than sitting in the occupied territories and waiting for peace to come. An ad hoc committee of Jewish activists called upon Israel to accelerate the peace process. Some Jewish leaders supported the Israeli government's actions publicly, but in private passed messages to Israeli leaders asking that something be done to end the tension. Many American Jewish leaders feared the erosion of public support for Israel, from which derived an annual American aid programme of over $3 billion. They felt a little uneasy that a country in which they had taken so much pride and which had made them feel comfortable as an ethnic minority in the US was now acting undemocratically. Some were truly worried about the moral and demographic consequences for Israel of its continued occupation of the West Bank and Gaza. The support of American Jews for this policy had been shaken.

In public statements, US government officials demonstrated displeasure. At the State Department, spokesman Charles Redman said that the US 'had always counselled against the use of lethal arms in circumstances such as this'; Phyllis Oakley, also representing the State Department, expressed the government's grief at the 'violence that has resulted in the loss of life and injury in the West Bank, Gaza, and East Jerusalem'.[92] To underline its unhappiness, the administration issued a travel advisory, warning Americans to be careful when visiting Israel and the occupied territories.[93] It officially demanded that Israel not deport

Palestinians suspected of complicity in the demonstrations.[94] On 4 January 1988, it voted with other members of the UN Security Council for a resolution requesting that Israel cancel its decision to deport Palestinians – the first time since 1981 that the US had voted against Israel.[95] Yet the Americans were not ready for an open rift with Israel. During this period, through the third week of January, it abstained on two other Security Council resolutions and vetoed a third.

Strong protests also came from Western Europe, where opinion was generally more sympathetic to the Palestinians. The EEC had for some time treated Israel and the occupied territories as separate entities, and had worked in small ways to help the Palestinians.[96] Direct export was one way. Claude Cheysson, EEC Commissioner, had for two years worked to persuade Israeli authorities to permit Palestinian farmers to sell their fruits and vegetables directly to European importers. In mid-December 1987, Israel finally agreed, since it desperately needed its own trade accord with the EEC following the entry of Spain and Portugal into the Community. The new agreement would give Israel greater access to the European market for its agricultural goods and also provide tariff cuts. However, as time passed, the EEC became more critical of Israel's handling of the demonstrators. Claude Cheysson called Israeli actions 'shameful'. He sent almost $3.6 million in aid to Palestinian authorities in the West Bank and Gaza. On 18 January the European parliament postponed the vote on the ratification of the trade agreement with Israel. On 8 February, after issuing a strong statement condemning Israel's measures in the territories, the EEC again deferred approval of the trade agreement until later in the year.

The Israeli government was right to treat the Intifada as an image problem. Israel was vulnerable. It had one of the highest per capita national debts in the world. With the exception of the armaments it exported, Israeli goods, inefficiently produced and marketed, could not compete well in the international market. About 87 per cent of Israel's trade deficit lay with the European Community, and this would only increase after 1992.[97] In the US, Israel enjoyed a large and willing market among American Jews, and had come to depend upon annual outlays of US government aid, much of it written off, to support its relatively high standard of living. Israel also relied heavily on tourism. Officials were privately furious at the US government for issuing its travel advisory on the eve of the holiday season – an action that cost Israel dearly in tourist revenues. Israeli spokesmen attacked the media for applying double standards in its handling of the revolt. But criticism is not the same thing as pressure. Israel's economic well-being was not threatened. Far greater was the challenge from within – the challenge to the status quo posed by the Palestinian Intifada.

The Intifada shattered the idea that the occupied territories could be assimilated to Israel, and that armed force would indefinitely suffice to maintain Israeli rule over a hostile Palestinian population. The folly of the policies pursued by Labour and Likud since 1967 now lay exposed. But what to do? Israel's leaders responded to the challenge posed by the Intifada with confusion, division, a profound misunderstanding of what was happening, and shopworn solutions irrelevant to the situation. No new ideas or plans were advanced to deal with the Intifada in its political dimension.

Israel's leadership was not sure how to define or even what to call this new threat. To Rabin, stone-throwing demonstrations were 'terrorism and violent disturbances'. Others applied the words 'unrest', or 'riots'.[98] Everyone tried to avoid using 'rebellion', 'uprising', or 'revolt', which implied oppression. At first, some leaders charged that the demonstrators were externally directed by the PLO. In early January, Rabin said the rioting had nothing to do with the PLO, which, he claimed, had lost its leadership role in the occupied territories.[99] Israeli officials always saw a lull just around the corner, and were then surprised by a new flare-up of fighting.[100] When the revolt began, Chief of General Staff Shomron predicted that it would end in a few days; in early January, Commander of the Central Region Amran Mitzna declared that most of the main activists had been caught; a week later, Israeli military experts were saying that the Palestinians were tired; and so it went on.

The Intifada added to the tensions already existing in Israel's coalition government, divided between Labour and Likud. At one stormy Cabinet meeting in mid-January, Sharon and Peres got into a shouting match and called each other liars after Peres had proposed that the cabinet discuss a political solution.[101] Shamir accused his Labour Party colleagues of encouraging the

Palestinians to increase their 'violent' agitation.[102] Labour
officials reproved Shamir's 'rejectionism'. Rabin restated the
Labour Party's solution: King Hussein should rule over part of
the West Bank.[103] A political settlement was needed, Rabin said,
but there was no one to talk to on the other side. Not to be
outdone, Shamir rediscovered 'autonomy'. Never mind that he
had vigorously opposed this idea when it was formulated and
presented as part of the Camp David Accords in 1979.
'Autonomy', whatever Shamir meant by it, was an old idea
hardly suited to the new conditions.

The Prime Minister in fact seemed to rule out any concessions.
The issue, he explained, was not the borders of Israel, but the
people's right to the land of Israel, their presence in it and
government of it. Nothing, he said, could prevent the settlement
of people of Israel in the land of Israel.[104].

By mid-January, some Israeli leaders began to realize that they
had misread the situation. In the past, manifestations of
Palestinian resistance had come in short waves, been confined to
certain areas, and were mostly the result of external planning or
internal action by PLO resistance groups. Arrests and deportations had put an end to them. They had not lasted long. 'It has
apparently taken Defence Minister Yitzhak Rabin five weeks to
recognize that what we are witnessing in the territories is not a
passing phenomenon,' wrote the *Jerusalem Post*'s Hirsh Goodman,
'but rather one that will require weeks or even months before
stability is restored.'[105] Rabin's current pessimism, Goodman
noted, stood in marked contrast to his predictions in December.
The Intifada had demonstrated the limits of relying upon force
alone. But this was not the lesson drawn by Israel's political
establishment. Neither Labour nor Likud was willing to hand
over the occupied territories to the Palestinians who lived there.
Both opposed Palestinian nationalism and were determined to
fight it with all the strength they possessed. Palestinians, many
Israelis believed, only understood force. Fear would have to be
re-instilled in the people of the occupied territories. The
disturbances would have to stop. They were too much of a threat
to Israel's international position, to its social peace, and to the
stability of the ruling establishment, already on the verge of a
deep political crisis.

Accordingly, a plan was formulated. Hold shooting deaths to

an 'acceptable' limit. Avoid massacres. Attack the press for its unfairness, but restrict it in order to limit the coverage of events. Wait for the world community to focus its attention elsewhere. Go all out to crush the Intifada by every means short of the use of massive firepower. This was a tall order. Beatings would have to replace, at least in part, the use of live ammunition. A host of collective punishments – administrative detentions, mass arrests, the sealing off of camps, house-to-house searches, curfews and even deportations – would have to be instituted. In January 1988, Rabin described the government's new policy as one of 'force, power and blows'. The beating-up of Palestinians thus received official sanction. Unwittingly, Israel's political establishment had played right into the hands of the Intifada's leaders, who in their leaflets were trying to expand their revolt. By punishing everyone, the Israelis caused the Intifada to spread to every social class and age group until virtually all Palestinians had become one with it.

4

'The IDF will not be a mob army'

The decision by Israel's leaders to crush the Intifada was the crucial factor behind its spread to all sectors of the Palestinian population. By adopting a harsh policy of collective punishment and applying it arbitrarily, Israel's political establishment declared war against everyone – young and old, rich and poor, women and children. Most of those hit by this new 'iron fist' policy had not themselves been directly involved in the revolt. 'We are aware that these actions also affect those who do not take part in the disturbances . . . ,' commented Chief of Staff Shomron, 'In the present circumstances, however, this is an unavoidable price.' The aim, he said, was to instil 'deterrent memories' in the consciousness of Palestinians.[1] The result was the opposite of what he and the rest of the leadership had intended. Israel's policies made it impossible for Palestinians to stand aside. 'In the beginning,' explained Dr al-Jarbawi,

many Palestinians from the upper and middle classes did complain about the Intifada, which was a major change. 'Why shouldn't my children go to school? Why can't I shop in Jerusalem?' But the harsh measures of the Israelis changed this.[2]

The Israelis tried to make their will prevail even in the smallest of things. Every manifestation of Palestinian protest from graffiti to the 'V' sign flashed by children had to be eradicated. The trouble was that the Israelis possessed neither the manpower nor the means (its army was not trained to deal with civil strife) to achieve this. 'The Israelis go in twenty convoys to twenty different places,' commented Dr Kamal Abdulfattah, Professor of Geography at Birzeit University, 'and take down flags and paint over graffiti. They stay three hours, and within five minutes after they leave, there are Palestinian flags and slogans.'[3] Israel could not prevent Palestinians from conducting commercial strikes nor could it protect its own Palestinian agents and collaborators. These two failures helped convince many Palestinians that the Intifada had come to stay. 'All of a sudden,' Dr Abdulfattah continued,

the common people – shopkeepers, peddlers, farmers – realized how strong the Palestinians were and how weak Israel was. Always Israel had made propaganda that it had the strongest army in the Middle East. People discovered that the Israeli intelligence services could be beaten, that Israel could not prevent people from making strikes.

Part of the mythology of the Intifada is the idea that Palestinians were united and rose as one people in December 1987. True, the revolt spread fast through the West Bank and Gaza, but it did not break out in every area. The 400 plus West Bank villages, comprising almost two-thirds of the area's total population, did not join the Intifada until later. (A few villages, however, did participate in it at an early stage.) Nor did every age group and social class participate from the start. As previously suggested, the Intifada was to a certain degree a revolt of youth against the elders, many of whom held back and counselled moderation. 'At the beginning,' said Nasser Hamammreh, a resident of the central West Bank village of Husan, 'the older persons laughed at the young people throwing stones and said "how silly."'[4] A Gaza youth put it differently. 'Some people didn't have courage at first,' he said.[5] 'The Intifada,' summarized Dr Bishara, 'started with the youth only. The entire society was brought into it through collective punishment.'[6] Coercion, it must be added, was also used by some Palestinians against others in the beginning.

The Israeli authorities were aware of the hesitancy of the elders and appealed to them to maintain calm, to control the kids. At first their tone was conciliatory. If things calmed down, they said, Israel would help with their taxes and in obtaining licences. Later, their talk became threatening, as they became fed up with the Palestinians.[7]

Israel's decision to apply collective punishment techniques to the entire Palestinian population arose from the failure of tough measures taken in late December, described at the time as the largest military sweeps since Israel took control of the occupied territories. Mass arrests, curfews, house-to-house searches, road blocks, the blockading of entrances to refugee camps with barrels and barbed wire, a massive military presence (troop strength was tripled) and helicopters – as many as five over one area at a time – scattering tear gas canisters and smoke grenades over demonstrators had only led to greater outbursts, especially after the deportation on 4 January of nine Palestinians.[8] 'Either new "troublemakers" were blossoming as fast as the old ones were being plucked off the streets,' wrote Hirsh Goodman, 'or the wrong people were being detained.'[9] Nothing seemed to be working.

A debate occurred in the Cabinet.[10] Almost alone among the ministers, Peres argued that the government should undertake a political initiative. Yet to have formulated a political programme would have been extremely difficult given the sharp ideological and personal divisions within Israel's national unity government, which since its formation in 1984 had been incapable of reaching a decision on the question of peace with the Palestinians. And even if agreement had been possible between Labour and Likud, Prime Minister Shamir would probably have been unwilling to launch a diplomatic initiative since he believed that the status quo favoured Israel.

In mid-January, the Cabinet approved new, tougher proposals. Violence by Palestinians would be confronted by the power of the Israeli army, Rabin stated, overlooking the fact that between 60 and 70 per cent of the actions taken by demonstrators involved stone-throwing and not one Israeli had yet been killed.[11] The centrepiece of the new plan, not all of whose details became public knowledge, was the extensive and massive application of curfews – 'environmental punishments', as they were euphemistically called. Their purpose was not just to contain the demonstrations, but also to apply economic pressure, that is, to prevent Palestinians from working in Israel, to cause a shortage of money, to impose hardships. Orders prohibited food convoys from entering refugee camps.[12] Chief of Staff Shomron explained: 'They will not go to work, they will not earn a living, and they will not receive travel permits and business licences until they realize that peace is as vital for them as it is for us.'[13] A war of attrition had been declared. These new collective punishments, Shomron added, would bring about calm within two or three weeks.

A policy of 'force, power and blows' was also put in effect. Israeli troops were to gather at trouble spots, shoot rubber bullets, charge the demonstrators, beat them with clubs, and detain the leaders.[14] This was regarded by the Israelis as more effective than a simple arrest. An arrested person, once freed, could throw stones again, but if soldiers broke his hand, it was argued, he would be unable to throw the stones for a long time. The aim behind this plan was to reduce casualties from the use of live ammunition, not only to improve Israel's image in the West but also to bring calm to the occupied territories. Israeli leaders knew that the rising Palestinian casualty toll had been one reason for the escalation of demonstrations earlier.[15] In mid-December, they had instructed the army strictly to obey the open fire orders, that is, to shoot only as a last resort. These orders had not been followed in a satisfactory way.[16]

Other measures were also being readied, including curbs on the press. In late December, the Commander of the Central Region, Amran Mitzna, had set a precedent by ordering the arrest of an army radio correspondent for the way in which he had covered the demonstrations.[17] Joshua Brilliant was twice refused requests to join soldiers on patrol. Soldiers placed their hands in front of television cameras and the IDF barred reporters from operation zones.[18] 'It is as if an army which had no hesitation about reporters accompanying it to Beirut has something to hide about its behavior in the territories,' the *Post's* defence reporters wrote.[19]

The decision to wage a war of attrition against a civilian population placed a heavy burden upon the Israeli army, which was being asked to perform a riot control function for which it was not prepared. Some soldiers still did not have riot control equipment. Presumably, Joshua Brilliant observed, they were expected to kick Palestinians and hit them with bare fists and rifle butts.[20] An exaggerated and unnecessary use of force was bound to result. Military sources, Brilliant commented, had been critical of the excesses of the Border Police. Now the army seemed to be emulating the Border Police approach. The consequences of this decision would severely affect the IDF's reputation and Israel's public image.

The Palestinian revolt had exposed to the Israeli public the true face of the occupation. Many people, commented Yehuda Litani, had adopted a self-image designed to disguise the truth. They told themselves that Israel only occupied the West Bank and Gaza because it was forced to do so, that soldiers only shot at Palestinians when absolutely necessary. Now the veil of self-deception had been torn away.[21] 'The military government has lost its legitimacy,' explained Danny Rubenstein.[22]

Before, when there was trouble, the military government would isolate the problem, close down a school, but say 'the rest of you Palestinians are good people.' Now the Israeli governors punish the entire school system [by closing it down]. They care only about punishment, not about implementing the law and keeping order, the usual functions of government. They just don't give a damn.

This new Israeli policy also brought an end to mediation. The dependence of Palestinians upon the government for everything from licences to build houses to permits for family reunification had given rise to intervention by local people, who could make requests of the authorities on behalf of clients or constituencies, and who could complain when something went wrong. Mediation was essentially intervention to ensure the provision of services, which were controlled by the Israelis. It also implied conciliation, as for example, calming tempers and diffusing tense situations in order to prevent confrontations between Israeli soldiers and Palestinians. The people who performed this function were men who had a certain standing in their communities, as mayors of villages or towns, members of local councils, and the like. These men enjoyed regular contacts with the Israeli administration (which appointed or confirmed them), so it was only natural that they should represent local interests before the government. In order for them to render services to their constituents, a good working relationship with the Israeli authorities had to exist. Mediation, then, was a way of getting things done.

Even in the days of the Labour government, Israel's occupation of the West Bank and Gaza, as we have seen, had amounted to direct rule. Administrative autonomy did not exist for Palestinians. The single exception to this was the municipal elections of 1972 and of 1976. Authorized by the Israeli government in the hope of promoting an indigenous leadership that might counter the PLO's growing influence, the 1976 election led to the emergence of intensely nationalistic and pro-PLO mayors and municipal council members.[23] At first, they continued the practice of intervening with the occupation authorities on behalf of their constituents, dispensing the funds and services provided for by the municipal budgets, which the occupation authorities had drawn up. The Israelis had never been willing to give Palestinian representatives any real authority, except in the smallest of matters. No mayor or any other local office-holder could intervene with the Israelis to secure for a client the return of a piece of land which the Israeli military had confiscated. However, in return for a bribe (a very common practice), he might gain permission for his client's wife, in Amman, Jordan, to come for a visit.[24] Such 'business', though small in scale, meant a lot to many Palestinians. The mediating activities of Palestinian communal leaders, especially in the first decade of Israeli rule, had provided a kind of cushion or buffer between the Israelis and the Palestinian rank and file that enabled people to go about their daily lives with a minimum of direct contact with the occupation. And it had also helped serve to mitigate tensions between the two sides before they could erupt into conflict.

By the early 1980s, this working relationship was breaking down. The new pro-PLO nationalist leaders, particularly the mayors elected in 1976, became less willing to co-operate with the occupation authorities.[25] A university president or a trade union leader was no longer willing to 'deal' with the military government. And while certain traditional leaders who were also pro-Jordanian (as, for example, Elias Freij or Rashad al-Shawwa) tried to avoid confrontations in their relations with the authorities, these men too were becoming more nationalistic. The occupation authorities were also applying pressure. Beginning in 1980, many mayors were removed from their posts. In their place, the authorities appointed Israeli military officers or Palestinians completely beholden to the occupation and without any social influence.[26] Israeli authorities granted fewer licences and permits, and restricted the amount of funds available to the municipalities. They also made their rule more direct. Control over natural resources (land, water), construction, industry and other Palestinian sectors became vested in the hands of ministries in Israel proper.[27] With tension mounting between the two sides, each cared less about maintaining the old working relationship. Mediation became ever more difficult to achieve, as those who had earlier performed this function were weakened and rendered ineffective.

When the Intifada began in December 1987, Palestinian society thus stood face to face with Israeli military power. One example suffices to illustrate the change that had occurred. Prior to the Intifada, when school children had rioted and raised Palestinian flags, an IDF force would lay siege to the school but permit the principal or local authority to negotiate its withdrawal so that the pupils could go home quietly. Then the school janitor or someone would remove the flag.[28] After December, and in accordance with the new tough policy, soldiers were ordered to stop disturbances immediately. Where this could lead became clear in an incident in the northern West Bank village of Anabta on 1 February when schools reopened after their winter recess. After an altercation broke out in the village, troops surrounded a school and fired tear gas grenades into the classrooms.[29] Two young men were hit by live ammunition fired by the troops. News of the shootings set off a wave of protest in the village and in its other schools. According to military sources, troops entered schools and used force to remove pupils who were throwing rocks at them and at the mayor who was trying to supervise the exit of the pupils. One of the women who converged upon the schools to rescue their relatives was shot in the head. Two young men were killed, one while standing on the school veranda.

Not all mediators were lost or gone. Attallah Musleh, the respected nationalist mayor of Beit Sahour, a town of Palestinian Christians located at the site of Biblical Shepherds' Field east of Bethlehem, performed valuable functions for his community until his death in December 1988. Because of his ripe age and wisdom, he could calm down an Israeli soldier who was angry or if he saw a Palestinian youth who wanted to pick a fight with a soldier he would talk with him. 'We do not have many like him, because people are afraid of playing this role,' commented one prominent resident of the town.

Mediators are being eliminated by the feeling of helplessness and fear among the population, and by Israeli pressure. The Israelis are not thinking of the future. They are destroying this class of intermediaries. They do not take into consideration that someday they will have to meet with us and sign an agreement.[30]

* * * * * * * * * *

Israel's policy of collective punishment, which produced widespread misery and suffering, provided a negative reason for Palestinians to join the Intifada. It engendered feelings of rage and hatred among those who had tacitly supported the actions of the youths, but had not yet committed themselves actively to the struggle. Alienated by the occupation, distrustful of the Israelis, and coming under increasing pressure from the militant youths, Palestinians decided to participate in the revolt when it became clear that everyone was to be punished for the acts of the young. Palestinians also had positive reasons for joining the Intifada. The sense of a capacity to stage and sustain a revolt, and the noise which the Intifada had made in the world, were very important. Palestinians knew that when they closed their shops or took to the streets, their actions would be reported on the evening news. Radio broadcasts from London and from Monte Carlo, *Time* and *Newsweek* magazines: all were full of stories about the Intifada.

The policy of collective punishment existed on two levels. There were closures and restrictions of a broad and general nature that isolated large numbers of people and prevented them from going about their daily lives. And there were specific acts of an aggressive and violent nature which were carried out by Israeli soldiers and individual IDF units. It is not sufficient therefore to know what a curfew was or did. Equally important for our understanding is the behaviour of the soldiers who, like the Palestinian militants, regarded this conflict as a war and were quite often acting under orders. 'There was no doubt,' commented Yehuda Litani, 'that once the minister of defense gave the green light to the IDF to beat the rioters ['no one ever died of a beating', he said], brutalities had to follow.'[31]

In January 1988, the Israeli government moved against local institutions. Two Palestinian press offices in Gaza were closed, and five journalists detained.[32] In March, the Palestine Press agency in East Jerusalem – a principal information source for the foreign press – was closed. In the West Bank, the Israelis shut down all universities, and on 3 February temporarily closed all primary and secondary schools. (These schools, except for those in areas under curfew, remained open in Gaza.) The government argued that the schools were centres of unrest – a perfectly true statement. High school and university students had participated in, and even helped lead, the revolt in the West Bank. However, what gave this measure a punitive rather than preventative quality was Israel's decision to close all schools, rather than just those where disturbances had taken place, and to declare illegal compensatory classes for small groups of students whose meetings in private homes exposed the owners to government raids and imprisonment (chalk and blackboards found in homes became evidence against the accused). The Israelis were well aware of the value that Palestinians placed upon education.

Israel also clamped down upon the Palestinians through closures and curfews. By declaring an area to be a closed military zone (closures were more frequent than curfews, but of shorter duration), the IDF could sever contact between it and the outside world.[33] In January, the Israelis enacted a new law delegating the power to declare a curfew or closure of an area to the senior officer present, rather than the area commander in whom this authority had previously resided. Closures were used to prohibit media coverage of trouble spots, as, for example, had occurred in Nablus and Jabalya camp in January and February. After the first month of the Intifada, the West Bank and Gaza were almost entirely cut off from each other (political co-ordination between them, however, remained good).

Curfews were Israel's main weapon. During them, families were usually confined to their homes. No one was allowed even to peer out of the window. Commonly regarded as temporary measures, curfews were used by governments in many parts of the world to deal with situations of imminent danger, such as *coups d'état* or civil strife. Israel, however, applied curfews on an unparalleled scale, until they had become, in fact, 'routine'. According to al-Haq, a Palestinian civil liberties organization, 1,600 curfews were imposed upon areas in the West Bank and Gaza during the first year of the Intifada.[34] Of these, 400 were prolonged curfews, running 24 hours a day and lasting between three and forty days. Almost every Palestinian was confined to his or her home at least once.

On 13 January, a curfew was clamped upon all refugee camps in Gaza, involving over 300,000 people.[35] Israeli authorities quickly extended these to other places. They imposed a 24-hour curfew upon the village of A-Tur – the first time since 1967 that a curfew had been imposed in East Jerusalem. By the first week of February, Shuafat refugee camp, also in East Jerusalem, was under curfew. On 10 February, Jericho was closed to West Bank residents. 160,000 persons on the West Bank were living in curfewed areas, most of them in the Tulkarm–Nablus region.

The impact of prolonged, round-the-clock curfews upon a civilian population not prepared for them was enormous. Jabalya camp (64,000 inhabitants) had already spent 22 days in such confinement, Balata camp 26 days, when curfews were reimposed on 13 January.[36] Curfews hit shopkeepers, already operating on reduced schedules; wage labourers, who could not travel to work in Israel; farmers, who were prevented from tending their crops – everyone. Food shortages grew. 'The fresh things go first,' explained a spokesman for UNRWA in Jerusalem, 'then canned foods. People survive by eating bread and things like that.'[37] In January, the Israelis were permitting residents of some areas to leave their homes for an hour every one or two days in order to buy food and necessities, but this hardly gave enough time to replenish their stocks.[38] Troops were stationed at every inter-section, and checkpoints had to be passed every few kilometres.

Despite severe food shortages, Israeli authorities in Gaza refused to allow UN relief vehicles to transport food and other supplies to Palestinians. Food could only be delivered once the curfews were lifted, they said.[39] In response, UNRWA officials announced plans to drive trucks with emergency food supplies to the gates of the refugee camps and leave them there. The trucks would arrive, the acting director of UNRWA in Gaza told Reuters news agency, carrying food for children, for pregnant women, and for nursing mothers. 'The vans will stand there,' she said, 'until the army lifts the curfew for people to come and get their rations.'[40] Several days later, the IDF turned back a food convoy organized by Arabs and Jews in Israel.[41] Palestinian women carrying food into Nuseirat camp had it dumped on the road by Israeli soldiers who trampled on the bread and vegetables.[42]

Another problem was the deterioration of health conditions and services. 'Our health programmes,' the UNRWA spokesman continued,

> are destroyed by curfews. Sewage piles high in the streets and clogs open sewers. During curfews, we can't get our maintenance men into the camps. Our supplementary daily feeding programme for children suffering from malnutrition and our mother-child programme have also been disrupted. Mothers are afraid to come to our clinics. Children do not receive their inoculations and the basic care provided by the clinics.

Nor, one might add, could injured or seriously ill persons be transported freely by ambulances to hospitals (streets, alleyways and entrances were blockaded or sealed), or help be sought in health crises requiring immediate attention (residents found outside their homes could be shot). Everyone suffered, the vulnerable members of society most of all. Other measures were applied. In January, Israeli military authorities compelled men between the ages of 15 and 45 in certain neighbourhoods to leave their homes and stand outside in the cold and rain for several hours so that they would be too tired to demonstrate the next morning.[43] Water, electricity and even telephone links were sometimes cut. Jabal Mukabber – a village within the Jerusalem area – lost its electricity by an Israeli government order of 7 February. In March, Israeli authorities blocked international telephone contact with the territories.[44] Israel also stopped the transfer of social security pensions to the bank accounts of East Jerusalem residents who were required to appear before the authorities and present their identity cards before receiving their entitlements.[45]

Palestinian society was also harmed by Israel's decision to limit the amount of money that people coming from Jordan or abroad could bring into the occupied territories. In February and March, foreign currency regulations were amended. Any Palestinian wishing to bring in sums larger than 400 Jordanian dinars had to apply for a permit.[46] Israel's goal was to prevent the entry of financial aid (especially PLO money) for the revolt, but this measure hurt thousands of Palestinians who depended for support upon family members working abroad, not to speak of Palestinian exporters–importers, many of whom had close ties with Israelis and who must have felt as if they were being cut adrift. More serious was the blow dealt to local relief and other organizations whose liquid assets were in Jordanian dinars and which had bank accounts in Amman. 'The limits upon the amounts of money each person could bring across Allenby Bridge hurt a lot,' said a spokesman at Ittihad al-Nisai hospital in Nablus. 'We relied upon donations from people in Amman; institutions cannot bring anything across the Bridge.'[47] An official at the boys' orphanage in Tulkarm voiced a similar complaint. 'If you bring more than 400 Jordanian dinars across the Bridge, it is confiscated. At the beginning of the Intifada, this really hurt us.'[48]

Rabin's policy of 'force, power and blows' also hurt and angered Palestinians. The aggressive use of force was an important change in Israeli army tactics. Soldiers were ordered not only to charge rioters in street confrontations, but also to enter areas under curfew in order to 'demonstrate a presence'.[49] Benefiting from a change in the rules, officers in IDF units could declare areas closed military zones, set up roadblocks, seal them off, go in and do more or less what they wished. But Palestinians were vulnerable anywhere. Tahir Sharita, a part-time *Jerusalem Post* and Reuters correspondent in Gaza, was in his car when soldiers ordered him to bring water to put out burning tyres near his home. When he drove away, he was pursued, arrested (along with his brother), and forced to stand in the rain and the cold for four hours, blindfolded, his hands tied behind his back. He was then taken to Ansar II prison. When the IDF learned that he was a journalist, Sharita was released.[50] In another incident, a Palestinian boy walking near a bus that had been hit by a stone was seized by soldiers, hustled into a command car, kicked, butted and beaten until his mouth was a bloody pulp, then driven away.[51] 'My son was reading on the roof of our house,' explained 'Ali', a resident of Jenin:

The soldiers came and beat him because they thought that he knew who had thrown stones at them from a nearby street. Two other youths were also taken from their homes. The three were in front of our house, when about 15 women – mothers, sisters, and so on – came out to stop the soldiers from taking them. The soldiers threw three canisters of tear gas on the ground amidst the women.[52]

The entry of troops into camps, town quarters and villages

might be preventative, designed to head off trouble, or punitive, to punish a community for the actions of youthful demonstrators. Civilians were beaten in their homes or more commonly taken outside, frequently to the edge of a camp or village, and clubbed. Blows were adminstered to the limbs, joints and the head with the aim of causing muscle tissue injuries and fractures.[53] Some Palestinians were returned to their homes; others who had been beaten were taken away and placed in administrative detention. (Mass and indiscriminate arrests of people were also made during these IDF raids.) Naturally, some beatings were carried to excess, and people died. Soldiers broke into a home in Gaza's al-Burayj refugee camp, arrested Iyad Akel, 15 years old, and his cousin and beat them. They then took the two youths, handcuffed, to the edge of the camp. Iyad's cousin's arm and leg were broken, and he was dropped into an orange grove. Iyad was left lying near a cemetery. On 8 February, Iyad died at al-Shifa hospital.[54] (The IDF denied that he had been beaten to death.) By late February, the International Committee of the Red Cross stated that it had 'irrefutable' evidence that three Palestinians had died as a result of such beatings.[55]

Israel's beating policy was a collective punishment that fell indiscriminately upon all age groups and classes. By 24 January, two hundred cases of broken limbs requiring casts were reported in Jabalya camp alone.[56] In Shuafat camp, a 70-year-old crippled man was beaten; in another incident, an 80-year-old was clubbed and beaten with rifle butts.[57] In Gaza, women defending their sons from beatings by soldiers were attacked by an IDF bulldozer. A one-and-a-half-year-old girl had to have stitches taken after she was hit by a policeman when she tried to follow her father who was being taken away.[58] Soldiers pursued the injured to hospitals and even took them to Israel to interrogate them.[59] 'Israeli troops attacked our hospital five times,' said the spokesman at Ittihad al-Nisai in Nablus. 'They entered with guns and ordered five injured people to go with them to hospitals in Israel.' Jerusalem's Maqassed hospital was luckier. 'The Israelis entered only once,' a spokesman there stated. 'They were looking for people who were visiting patients. They collected ten persons, all visitors.'[60]

The use of such force was not confined to beatings. During the raids, troops shot canisters of CS gas into homes and vandalized and destroyed much private property.[61] In Shuafat camp, the *Jerusalem Post*'s Andy Court reported, the visitor could see spent bullets, tear gas canisters and the remnants of flares used to illuminate the place at night.[62] Its UNRWA director had kept a record. The police, he said, had vandalized the cars of ten residents when the camp was under curfew. In addition, 200 small solar water tanks had been shot up by live ammunition. During a police raid on 28 January, some 50 persons were sent to Maqassed hospital with beating injuries; another 20 were treated by the UNRWA doctor in their homes. About 85 per cent of the families in the camp had felt the heavy hand of the police, one camp resident added. The reason for such behaviour, another observed, was the inability of the police to catch the demonstrators. They lashed out at all the residents, thinking that collective pressure would cause the adults to restrain their children. Shuafat, it must be added, was the only refugee camp under Israeli sovereignty, that is, within Jerusalem's borders, hence presumably under the protection of Israeli law.

Woe be to the owner of property which happened to be located near the site of a stone-throwing attack. The *Jerusalem Post*'s Andy Court and Bernard Josephs described one such incident. A thick haze of tear gas filled a house in Sur Bahir, a village near Jerusalem. One could not enter the rooms without gagging. In a nearby home, a woman cradled a child whose eyes were still swollen, two hours after the police attack had occurred. Nearly all windows had been smashed. Furniture was overturned, and tear gas canisters lay about two rooms. A tape deck, a cupboard and an iron had been broken. Earlier in the day, near this house, policemen had been attacked by youths with stones and marbles fired from slingshots. Eighteen children were in the house when the police entered. "' . . . the adults of Sur Bahir should control their young people and then no one's property will be damaged," a police spokesman said. "The people who did this may have been in police uniforms," a relative of the home owner declared, "but they acted like the Mafia."'[63]

Such behaviour by troops only inflamed Palestinians. 'Most of the people are angry now,' commented one resident of Shuafat.[64] Incidents multiplied, as civilians confronted troops entering their areas. Shooting deaths did not significantly decrease. When troops began entering Tulkarm refugee camp under cover of a curfew, residents confronted them directly. One youth was shot and killed in the mêlée.[65] The total number of casualties from such incidents will probably never be known. Carmel Shalev, author of the West Bank Data Base Project's report on civil rights in the occupied territories, estimated that one out of every 15 males over the age of 18 had been physically affected by the uprising.[66] The International Committee of the Red Cross, in an unusual departure from its normally subdued tone, declared that thousands of persons had been the victims of brutality and grave ill-treatment by soldiers.[67] Many of these actions, it said, had been perpetrated against 'innocent victims' – young children, pregnant women and the elderly. A report by a fact-finding team of US physicians spoke of an 'uncontrolled epidemic of violence' in the occupied territories, on a scale and of a degree of severity not realized by the public.[68] ' . . . we are not dogs,' said a badly bruised father of four from the village of Halhoul, 'we are people with dignity.'[69]

The treatment meted out to those Palestinians who had been arrested or detained, and the damage done to people by the use of CS gas, were equally disturbing. By May, an estimated 1,900 people were being detained without trial.[70] Many detainees were older men, professional people – journalists, physicians, lawyers. Prisoners were held in primitive conditions of overcrowding and poor sanitation.[71] Many were subject to insulting and humiliating treatment by prison guards; some to brutality and even torture.[72] 'The moment I arrived [at Jerusalem's Russian Compound prison],' said 'Mahmud', a physician arrested in the spring,

I was hit over the head with two chairs. The man who received me began saying terrible things, like 'I'll bring your sister and fuck her' . . . fifty-five of us were in one small room, which contained 12 beds. Three of the prisoners had been shot in the stomach. They had been removed from their hospital beds by Israelis and dumped into jail here . . . There were also men who had been hit by soldiers and not treated. One man had an artificial leg which had been broken by the Israelis. Many were suffering from trauma and needed treatment.

When Dr 'Mahmud' was transferred to Dahariya Prison (south of Hebron), conditions were no better.

People were all ages, from 10–11 years to 75 years old . . . Many had been beaten. Our clothes were filthy. Once a soldier brought water in a rubber can and threw it all over us. At first we were happy because it was like a shower. But then another Israeli entered and threw cement powder upon us, in our wet clothes. Some of us vomited, everyone was scratching and itching. One soldier wanted to bring in the urine jug and throw that on us, but another said 'It is enough for today.'[73]

Palestinian detainees also faced irregular trial procedures. A number of prisoners did not even see a lawyer before coming to trial. Some lawyers were neither informed of their clients' transfer from one prison to another, nor given sufficient notice of their trial dates.[74] Frequently, a prisoner was brought into court so abruptly that he did not understand what was going on. Charge sheets were drawn up in Hebrew, without written translation into Arabic. Judgments were often made on the basis of confessions (sometime extracted by force, or made from a desire to leave prison as soon as possible), also frequently written in Hebrew.

The ACRI [Association for Civil Rights in Israel] [related Carmel Shalev] observed one session in the Gaza military court, and reported standard sentencing of 3 months imprisonment with NIS [Israeli shekels] 750 in fines in 8 cases that were heard in 35 minutes. None of the defendants were represented by counsel.[75]

In March 1988, new legislation deprived Palestinian administrative detainees of an automatic judicial review. Previously, they had had periodic review every three months. After March, the only way they could come before a court was to ask for an appeal, and then they came before a judge, not an appeals committee.[76]

Parents and relatives faced big problems in communicating with imprisoned family members. Many parents were not even notified that their children had been arrested even though, by a law issued in February, they were to be so informed without delay.[77] And once they had learned, people did not know where an arrested relative was being detained. Fathers and mothers spent days and weeks searching for their sons, visiting one detention camp after another. Prisoners were being transferred from one prison to another so often that it was hard for anyone to know what was happening. In April, the Israelis announced new rules for family visits. Previously, visits through the

International Committee of the Red Cross had been almost unlimited. Now families had to obtain permits from the Civil Administration that were good for one visit only. According to Shalev, the Israelis wanted to monitor the identities and numbers of visits and to use permits as a tool of punishment.[78] The families of detained youths were 'punished' in another way. In April, parents were required to post a bond to guarantee the good conduct of their children.[79]

The firing by soldiers of CN and CS gas into schools, shops, homes and other closed places had a pernicious effect upon a society where women, children and the elderly enjoyed a protected and special status. From the beginning, troops had shot gas canisters into crowds of demonstrators to disperse them or to slow down fleeing youths. Some of these projectiles had by accident entered buildings in the vicinity. However, gas canisters were also deliberately fired into places where entire families were living. Introduced in January, CS gas had been used in South Africa, Northern Ireland and France (during the 1968 riots), but in open places – not closed areas, where its effects could be catastrophic.[80] Infants, children and people suffering from heart or respiratory problems might die if exposed to more than ten minutes of this toxic substance.[81]

The majority of people treated here for tear gas until now [said a spokesman at Maqassed Hospital] have suffered from CS gas, not CN. The Israelis put it in cartridges or drop it from helicopters. Occasionally, they use mace, which is CN . . . People who have asthma may suffocate. It can cause coronaries, and affects the skin too. It causes severe blisters, and first and second degree burns which may become chronic. We have had two or three cases of people exposed to it whose central nervous systems were affected. They went into convulsions and had nightmares. As for women, the rate of abortions at Maqassed for the first eleven months of the Intifada has been greater than the rate of the preceding eleven months, but we cannot prove that the abortions were caused by tear gas. Out of our 4,500 Intifada casualties, tear gas victims numbered 1,800 in the first eleven months.[82]

In mid-January, stories began to surface about the effects which gas was having upon women, children and the elderly. The *Jerusalem Post* related claims that in some refugee camps a new form of gas was causing dizziness and nausea.[83] The Israeli daily

Davar reported that a woman and her one-year-old child had died of tear gas inhalation.[84] In February, Joel Greenberg of the *Jerusalem Post* described women in refugee camps standing in homes that reeked of tear gas and relating stories of how their small children had been hospitalized by inhaling the fumes.[85] Formal complaints were lodged and reports issued. UNRWA's medical director complained of the IDF's use of new, highly toxic gases.[86] A team of six Israeli doctors checking on casualties in Gaza reported that tear gas used in closed areas had almost certainly caused some 30 miscarriages and adversely affected the health of infants, the elderly and persons suffering from heart or respiratory disorders.[87] UNRWA casualty statistics from Gaza suggest the impact that tear gas was having upon children. As of 30 June 1988, 1,628 Palestinians had been treated at UNRWA clinics for tear gas inhalation. Of these, 1,145 were children (youths under the age of 16), of whom over a half were aged five or younger.[88]

The war, as Joel Greenberg remarked, had indeed taken an ugly turn. No longer was it hidden by the façade of daily routine.[89] The soldiers' violence, he added, seemed like pointless thuggery. 'How can you do these things,' a Palestinian woman asked him. 'Isn't it a pity, taking people out of their homes, beating them, and dumping them like that in the hills. You're a Jew and I'm an Arab. Don't I deserve to live like you?' Many innocents had been punished. More people than ever were now willing to take action. 'We are ready to starve,' said a worker from Nusseirat camp.[90] 'We are ready to suffer – but we won't give up. This wave of unrest will continue.'

The violence unleashed against Palestinians constituted a painfully tragic episode in the history of the Palestinian–Israeli encounter. Of all peoples, Jews had experienced so much suffering themselves at the hands of others. How, then, can such behaviour be explained? As we have seen, the conduct of IDF units was a function of the objectives of the Israeli authorities. General orders had been issued by Rabin for soldiers to use force against Palestinians, but under what conditions could violence be perpetrated? According to official guidelines, force was permitted during a violent incident in order to break up a riot, overcome resistance to arrest, or in the pursuit of rioters or suspects.[91] But force could not be used following the dispersal of a demonstration or after a person had been apprehended and was not resisting. It was also illegal to use force against property, or for the purpose of punishment, deterrence or humiliation. All too frequently, however, these rules were ignored. In February, the Attorney-General declared that in light of the large number of complaints that had been made, violations of these guidelines could no longer be regarded as exceptions.[92] What, then, was the problem? A fundamental contradiction existed between the rules themselves and Israeli policy objectives, which were: (1) to effect 'deterrence' by reminding Palestinians of the price to be paid for the actions of their youth; and (2) to locate and neutralize the organizational leadership. Through arbitrary and mass arrests, by declaring curfews and closed military zones, and by taking other measures (for example, shutting down Palestinian institutions), the authorities hoped to disrupt the plans and activities of the leaders and terminate the Intifada. However, if 'deterrence' was to be re-established, soldiers could not limit their use of force only to those persons who were fleeing from them, or resisting arrest. In the view of the authorities, fear had to be reinstilled in the population. Palestinians had to be taught a lesson. Given this, widespread violation of the rules was inevitable. This helps explain the glaring discrepancy between the official guidelines and the reality on the ground.

These policy objectives, however, only partially explain the violence meted out to Palestinian civilians by IDF soldiers (and, occasionally, Israeli settlers). Shooting deaths of Palestinian youths sometimes occurred as visceral reactions by soldiers to stone-throwing and other incidents. Vandalism of personal property and the firing of toxic gas into enclosed spaces often reflected frustration, vindictiveness and deep-seated anger. Soldiers beat up Palestinians to 'let off steam'.[93] An Israeli soldier would single out a Palestinian who had been arrested and, in a rage, beat his face into a bloody mess. Why? The underlying reasons for this (and other kinds of behaviour) are complex and go to the very heart of the dispute between Israelis and Palestinians. For a start Israeli youths saw nothing particularly wrong with abusing Palestinians. 'The territories have been occupied now for 20 years,' explained Tom Segev, reporter for the Hebrew-language *Haaretz*.[94]

There is democracy in Israel but none in the territories. A whole generation of Israelis grew up with a non-democratic system next to them, as non-democratic rulers. There is a difference between the arrest of Arabs and Jews. When you [a Jew] get arrested, the police or the secret service people will say 'We will give you Jewish treatment.' You will be slapped around perhaps, but not tortured. Arabs who are arrested are beaten and tortured. It is difficult to convince Israelis that this undemocratic way of ruling and treating Arabs is wrong or evil. Israelis see it as normal practice [towards Arabs, not themselves].

As David Shipler has shown, Israel's long occupation of the West Bank and Gaza had induced in many Israelis attitudes of contempt and disdain for Palestinians, who held similarly negative views of Israeli Jews.[95] Jewish school children could be heard making bigoted remarks about Arabs, who were stereotyped as violent, bloodthirsty and savage. Jews serving in the occupied territories spent their time vilifying Palestinians and their tough macho talk aimed at reinforcing the image of Jewish power and control. Any Arab 'uppityness' or challenge ignited a deep fury. Such attitudes reflected an unwillingness to recognize the reality of Palestinian nationalism because this would conflict with Israeli claims to the same land. Until the Intifada, Palestinians had generally acquiesced in Israeli rule and Israelis became accustomed to a passive and relatively docile subject people. Beginning in December 1987, crowds of local Palestinian youths baited and taunted Israeli soldiers, who were outraged at the 'effrontery' of a formerly 'subservient' people, and who saw in this challenge a threat to their own well-being. As Carmel Shalev has noted, the failure of the authorities to take serious punitive action against soldiers (and settlers) for violence against Palestinians only helped legitimize this kind of behaviour.[96] Israeli Jews received lighter sentences and easier treatment than Palestinians who committed crimes – a double standard of justice that pre-existed the Intifada and continued during it.[97] Widespread violence thus occurred, which not only provoked international condemnation of Israel, but also brought a sense of shame to some Jews, including soldiers and their families.

* * * * * * * * *

Without fully realizing it, the Israelis were helping bring Palestinians closer together, forcing them to become more self-reliant, to co-operate as perhaps they had never done before. Rabin's policy of 'force, power and blows' facilitated the very disengagement which the UNL had been trying to achieve through its leaflets.

As winter wore on, Palestinians found some reason for hope. In two key tests of strength with Israel, the uprising was able to make its will prevail. In February 1988, it became clear that the Israeli authorities could not prevent Palestinians from engaging in commercial strikes. By spring, these had become a fait accompli. The uprising also succeeded in bringing its power to bear against those Palestinians who, paid and armed by Israel, worked as informants and intelligence gatherers throughout the occupied territories. On 24 February, a collaborator in the West Bank village of Qabatya was besieged in his home and killed by fellow villagers. The Israelis failed to rescue him, even though they had military garrisons close by. Thereafter, many Palestinians who had collaborated with Israel joined the revolt. These two 'victories', along with other developments, such as the media attention paid to the Intifada, gave Palestinians more confidence. The success of the commercial strikes and the Qabatya incident showed that the Israelis could not be everywhere at once. If many people in different locations decided to do something, Israel could not stop them. The Intifada might have a future after all. Palestinians were thus given positive reasons for joining the revolt.

Commercial strikes had begun in Gaza and in East Jerusalem, Ramallah and al-Bireh in the West Bank almost from the first day of the revolt.[98] These involved businessmen and shopkeepers of all kinds – green grocers, haberdashers, tobacconists, florists, butchers – and affected wholesalers and even the farmers who brought fruits and vegetables to market. By mid-January, strikes had become an ubiquitous phenomenon in the towns and cities. Many retail shops remained closed all day. Pharmacies and bakeries, on the other hand, were kept open. In certain places, shops were closed for long periods: 24 consecutive days in East Jerusalem, for example, and 50 days intermittently.[99] These strikes hurt Israel, which used the occupied territories as a market for its manufactured products and a source of revenues through VAT and other taxes. With the exception of East Jerusalem, where commercial establishments were spared Israeli violence until mid-January,[100] Israel employed coercive methods to reopen the shops. In Nablus, shops were forcibly opened by soldiers, but closed again by Palestinians.[101] Shopkeepers on strike during morning hours in Bethlehem, Qalqilya, Jenin and Tubas were compelled to reopen. In some parts of Gaza City, troops welded shut the locks that merchants had placed on their shops, as a punitive measure. During the first month, however, IDF troops were preoccupied mostly with clearing roadblocks, extinguishing burning tyres and confronting crowds of stone-throwing youths.

The Palestinians who launched these strikes were an important part of the middle class. Retailers mostly, this petit-bourgeoisie may have had less formal education than the urban professionals, but because of their place in the local and regional economy they possessed great collective influence. These men had wide-ranging contacts with wholesalers, exporters and importers and other suppliers, and with the general public. Having borne the brunt of Israel's imposition of the value-added tax, they resented having had to finance a large proportion of the military administration's budget. An important distinction, however, must be made between businessmen and shopkeepers in the towns and cities, who were the middle class, and those in the villages, who were not. (As village stores were very small, landowners rather than shopkeepers formed the middle class there.) From the outset, the majority of shopkeepers supported the Intifada, but a small minority did not. In order to achieve solidarity, the youthful organizers applied pressure on them. Masked youths appeared, warning shopkeepers to keep their stores shut.[102] Telephone threats were also made against the homes and cars of some shopkeepers. Leaflets appeared with the names of Palestinians who had co-operated with Israel. A PLO radio station broadcast intimidation. Through contact numbers in Europe, PLO members in the occupied territories could call in the names of storeowners who had opened their shops. The vast majority of shop closures, however, were not dictated by threats or any other act of intimidation. 'Shopkeepers are grown-ups,' commented Dr Abdul-Fattah, 'and many went along with the Intifada from the first day. Some were forced, but most were certainly willing to support it. If not, strikes could not have occurred.'[103] In Ramallah and al-Bireh, owners opened their shops, and then went home. Youthful participants in the revolt prevented them being entered (almost no shops were looted), and locksmiths waited to repair free of charge any damage done by the Israelis.

During the first month or so, life was hard for the striking petit-bourgeoisie. Many drew from income stored in bank accounts, but this source was quickly depleted. In January, Israeli banks were no longer accepting cheques from some merchants.[104] PLO strike funds helped shopowners, but not very much. Relief did come, but not from the Israelis. At the end of January, the UNL announced that shops and stores could open for three hours each day (except for days on which general strikes had been called).[105] Shopowners received designated opening times. In East Jerusalem, opening hours were 3:00–6:00 p.m.; in Ramallah and al-Bireh, 8:00–11:00 a.m.; in Tulkarm, 9:00–12 noon; and so on. At other times, strikes would continue. Done partly to deprive Israeli businesses in Jewish West Jerusalem of Palestinian customers, these restricted opening hours were a godsend to the storekeepers. Some made almost as much in three hours as they had all day prior to the Intifada, owing to the greater volume of business.

About this time, some merchants began issuing public statements supporting the revolt. On 2 February 1988, a committee representing merchants in Ramallah and al-Bireh held a press conference at the National Palace Hotel in East Jerusalem.[106] The merchants pledged to continue their strikes until all 'national demands' had been met. They listed nine objectives of the strike – among them, the convening of an international peace conference, with the participation of the PLO; the cancellation of all taxes imposed upon Palestinian merchants since 1967, especially VAT; and the cessation of efforts by Israel to break the strike through violence. Shopowners had become better organized, they said, and were learning to help one another financially. Acknowledging that much money had been lost, they were willing to accept these losses, they declared, in order to achieve national independence.

Merchants *had* to help one another and become better organized, because Israel was intensifying its pressure upon them. On 18 January, police in East Jerusalem for the first time tried to force open shops, without success.[107] Shutters slammed shut, and the few stores that were open closed down immediately. Israeli officials attributed the merchants' refusal to open to a fear of reprisals by other Palestinians. Some merchants blamed it upon the Israelis. 'They got smart with me,' a pharmacist said. 'I was open, but I had my shutters half-closed. The plainclothes police told me I had to open my shutters all the way. So I closed.'[108] The merchants who met at the National Palace Hotel claimed that since the beginning of their commercial strike on 12 December, over 200 shops in their towns had been damaged by Israeli soldiers. Seventy shops had had their shutters broken more than three times, they said. Soldiers had smashed display windows and even looted shops.

In mid-March, the authorities redoubled their efforts against the strikers. They wanted to have the shops open, but not at the hours decreed by the Intifada leadership. In Nablus, Tulkarm, Jenin and Qalqilya, soldiers tried to prevent storekeepers from opening in the morning, then worked to force open the shops during their afternoon closing hours.[109] In Jericho, jeeps patrolled the streets to make sure that shops and the main agricultural wholesale market would not observe their morning hours of opening.[110] Here and there in West Bank communities, shops were prized open with crowbars, then left to stand open when the owners were absent. Soldiers sometimes entered the stores, stomping on bread, breaking eggs, mixing bleach with flour, smashing refrigerators and overturning fruit stands.[111] One angry soldier slammed his jeep into two locked shops doors, destroying them completely.

Palestinian shopkeepers fought back. In Nablus, Jenin and Tulkarm, Israeli orders to open and close shops at certain times were not heeded. Storekeepers just shut down their shops completely.[112] In East Jerusalem, shopkeepers on Prophets' Street defied an order to remain open from 7:30 a.m. until 7:00 p.m. When the Israeli authorities issued a new order directing stores to close beween 2:00 and 7:00 p.m., merchants simply refused compliance. Fourteen shopkeepers were arrested.[113] Some merchants stopped paying their taxes – one was in jail for over three weeks for this.[114]

Merchants, however, did not have to fight their battles alone. Increasingly, they drew support from local society. Some landlords decided not to collect their rents – a sacrifice that was being advocated by the UNL in its leaflets. Groups of locksmiths were set up to repair locks on shops that had been opened by force.[115] In Gaza, locksmiths stood by to repair shutters and locks as soon as the soldiers had left.[116] In some places, special committees were organized to help shopowners conduct their strikes, and to watch and defend shops that had been forced open by Israelis and left unattended.[117] Commercial strikes thus continued without any let up. On 16 February, a general strike paralysed East Jerusalem. Shopkeepers did not open from 3:00–6:00 p.m., as they had been doing; Arab bus and taxi companies did not operate. This was part of a general strike that closed down the entire West Bank. 'I've never seen it so dead in East Jerusalem,' one Israeli city official commented.[118]

The crucial factor in the success of the commercial strikes was the willingness of shopkeepers and other businessmen to accept a lower standard of living. Israeli actions had exacted a heavy financial toll, but many Palestinians had come to feel that this was not too high a price to pay for the achievement of their goals. 'Deep down, I feel happy,' a car dealer said. 'Money isn't everything. All the world is looking at this place now.'[119] A merchant from al-Bireh expressed similar sentiments:

We want the world to see us [he explained]. And it [the strike] is hurting the Israeli economy because their products are not coming into the West Bank, and they are not collecting [sales] taxes. You can't tax someone if he's not selling anything.[120]

It was the Israelis who sounded tired. On 16 February, Deputy Chief of General Staff Barak was asked if the IDF had decided not to force striking shopowners to open their businesses. 'We do not perceive the strike as a direct threat to public order,' he replied.[121] About the same time, Chief of Staff Shomron declared that soldiers would no longer force open shops.[122] This was not quite true. Israel's efforts to break the strike continued throughout March and April, but the battle had essentially been lost. By mid-May, Palestinians were free to open and close their shops at the times of their own choosing, in compliance with UNL instructions, and with little interference from the army.[123] The Israelis just did not have enough troops to force and keep open every store. 'You can open up one shop by force,' a Palestinian businessman said, 'but you can't open up a whole city.'[124]

The uprising won a victory of quite another sort on 24 February 1988, when Muhammed Ayyed, a Palestinian collaborator, was hanged by his fellow villagers in Qabatya, near Jenin. When the Intifada began, Israeli security services had in place thousands of Palestinian agents and informants in the West Bank and Gaza. 'Collaborators come from marginal social groups,' explained Dr Bishara. 'They are people without professions; people who have been humiliated in society; some are criminals.'[125] Some had special licence plates on their vehicles, and many had been assigned weapons by the Israelis. Muhammed Ayyed, for example, was licensed to carry a Uzi submachine gun – a rare privilege for a Palestinian agent of Israel.[126] Like all other Palestinians, these collaborators went about their daily routine, but at night they communicated by radio to their Israeli employers the news of the day. Quite a few were already known as Israeli agents; others were merely suspected collaborators; and some, of course, went undetected by their fellow Palestinians. After the Intifada began, the question arose as to whether or not these men could still function usefully for Israel. Their continued loyalty would depend in large part upon Israel's ability and willingness to protect them. As the revolt gained strength, pressure was applied to Palestinians who worked for the occupation authorities. In late January, leaflets appeared, signed by the Islamic Jihad, which listed the names of Palestinian policemen, suspected political informants and others who had allegedly co-operated with Israel.[127] At Salfit, near Nablus, Palestinians tried to burn down the house of a village mayor suspected of collaborating with the authorities.[128] On 7 February, Jamil al-Amleh, Head of the Hebron area Village Leagues (an Israeli-sponsored programme for Palestinians designed to counter PLO supporters in the occupied territories), announced his resignation and the dismantling of his organization.[129] Some Arab mayors also came under pressure to resign.[130]

The incident at Qabatya was a turning-point.[131] Hitherto, few if any collaborators had been hurt, despite intensifying pressure. While keeping a lower profile, the vast majority of them had remained loyal to their Israeli employers. After Qabatya, matters would be different. Muhammad Ayyed was a known collaborator, one of many in the Jenin area. On 24 February, a protest demonstration in his village passed close by his house. An argument broke out between him and some of the villagers, who asked him to surrender his weapon. He refused. Tempers flared. A fight erupted. Ayyed pulled out his firearm and began shooting. One shot hit and killed a four-year-old child. The villagers became enraged. For three hours, a reported 4,000 people besieged his house, throwing stones and petrol bombs. (Villagers did evacuate his wife and children from the house, however.) Ayyed continued to fire upon the villagers, wounding 13. He (or his wife) also called upon the Israeli authorities for help. The report was received at the Jenin regional command, and the authorities sent a helicopter to fly over the village and drop tear gas canisters upon the crowd. This action, however, did not deter the villagers. Eventually, they apprehended Ayyed, and hanged him.

One Palestinian in the Jenin area has related the story of how IDF units tried and failed for three hours to rescue Ayyed. The Israeli helicopter operator, according to this popular account, feared that his machine would be hit by stones, so he did not land. Military garrisons nearby could not rescue him because all the mainroads had been blocked with stones. This account, however, seems exaggerated at the very least and may be an attempt to romanticize the Intifada. Media reports of the incident strongly suggested that the Israeli authorities did not really try to rescue Ayyed. One explanation offered for the failure to intervene was that the authorities feared a bloody battle might develop as a result of fighting with thousands of people in the narrow village alleyways. Whatever the reason, the IDF had to give an account to the Knesset Foreign Affairs and Defence Committee. It excused its behaviour by arguing that two hours between the receipt of the first report and the fatality did not provide sufficient time for it to act.

One Israeli source described the Qabatya incident as a serious escalation. The villagers' success, the Hebrew-language daily *Maariv* reported, could encourage other attacks against known collaborators. The system of intelligence so carefully built up by the Israelis over the years, it said, might even collapse. Palestinians throughout the occupied territories were also watching and following the Qabatya affair. An armed collaborator had been besieged by unarmed villagers and the Israelis could not – or would not – do anything to stop it. 'You [Israelis] are capable of risking whole units, pilots and equipment to rescue a single wounded soldier, but when it comes to Arabs you do not care,' said one disgruntled pro-Israeli Palestinian Village League elder. 'This [incident] gave people confidence to be more daring,' declared Dr Abdulfattah. 'Suddenly, people realized how much power they had in their hands.' Following this, four other collaborators from Qabatya turned in their weapons to the village mayor. Collaborators in other places also began handing in their firearms and joining the revolt. Israeli efforts to restore 'deterrence' by closing down Qabatya (disconnecting electricity, telephone lines, water supplies) for 40 days afterwards had no effect on this turn of events.

* * * * * * * * *

The revolt was now spreading to all age groups and sectors of the population. On 31 January 1988, Greek orthodox Christians led a protest march from the Church of the Holy Sepulchre – the first of its kind since Israel's 1982 invasion of Lebanon.[132] This, however, was just one of many marches which occurred that day following Sunday services, as Christian Palestinians, Orthodox and Catholic, responded to calls in the UNL's Leaflet Five (distributed 28 January) for protests to come from churches as well as mosques. Demonstrations broke out among Christians in Bethlehem, Ramallah and Beit Sahour, in addition to Jerusalem. The heeding by Christian Palestinians of calls in the UNL's leaflet was dubbed a new development by the Israeli press, but in fact many Christians had sympathized with the Intifada and had even been part of it from the outset. Shopkeepers in places like Beit Sahour and Beit Jala had participated in the early commercial strikes, and some Christians had gone into mosques, waited for services there to end, and then joined with Muslims in demonstrations. In Gaza, whose Palestinian Christian community was composed of a few extended families, all interrelated, the beating to death on 9 February of nineteen-year-old Elias Tarazi by IDF soldiers fuelled the growing outrage.[133] A member of a very prominent family, Tarazi had left his home on a bicycle and had somehow become involved in a disturbance. His family searched for him for two days before receiving word of his death. Tarazi's funeral was turned into a nationalist demonstration, and he was eulogized as the first Christian martyr of the Intifada. 'It [his death] will prove to the world,' declared one of his relatives, 'that all Palestinians are participating in the uprising, even the Christians.'

The growing involvement of Palestinians in the revolt can be illustrated by two other developments. The first was the emergence in February of a new organization, the Islamic Resistance Movement (*Harakat al-muqawama al-Islamiya*), also known as Hamas.[134] Formed by younger leaders of the Muslim Brotherhood who had been radicalized by the Intifada, Hamas represented a sharp break with the quiescent and gradualist approach of the traditional Muslim Brotherhood leadership and was an acknowledgement that its earlier emphasis upon reform of the individual Muslim had failed. As we have seen, prior to the revolt, the Muslim Brotherhood had not advocated resistance to the occupation. The cause of 'liberating' Palestine was not its cause. The Intifada, however, confronted this organization with the choice of losing its position and influence in the occupied territories entirely, or of preserving itself and gaining legitimacy by joining it. From December 1987, some younger members of the Muslim Brotherhood had participated in the revolt, but as individuals only. In January, communiqués were issued which were supposed to have come from these young men, though no affiliation was claimed. On 11 February, the words Islamic Resistance Movement were used for the first time in a communiqué, pointing to a new activist orientation, and the organization presented itself as an expression of the Muslim Brotherhood.

Unlike Islamic Jihad, Hamas would prove unwilling to subordinate itself to the UNL. 'Palestinians have a practical dispute with Hamas,' Dr Bishara observed in September 1988:

They [Hamas' leaders] have tried to organize independent actions to test their strength among the people and to use the uprising to get more support for themselves. They sometimes introduce different suggestions from those of the national leadership.[135]

Hamas would subsequently introduce its own strike days and, according to its Covenant (issued in August 1988), even claim that it had started the Intifada. It would publish its own leaflets, and assign them serial numbers higher than those of the UNL in order to claim precedence over the UNL. Hamas essentially saw itself as a competitor of the PLO for the leadership of Palestinian society. Joining the Intifada, then, was a way of making gains for itself and for the Muslim Brotherhood, of which Hamas was an integral part. Hamas' goal was the achievement of an Islamic state in the whole of Palestine, including the area 'occupied' by Israel, through holy war. In its view, Palestine was an Islamic trust in perpetuity. No part of it could ever be ceded.

The overwhelming sentiment among Palestinians in the occupied territories was certainly for independence, but as we have seen, many West Bankers and Gazans had been willing to accept a two-state solution even before the Intifada. Moreover, the vast majority subscribed to a secular, not Islamic, state. To grow and develop, then, Hamas would have to find a way of gaining support from, or at least the respect of, the overwhelming majority of Palestinians who were part of the nationalist camp. Herein lay a dilemma. To gain a wider following, Hamas could not go too far in separating itself from the national movement. Hence its decision to participate in the Intifada with stones, not with firearms. Hence, too, its decision to appeal to fellow West Bankers and Gazans with Palestinian slogans, and not strictly religious ones.

The emergence of Hamas was a very important development. It came at a time when the Islamic Jihad was being weakened by arrests and the deportation of key leaders. The Islamic Jihad had not yet made the transition from an élite to a mass organization, and it was therefore unable to absorb the blows dealt it by the Israeli authorities. By March 1988, it had been practically crushed. Months would pass before the Islamic Jihad could rebuild itself. Hamas and, through it, the Muslim Brotherhood thus became the leading Islamic organization to participate in the Intifada. (The only other politically active Muslim group was the Islamic Liberation Party.) Determined to prove themselves on the field of battle (e.g., in street confrontations with the Israeli authorities), and already enjoying support among young people in the refugee camps and lower-class sections of towns, its members would gain new followers as the revolt spread into the rural areas.

In February and March, villagers all over the West Bank erupted in protest demonstrations – the second key element attesting to the spread of the revolt. Men, women and children marched, sang songs and went out into the streets.[136] Palestinian flags were run up electricity poles and flown from rooftops. Roads were blocked, automobile tyres set alight and buses stoned. Israeli troops rushed from one village to another, erasing graffiti, pulling down flags and dispersing crowds of stone-throwing youths.

One such place was Taibeh, a village perched on a mountaintop northeast of Ramallah. A strike had occurred in December; in January, people began boycotting Israeli products and stopped working in the Jewish settlements, but no violence had broken out. In March, however, a three-hour confrontation occurred in which the majority of its 1,400 inhabitants, and not just young people, participated.

The expression of our demonstration [recounted 'Antoun', co-founder of Taibeh's popular committee] was a Palestinian flag that we had erected on the crest of the mountain. The aim was to keep the flag flying as long as we could. All streets, alleyways and trails going up to the mountain-top had been blocked with tyres. After mass on Sunday, the youths began to demonstrate. They burned tyres, hurled rocks and threw about 30 petrol bombs. The Israeli soldiers tried and tried to go up the alleyways but each time they were turned back by the children with stones. This was the revolt. For three hours, the villagers held out. Then a helicopter came and the Israelis took the flag down. We lost one boy dead. Some people were wounded, but not seriously. The troops used rubber bullets, and after that some light ammunition, and tear gas.[137]

The entry of Jewish settlers into villages was a sign of how fast the revolt was spreading in the countryside, and how intense it was. Jewish settlers could not drive their cars without having stones thrown at them. They tried to protect themselves by taking matters into their own hands. Possessing army jeeps with two-way radios and an adequate supply of weapons, settlers (sometimes accompanied by IDF soldiers) entered neighbouring Palestinian villages and towns, puncturing car tyres, smashing the windows of vehicles and homes, burning olive trees, firing their weapons and creating havoc.[138] Villagers greatly feared the settlers – and with good reason. During the first ten months of the revolt, Jewish civilians shot and killed ten Palestinians.

The rising casualty rate was another indicator of the spread of the Intifada. During the first week of February, four Palestinians were shot dead; in the second, 15 died; during the third, the figure was two dead; 15 were killed in the last week of the month.[139] 'The relatively high number of gunfire casualties,' wrote *Jerusalem Post* reporters,

indicated a reversion by troops to the use of live ammunition to repel rioters. Many of the incidents occurred in relatively remote villages, indicating a trend in which the unrest is spreading from the cities to the countryside.[140]

The revolt assumed greater intensity everywhere. On 16 February, a general strike paralysed the West Bank.[141] Few workers arrived at their jobs in Israel. Public transport was non-existent. Residents stayed inside their homes. Palestinians were confronting IDF troops by night as well as by day. In Tulkarm and other places, families turned off all lights in the evening in order to provide better cover to the youths who engaged troops in the streets. 'The Palestinian–Israeli war,' wrote Joel Greenberg, 'is being fought in the territories with the greatest intensity in 20 years.'[142] An entire population was now involved.

With virtually all of Palestinian society engaged in the conflict, the Intifada could now move from stone-throwing and strikes to a much broader and more effective form of resistance. Siniora and others had made a start. The Palestinian people would do the rest. Civil disobedience, as we shall see, would not only be a means for Palestinians to disengage from Israel, but also a way to deepen the Intifada.

5

'All the fish
are in the water'

In spring 1988, a shift in focus was taking place. The revolt had begun as a spontaneous movement of local resistance, consisting mainly of large-scale demonstrations that broke out in dozens of places simultaneously. Work stoppages, peaceful marches and commercial strikes had also occurred, but the main emphasis was on street confrontations. These demonstrations continued, of course. However, they now began to be supplemented and even surpassed by another kind of resistance, made possible by the mass participation of the entire society, which in spite of economic hardship and pressure was showing great adaptability in adjusting to the new circumstances. The boycott of Israeli products, coupled with efforts to increase Palestinian self-reliance, had already begun (production of Palestinian cigarettes, for example, increased by 25 per cent in January).[1] What had been lacking, however, was a willingness among Palestinians of all ages and classes to participate actively in resistance. By March, this was no longer true. Infuriated by Israel's policy of repression, Palestinians en masse were now ready to carry out the acts of civil disobedience called for in the UNL's leaflets. Throughout the occupied territories, Palestinians began cutting their ties with the structures that had maintained Israel's domination and perpetuated its control over them. Many refused to pay their taxes. Others resigned their positions in the Civil Administration. A few burned and destroyed their identity cards. People also began organizing themselves in their neighbourhoods, towns, villages and camps for the purpose of achieving self-sufficiency. This carried civil disobedience beyond mere disengagement from Israeli control and toward the creation of a new order by the Palestinians themselves. As people sought to take charge of their lives in order to rid themselves of the hated occupation, alternative economic and administrative structures arose. This development was of grave concern to the Israelis, who saw it as a threat to the authority of the Civil Administration and as a vehicle for the achievement of de facto Palestinian autonomy. This new form of 'quiet' resistance would not only weaken the power of the Civil Administration, but also extend the Intifada and guarantee its survival.

The UNL's political strategy aimed at crippling the Israeli government in the occupied territories and replacing it with a new national authority. The UNL had already succeeded in demonstrating its power in street demonstrations, commercial strikes, and in other ways. The move to civil disobedience, with its emphasis upon community-based economic organization and the formation of new popular committees, thus represented a qualitative development of the Intifada.[2] According to the author of an article in an Arabic-language weekly published in Cyprus, whose information came from PLO sources on the island, the UNL hoped that by uprooting the occupation authorities' structures and instituting alternative local bodies, it could prepare the ground for an interim stage of autonomy which would be controlled by the PLO and which, it was hoped, would lead to the end of the occupation and the establishment of an independent Palestinian state.[3] As we shall see, however, the extent of civil disobedience and Palestinian self-sufficiency would depend upon more than one factor – not least of them, Israel's own response.

From the beginning, the UNL's leaflets had urged the population to carry out acts of partial civil disobedience.[4] Its first numbered leaflet (10 January) called for the disbandment of all Israeli-appointed municipal councils, village and camp committees, and the cancellation of VAT. Leaflet 4 (21 January) asked Palestinians to boycott Israeli goods, set up popular committees in their localities, work the land and develop home production. Merchants were also requested not to pay taxes. Subsequent leaflets called for the resignation of Palestinian policemen, the contesting of Israel's closure of educational institutions, and overtime work in Palestinian factories to increase production. Leaflet 18 (29 May) stipulated a wide range of civil disobedience measures, including a tax revolt. Through its leaflets the UNL explained to the population the significance of civil disobedience. It meant separation from the occupation authority, rejection of its rules and regulations, and defiance of its laws. A more austere life would be the result. Israel, it said, could be expected to do everything possible to stop this movement. It would cut off fuel, water and electricity, and prevent the transport of goods. Palestinians were thus urged to make do with the basics, to make sacrifices and care for one another.

There was, however, an ambiguity to this call for civil disobedience. Statements in some leaflets seemed to indicate a desire for a total break. Leaflet 5, for example, requested that Palestinians not work in Israeli factories, farms and projects.[5] Leaflet 9 called upon those employed in branches of the Civil Administration to resign at once – a demand which, if acted upon, would have affected between 17,000 and 20,000 Palestinian employees.[6] In late May, a leaflet asked people to refrain from dealings with the organs and bodies of the occupation – the civil courts, petitions, the Civil Administration proper, and all appointed committees and councils. Popular committees were to replace the police and other services provided by the Israelis. Palestinians were not to pay taxes or fees to Israeli authorities. Identity cards were to be burned, though at a later stage.[7] In June, leaflets again urged the severing of all ties with Israeli authorities.[8] However, other statements suggested that the UNL was not prepared to go as far as comprehensive civil disobedience. Demands for Palestinians to cease working for Israelis were later modified; Palestinians could work in Israel, except on strike days. (They were not, however, to work on Israeli settlements.)[9] A call for Palestinian civil servants to resign was subsequently explained as applying to policemen, tax collectors, and VAT, motor vehicles and housing employees, but not to Palestinians employed in social work, education, agriculture, health and postal services, who were to remain in their jobs.[10] A call for the resignation of all West Bank deputies in the Jordanian parliament (Leaflet 10) was subsequently reversed. And so on.[11] Several days after Leaflet 18 had called for an extensive campaign of civil disobedience, Yasser Arafat stated in an interview that he had not yet decided whether to embark upon comprehensive civil disobedience. 'We are now at the stage of partial strikes and partial civil disobedience,' he said.[12]

How are we to account for this ambiguity? In the first place, the leaflets were a response to a changing situation, of which the UNL was trying to take advantage, rather than the result of a clearly considered and pre-planned strategy. Second, a certain slackness of co-ordination existed among the factions in the drafting and issuing of the leaflets. Representatives of the four PLO factions comprising the UNL would meet and reach general agreement on the contents of a leaflet. But it was the responsibility of individual factions to draft and print up the actual leaflets themselves. According to the Palestinian scholar Dr Abu-Amr, this gave each faction an opportunity to introduce its own rhetoric and make marginal changes in the texts.[13] It was even acceptable for a faction, if it disagreed strongly with the contents of a particular leaflet, to issue a leaflet under its own name, stating its position without disavowing that of the UNL. Yet this did not mean that the leaflets differed from one another. There was a broad consistency throughout, the most notable exception being the double leaflet (10) which first called for the resignation of Palestinian members of the Jordanian parliament and then reversed itself.

More to the point, within the UNL and the factions outside, a debate was underway as to the pace and extent of civil disobedience.[14] One side, composed of pragmatic elements inside and outside al-Fatah (Arafat's supporters), urged a measured, gradual approach. The objective constraints, they argued, were too great for the population to move quickly to full civil disobedience. Israel could considerably hamper the flow into the occupied territories of the money needed to compensate for anticipated financial losses, and the Palestinian economic infrastructure was too weak to provide for society's basic needs. People's expectations should not be raised too high, they said, because statehood was not around the corner in any case. These men represented that tendency in the national camp for which the Intifada was a means of enhancing the PLO's status internationally and enabling it to negotiate a settlement of the dispute. The other side, composed of members of the PFLP and perhaps some elements in al-Fatah and the DFLP, wanted to move to full civil disobedience. These men reflected the tendency which held that the uprising should itself be the vehicle for achieving Palestinian national goals. Their opponents argued that

the Palestinian people would be unable to respond to over-
ambitious goals and that full civil disobedience would be self-
defeating. Most of the earnings of Gazan workers in Israel went
to provide for their daily needs and those of their families. How
could they be expected to give them up? Similarly, Palestinian
factories whose owners refused to pay their taxes would be shut
down. How, the gradualists argued, would that help the
Palestinian cause? In the end, the leadership of the uprising
decided not to proceed to full civil disobedience, but rather to
adopt certain elements of it and prepare the way for greater civil
disobedience at some later date through the development of
home production, the build-up of an economic infrastructure and
the expansion of the role of the popular committees.

It would, of course, be up to the people themselves to decide
how and when to respond. By March 1988, Palestinians had
collectively decided to sever ties with the military government in
a dramatic way. The boycott of Israeli products would be
accelerated, but something new was to be added: a tax revolt and
the mass resignation of Palestinians working for the Civil
Administration. When this happened, the Intifada became a
movement of the entire society, which became mobilized on a
scale unprecedented in twenty years of occupation.

On 6 March, Palestinian employees of the Gaza Income and
Property Tax division resigned.[15] Only two of its 40 Palestinian
employees remained on the job. Shortly afterwards, bookkeepers
in the Jenin area decided to stop handing over their tax returns to
the income tax officials. On 12 March, the Israeli press reported
that most of the 300 or so Palestinian policemen in the Judaea
district of the West Bank had quit. One day later, it was
announced that almost half of the 1,000 Palestinian policemen in
the occupied territories had resigned, and that many police
stations would be closed. In East Jerusalem, eight policemen,
representing 10 per cent of the Palestinian police in the city, left
their jobs. Palestinian internal revenue service personnel and
customs officials also quit their posts.

Palestinians who resigned made it clear that they had done so
in order to support calls from the UNL and the Islamic factions.
The authorities, embarrassed by the magnitude of these resignations, disputed this. In their view, Palestinians had resigned only
under duress. They had caved in to pressures and threats from

the Intifada leaders. As in the case of the commercial strikes, coercion was applied by the leadership organizations. In particular, pressure was brought to bear upon the Israeli-appointed mayors and members of municipal, village and camp councils.[16] Some received letters requesting their resignations and warning of immediate but unspecified punishments in the event of non-compliance. Attacks were made on the property of some Israeli-appointed officials. Leaflet 10 even contained a death threat against municipal council members who remained in their posts. In one instance, an attempt was made upon a mayor's life. (This was Hasan al-Tawil of al-Bireh.) Coercion, then, was a factor in the resignations of some mayors and council and municipal members. However, such pressure cannot possibly explain why Palestinians broke with the occupation authorities in such large numbers and simultaneously. After all, in March Palestinians were also in full tax revolt against the authorities. Coercion could not have compelled so many Palestinians to act as they did.

The Israeli explanation contains a false assumption and overlooks crucial developments that occurred in January and February. The false assumption, held by Rabin and many in the political establishment, was that a conflict of interest existed between the vast majority of Palestinians, who only wanted to live their lives in peace, and a minority – the activists – who were preventing them from doing so.[17] The truth was quite different. On the eve of the revolt, virtually every Palestinian was opposed to Israeli rule and from its outset a general sympathy existed for the youthful protesters. Some Israeli observers understood this. It was not fear of punishment by Intifada activists that drove Palestinians to co-operate with them, observed a writer for *Al Hamishmar*, but rather a ' . . . genuine desire to be freed of the insufferable burden of Israel – the inevitable consequence of the Likud policy over the past 10 years, which has been continued by Defense Minister Yitzhaq Rabin's policy.'[18]

Developments in January and February were also an important catalyst. There was, first, Israel's own policy. 'You with your clubs are strengthening us,' a refugee camp youth told an Israeli reporter.[19]

When I see a soldier beat someone, lay his hands on elderly people or women, I, blind with rage, tell him: Wait a minute, he is no better than me. I, the cleaner of your toilets, look at the soldier and say: I am worth more. I am better and I can face up to him.

The continuation of the Intifada, a senior government official stated in a document, was the result of the brutality of IDF troops and their degradation of Palestinians.[20] Equally important were positive developments: the success of the commercial strikes, the world-wide media attention, the IDF's failure to save its collaborator at Qabatya, the sense of being able to sustain the Intifada. 'This gave people confidence that the Intifada was there to stay,' noted Dr al-Jarbawi. 'People saw that there were advantages in supporting it, that it might be a way to end the occupation.'[21]

By spring 1988, large numbers of Palestinians were refusing to pay their taxes. While it is impossible to gauge the precise extent of the tax revolt, it very quickly assumed large-scale proportions. Refusal of Palestinians to pay taxes was cited as the reason for the growing budget deficit of the Civil Administration.[22] In February and March, a decline of about 20 per cent had occurred in the amount of VAT collected in the occupied territories. This had been due not only to Palestinian non-compliance with the tax laws, but also to the decline of economic activity in the territories generally, owing in part to workers' absenteeism because of strikes and Israeli-imposed measures. The same reasons underlay the accumulating debts owed by Palestinian merchants and factory owners to their Israeli suppliers, which had reached $60 million by mid-February. The tax revolt gained momentum, as individuals and groups followed the example of the striking merchants and refused to pay. By mid-March, most Palestinians living in East Jerusalem had not paid their municipal taxes. Throughout Gaza and the West Bank, people quietly 'defaulted' on the payment of fees and taxes.

The non-payment of taxes was an important matter of principle for Palestinians. People knew that they were not only paying for their own occupation, but were also subsidizing the Israeli treasury. Palestinians paid an income tax, VAT on merchandise and services from Israel, property taxes, and customs duties on goods imported through Israel or from Jordan across the bridges. In addition, large deductions were made from the salaries of those who were officially employed in Israel. These sums, according to Meron Benvenisti, were transferred directly to the Israeli treasury without the workers being entitled to most of the benefits which Israeli workers received.[23] In toto, Benvenisti believed that Palestinians in the occupied territories contributed about $50 million annually to Israel. While his figure is only an estimate (Israeli defence officials put the Palestinian contribution to the Israeli consumer at $16 million per annum), the occupation clearly profited Israel. What better way to weaken it than to destroy the profits from it!

The Civil Administration faced a serious crisis. Tax losses were eroding its financial base and resignations of Palestinian employees were crippling its ability to function normally. Taxes were not so readily collectible from a hostile population without Palestinians who knew how to do it. The departure of local employees paralysed the Gaza tax division, whose annual returns exceeded the amount spent by Israel on Gaza's 'development', and made subsequent collections much more difficult. 'The tax division is the most hated department in Gaza,' said one departing Palestinian employee. 'Even the army officers who run the Civil Administration are scared to go into Gaza to try to collect taxes.'[24] The Civil Administration made cutbacks and reduced services. Police stations were closed in March.[25] Teachers in government schools received three weeks leave of absence in April. In May, the Civil Administration announced the impending lay-off of 25 per cent of its West Bank employees. During the summer, health, education, veterinary medicine, agricultural and other services experienced cutbacks. West Bankers employed by contract or on a daily basis were dispensed with. Palestinians who remained at work in the Civil Administration had their salaries reduced by 10 per cent. Civil disobedience was indeed having an impact.

As noted, however, Palestinians did not proceed to a complete break. They did not shut down everything. The non-payment of taxes and resignations of officials were not absolute. Some Palestinians who had quit returned to work, though not in very large numbers.[26] Many mayors remained in their posts, though some members of the Israeli-appointed councils resigned.[27] The mass burning of identity cards, which every Palestinian male over the age of 16 had to carry, never materialized. Some Palestinians did destroy or give up their cards.[28] The most publicized incident occurred on 7 July in Beit Sahour when several hundred residents handed in their cards after soldiers and tax collectors had raided the village, impounding cars for the non-payment of licensing and other fees, and entering homes where they seized the residents' identity cards to guarantee the payment of back taxes.[29] Beit Sahour's example was not followed on any significant scale elsewhere in the occupied territories. 'Without an ID card,' commented a spokesman for the International Red Cross in Jerusalem, 'a person can do nothing. It is forbidden not to have one, so a Palestinian can be arrested and put in jail. He cannot apply for anything or visit his relatives in jail, or pass through any checkpoint.'[30] Identity cards were required to obtain permits for nearly every public act, from marriage to driving a car. At this stage at least, Palestinians were not ready to break totally. But they did not need to. A measure of the damage inflicted on the power of the Civil Administration is revealed by the fact that one year after civil disobedience had begun only six or seven police stations were operating in the whole of the territories. Eleven of the Civil Administration's nineteen employment exchanges had been set on fire, as had 41 bus stations.[31]

Disengagement on this scale imperilled services from water supply to street cleaning and to garbage collection. Elias Freij seems to have feared the worst: the resignation of policemen, he said, would paralyse the civil courts. When quarrels occurred, there would be no help to call upon.[32] In a real sense, he was correct. When car accidents took place, no policemen or ambulances rushed to the scene. In Gaza, the Israelis sent judges away on unpaid leave because the civil courts were no longer functioning.[33] However, if Israeli observers saw paralysis, chaos and anarchy resulting, Palestinians found only opportunity.

* * * * * * * * *

Palestinians could survive their partial disengagement from Israel only by moving to a subsistence standard of living, and by organizing themselves economically and socially in hope of providing for their basic needs and reducing dependence upon the occupation authorities. A crucial step was taken when the upper and middle classes decided to lower their demands. 'In the beginning,' observed Dr al-Jarbawi,

the upper and middle classes complained, because they believed that the Intifada had no future. When the Intifada picked up momentum, this eroded internal complaining. 'I'll lower my expectations,' people began saying. 'Maybe something will come out of this.'[34]

For people of means, this not only involved postponing their children's education or letting one of their two cars sit in the garage, without a licence, but also meant considerable financial sacrifices. Many who owned buildings and other properties voluntarily renounced the collection of part or all of the rents due. 'My family owns property in the Jenin area,' said one middle-class Palestinian, 'and we have cut rents by $50,000.' This move was important. If the upper and middle classes had not done this, 'a struggle would have occurred between those with nothing to lose, like the Gazans, and those with too much to lose,' continued Dr al-Jarbawi.

Complaints that were first heard no longer existed, because the upper segments [of society] realized that the Intifada had a great magnitude and so they co-operated and not out of coercion. People began to say 'This is the way it should have been all along.'

The transition to a subsistence economy and organizing for greater self-sufficiency were going to require a high degree of co-operation among Palestinians. But this was precisely what conditions were forcing upon them. Owing to Israeli-imposed curfews and closures, as well as Intifada-inspired strikes and other actions, Palestinians were travelling less. People shopped only on certain days, and in markets close to their places of residence. With children home all the time, and male family members also spending more time in their homes, families and neighbourhoods were brought closer together. 'People now close at noon,' noted Dr al-Jarbawi, 'so they sit together, talk, get to know each other. People tend to come together, play cards, and discuss.'[35] Dr Abdulfattah concurred. 'I have gotten to know all the people who are poor and needy in my neighbourbood, which I did not know before.'[36]

Communities also learned how to deal with daily arrests, beatings and shooting incidents. Plaques and memorials were erected for those who had been killed. Palestinians released from jail received a hero's welcome from their people. Co-operation thus increased and support for the collective was raised to a high level. When an automobile accident occurred in Gaza, someone would emerge from the crowd to take the injured to the hospital. Women in town quarters began knitting woollen sweaters for the poor and needy and for the children. People became accustomed to helping one another.

I take home one kilo of potatoes [said a Gazan] and give some to a needy neighbour. I give part of my salary to a poor neighbour and consider it a loan. Everyone asks which are the families in need and everyone gives what he can. We have a nice emotional attitude towards each other.[37]

In the northern West Bank, a similar attitude was developing. 'By spring,' continued Dr Abdulfattah,

people had acclimatized themselves to the new way of life. There grew up a sense of mutual consciousness, so people helped each other by any means. If some shabab had to leave a village, people in a nearby village put them up. Everyone was ready to help each other. Efficiency in mutual relations was very high. Solidarity was growing. Differences and hindrances usually found were overcome.

This co-operative spirit did not mean that the entire society had come together as one unit. In central West Bank towns like Ramallah, where a large number of people originated from outside the area and many families had relatives who lived in the US, the co-operative spirit was less intense than in places like Jenin, Tulkarm and Qalqilya where people had rural origins and where outsiders were few. 'Jenin and Nablus are more closed societies,' explained Dr al-Jarbawi:

People are tied closely to each other. In these towns, which are more like villages, you find three or four major extended families. If someone is shot and killed, by necessity all family members must participate in the funeral and the demonstrations about the death. People pick on each other more.'Ah, you are drinking milk from Israel,' one will say to another. 'Why do you work on a strike day?' another will ask. 'Why is my son involved in demonstrations and your son not?'[38]

In central West Bank towns, by contrast, such intimacy and intense human relationships were found only in lower-middle-class areas.

In Gaza, co-operation was higher still. Living in an area that

was small, poor, hemmed in and easily cut off from the outside
world (there were only two exit and entry points), Gazans stood
face to face with the occupation. 'We in Gaza cannot hide in the
hills [as West Bankers could],' said one youth. 'We must be
stronger here. No one is wounded in his back.'[39] One mark of co-
operation in Gaza was the Central Blood Bank Society, a local
organization whose purpose was to ensure a supply of blood to all
Gaza hospitals and even some in Israel (Gazans were transferred
to Israeli hospitals). With the help of donors, this provided blood
for all needs, free of charge.

As Palestinians lowered their living standards and began
organizing within their own communities, they found strength in
their old traditions. The popular press began devoting more
space to articles on customary law and printed photographs of
pastoral scenes. The concept of *awni*, which conveys the idea of
being charitable, of helping others and sharing what you have
with those who are in need, experienced a revival. 'In the
nineteenth century,' explained Dr al-Jarbawi,

village land was collective land. Everyone helped you cultivate your land
and build your house. People were used to helping each other in all
facets of life. After the land registration law of 1858 [according to which
land was converted into private property] people still helped each other,
though the concept declined. You could, though, see examples of it. If
you had an excess of bread you just went and offered it. When you saw
someone in distress, you gave help. Today there is a reassertion of awni
in the towns and villages where people are still peasants. Awni is found
in the northern West Bank, in Jenin, for example, but in Ramallah only
in lower-middle-class areas.[40]

In some communities (Beit Sahour, for example), people formed
co-ordinating committees made up of members of the four UNL
factions and 'sectors': merchants, industrialists, doctors, engineers,
academics, and so on. These people would collect money from
others in their professions, who donated the proceeds of one
day's work a week to the co-ordinating committee. A social
worker then distributed this money to the poor and needy.[41]

Another traditional practice to undergo a revival was *atwi* – a
kind of mediation historically performed by clan members who
would gather to settle disputes. 'With the establishment by Israel
of civil courts,' explained Miss Nora Kort, a Palestinian social
worker,

this informal practice began to die out, but it was revived to a degree and has taken a strong direction since the Intifada. People are trying to solve their problems themselves. If a dispute occurs and someone is killed, people try to establish the identity of the murdered party and the murderer and find people who have influence in both families. The murderer's family passes the word to the family of the deceased that it is coming to take *atwi*. This family then receives the guests and often extends forgiveness. Most of the time, a monetary settlement is made.[42]

In Gaza, too, disputes were settled by *sulha*, or peace made between two parties, rather than through courtroom judgments and decisions.[43] The point is that the return to tradition derived from the Intifada, not just to help people survive, but also to reinforce resistance to the occupation.

The shift to a subsistence standard of living was associated with the re-emergence of the domestic economy. Production came to be centred upon the household, or a number of households, and consumption based largely upon what could be produced locally. Prior to the Israeli occupation of 1967, Palestinians had been mostly producers, but during the 1970s they became consumers, working for wages and spending their earnings to buy capital goods and other products made in Israel or imported from abroad. However, in villages located far from the towns, an old household economy continued in existence. Families kept some animals (chickens, rabbits, pigeons) and had small garden plots. Wages were supplemented by knitting and other kinds of domestic production. The transition to household production, while marking a radical change for many Palestinians, was not something foreign to the culture.

By spring, Palestinians were paring needs to the bare minimum. People stored up flour and milk, used oil and kerosene lamps, and for water relied upon catch basins, reservoirs and cisterns. Bread was baked on big stones over fires of dry tree branches, in the old Palestinian manner called *tabun*. If possible, families kept goats (for milk and cheese), a few laying hens (one egg a day for protein) and also cultivated garden plots. They preserved their surplus by canning and pickling processes. Olives, olive oil and cheese were stored away. Homes became centres of retail trade as well as production.

As noted, Palestinian self-sufficiency was part of a wider strategy of opposition to the occupation. The aim was to reduce dependence upon Israel for goods and services, to produce or buy Palestinian, at least whenever possible. 'Going into a grocery store and not buying Tnuva [Israeli dairy] products is now a kind of resistance,' Dr al-Jarbawi explained:

You ask 'Do you have an Arab product of the same kind?' If there is none, you buy the Israeli product but you also start reorganizing to [supply] the product that is missing from the shelf and which could be produced by Arabs.[44]

Palestinians would continue to make money by working and even producing for Israelis, but they would also compete with Israel by developing their own agricultural products and industrial goods, whose surpluses would be sold in the Palestinian market for less than Israeli goods. While Israelis would have greater difficulty marketing their products in the occupied territories, Palestinians would continue to earn some money. 'The idea,' affirmed Dr al-Jarbawi, 'was to let a Palestinian rather than an Israeli make a profit from this.' Though Palestinians would never be able to dispense entirely with external products, dependence could be significantly reduced if they bought only the basic items and returned to household production.

Of all the elements making up the household economy, vegetable gardens, appropriately dubbed 'Victory Gardens', were the most widespread.[45] 'I have counted 15 kinds of vegetables that we have grown since the Intifada began,' exclaimed Dr Abdulfattah as he examined the small garden in front of his home in Jenin:

We cannot feed ourselves on all of them but some that we grow provide all our needs. Eggplants can be used ten ways for cooking. I have just put dung in the ground, not fertilizers, in order to reduce dependence upon Israel. For every villager there is one small garden. Just think of it: maybe 200,000 gardens.[46]

In towns, little garden plots were to be found sprouting in the corners of courtyards or growing in the back and front yards of homes, where chickens scratched in the earth and rabbits and goats could occasionally be seen. In many places, neighbourhoods had communal plots to cultivate, sharing the produce and strengthening their solidarity as a result of their common labour.

'Most of the young men of Beit Annan, a village near Ramallah, are labourers,' Miss Kort commented, 'but they have planted vegetable gardens and are self-sufficient.'[47]

Such gardens, and the animal rearing that usually accompanied them, helped stimulate exchange within individual communities, since families used the surplus to add to their income. Some marketed eggs, or traded animal products, or constructed and sold hatcheries to meet local demands. The need for technical advice (on animal breeding, ploughing, etc.) was joined to the problem of supply. Ploughs were required, not to mention seeds and seedlings. In some districts agricultural committees were established that received donations from villages. One of these committees supplied Ramallah neighbourhoods with fertilizers, seeds and seedlings, and advice, 'One neighbourhood got implements from villages to do ploughing,' observed Dr Hanan Ashrawi, Professor of English Literature at Birzeit University. 'My neighbourhood got cauliflower and peppers, advice on where to plant and how to plant.'[48] Relief organizations like the Union of Agricultural Work Committee, and PARC (the Palestine Agricultural Relief Committee), which had been in existence before the Intifada, also helped small West Bank farmers. Possessing a large nursery and having contacts with agricultural engineers and other specialists, PARC distributed seeds and seedlings, produced cages and hatcheries, and arranged tours of towns and villages by technical experts who gave talks and offered advice.

A model of achievement was the town of Beit Sahour, blessed with an abundance of educated professional people and possessing a strong community spirit, though not deeply involved in agriculture prior to the Intifada. Following the resignation of the policemen, the residents of Beit Sahour began organizing themselves. Families started planting their backyard gardens with vegetables, and people began to see the need for greater co-operation in agricultural matters. In mid-March an agricultural centre, named the Shed, was established by a group of volunteer professionals who were also close friends. Its purpose was to provide the community with seeds, seedlings and equipment. Hundreds of thousands of seedlings (tomato, eggplant, pepper, cauliflower and lettuce) were sold. (These had been procured from nurseries in the West Bank and elsewhere.) The Shed also sold layer and frier chickens, fruit trees, lambs, fertilizers and pesticides, hoes, drip irrigation equipment and many other items to the community, often at near cost price. In April the centre began offering services to areas outside Beit Sahour.

Private homes increasingly became a favoured place for conducting retail trade and other business. Many merchants moved goods out of the shops and into their own residences. In Tulkarm, for example, some homes were turned into mini shopping centres. In communities placed under curfew, foodstuffs and other items were purchased and stored in one house, known only to the local residents. People entered through the back door to make their purchases. 'Neighbourhood shops', as these places were called, sold a great variety of items, even appliances. Some homes were turned into slaughterhouses, butcheries and bakeries. The home was indeed becoming a market-place.

Houses also were centres of industrial production. Food processing was done by women in their homes or in local workshops. One woman would make *kubbeh* (spiced ground lamb), put it in the freezer, and market it in the store; another would specialize in biscuits, baking and packaging them, and selling them in the supermarket; a third would spend two hours a day making *felafel* (deep-fried balls of ground chick-peas) for the neighbourhood; and so on. Small entrepreneurs like these were able to carve out little niches for themselves and become quite successful. Thyme, an important vegetable product, became very popular with West Bank Palestinians. 'Before the Intifada,' related Miss Kort,

thyme sold at 6–9 shekels per kilogramme and was a business restricted to people in the north. Since then, more and more women have been employed in processing it, and it now [December 1988] sells for 13–15 shekels per kilogramme. It is in great demand.[49]

Pickled products became very popular, replacing the Palestinian taste for Israeli jam. Women also made tomato paste in their homes, selling it to grocers. Textile production in West Bank homes, workshops and local co-operatives also increased. 'Before the Intifada,' Dr al-Jarbawi explained,

people would produce textiles in homes and send them to Israel where the product was finished, returned to the West Bank and purchased by

Palestinians. Now the mentality is 'we will still produce textiles for the Israelis, but on the side we will have our own products and compete with them too.' People are producing textiles quietly in their shops and homes and they are sold here on the West Bank where they are a local product and can be sold for less money [than Israeli-produced textiles]. At the same time, Palestinians are making money by continuing to produce for the Israelis, as before; but the Israelis have more trouble selling their textiles in the West Bank.[50]

During the Intifada, most industrial plants which had received licences before December 1987 continued in operation. Owing to a fall in Palestinian purchasing power and the population's decision to tighten its belt, total sales were down, but losses would have been far greater had it not been for the increased demand for local products. (Having the protection of an American or European company, like RC Cola, also helped Palestinian industries survive.) Palestinian companies were soon producing many of the pharmaceutical items and medical supplies needed locally, as well as many food items. Tnuva products faced growing competition from the dairy products of Jneidi and Mashrou companies, especially in the rural areas. A big rise in Palestinian entrepreneurialism had commenced.

* * * * * * * * * *

The home economy only formed one part of the Palestinian attempt to achieve greater control over their daily lives. In addition, there were local committees, which provided organization for society and a structure to sustain local resistance to the occupation. Popular committees, as we have seen, had begun to arise in December. But the spur to their growth was the need for protection consequent upon the resignation of Palestinian policemen.[51] Following attacks by settlers upon Palestinian homes and cars in Hebron, Palestinians in various places organized guard teams, erected observation posts on rooftops and formed roadblocks to impede settlers' cars.[52] Hebron's example was followed by other localities. In the central West Bank village of Husan, security guards watched for the arrival of settlers, soldiers or Palestinians working for Shin Beth (Israeli intelligence). Youths on bicycles scouted the area and reported any suspicious movements.[53] In many towns, night watches were done by older people, who also performed other kinds of guard duties.

The functions of these committees soon widened to cover a myriad of activities and services. In Beit Sahour, committees were formed to clean the streets; collect garbage; educate children; gather and store food, medicine and first-aid equipment; supply medical treatment; and provide assistance to the poor and needy.[54] (Popular committees did not make poor people feel inferior; members came late at night and left some kerosene or a food package near the door.) Each neighbourhood committee had subcommittees for agriculture, first-aid training, and so on. There was also a traffic committee, a social committee (to resolve disputes) and a relief committee.

Such groups were formed spontaneously by local people who were willing and able to help. 'Neighbourhood committees in Ramallah,' Dr Ashrawi observed, 'include practically everyone in the neighbourhood. They are not based upon political organization or sex. They handle all matters: arbitration, welfare, agriculture, medicine, education and security.'[55] Beit Sahour's agricultural committee was made up of five professionals who were all close friends: a teacher, a civil engineer, a dentist, a plant physiologist and an agricultural engineer.[56] 'After the death of our first martyr,' related 'Antoun', from the village of Taibeh, 'I and an older man decided to form a popular committee for our village. No one told us to do this. We just sat down and took the decision ourselves.'[57] Popular committees, however, could not have arisen so quickly, or functioned so effectively, had there not been a structure below. Many committee members came from organizations already in existence, that is, the political factions and the Islamic groups.

The committee we put together [continued Antoun] had one representative from each clan in the village. We chose individuals who were patriotic, clever, physically active, good listeners, and who could withstand beatings in the event of arrest. All were members of factions: al-Fatah, the Communist Party, and the PFLP, in that order.

Committee members unaffiliated to any of the organized groups were called 'independents'. 'These are the best men,' said a villager from Husan, 'because they say "we are all one people. Party affiliation is not important."'[58] Husan's popular committees, however, were almost entirely composed of members of al-Fatah and Islamic Jihad. Some independents ended up joining one or another of the factions; others never did.[59] By spring, genuine popular committees had come into existence, representing the entire society. 'Palestinians showed,' commented Dr Ashrawi, 'that they were capable of organizing their lives in the face of the occupation.'[60] Based upon the will of the people, the Intifada was being broadened and deepened.

Popular committees not only provided services; they also became the authority in their localities. One of their functions was the mediation of disputes. Peace (sulha) committees were organized by the factions to resolve problems of all kinds. 'The other day,' said Dr Abdulfattah, 'a quarrel between two families broke out in a village near Jenin. A man was killed. The committees put an end to the quarrel right away.'[61] While basing themselves in theory upon customary law, sulha committees rendered verdicts in new ways: fines were assessed for offenders and given to the poor and needy. And the village mayors? 'In the West Bank, if a mayor wants to preserve his position, he must co-ordinate his actions with the young people,' Dr Bishara remarked.[62] Another illustration of how the authority of the popular committees was asserted can be found in the way they dealt with collaborators. According to Dr Abu-Amr, collaborators were requested to turn in their weapons, publicly announce an end to their co-operation with Israeli authorities, and ask forgiveness in the mosques over loudspeakers. Some had to lead demonstrations. Those who refused saw their houses burned. A few, who turned their weapons against other Palestinians, were killed.[63]

The fact that many popular committee members were not just local residents giving aid and advice to their communities, but also representatives of the four factions comprising the UNL was very important. This lent a certain organizational strength and discipline to these structures, and guaranteed that they would serve as the local arm of the UNL, which had been encouraging their formation and considered them essential for the establishment of an alternative political-administrative authority in the provinces.[64] 'In our village,' said one local activist,

we have a secret committee which takes decisions for the entire community. It follows completely all the instructions from the UNL, but also issues its own instructions, which recently included asking a wealthy man to give some money to a poor family.[65]

Popular committees in the town of Qalqilya instructed its inhabitants to follow all UNL commands. They requested that merchants not pay taxes, that property-owners discount the rents of those who had little money, and that people not pay their water or electricity bills.[66] Popular committees thus formed the bottom part of the two-tiered structure of Intifada leadership, supporting and implementing the decisions of the UNL.

The presence of faction members on the committees also meant that a kind of communication could take place between the top and the bottom. Once a decision had been reached by the UNL, the members of each of the four constituent organizations would pass the word to their followers at the base. However, as Dr al-Jarbawi has noted, poor communications (owing to Israeli restrictive measures) reduced the degree of co-ordination between the summit and base, and for this reason local leaders were excluded from the decisions taken by the UNL.[67] Relative isolation, though, enhanced the influence of the popular committees, making them the only local authority in their areas.

Drawn from people at all levels of society and supported by a population ready to sacrifice for the sake of the collective, these popular committees could not be uprooted by the Israelis, no matter how many arrests they made. For every person jailed, a replacement emerged. The occupation authorities, as one Israeli security officer lamented, could not place a soldier next to every Palestinian.[68]

This did not mean that there was no friction between the popular committees and elements of the local population. One of the committees' tasks was to exhort people to greater sacrifices for the Intifada and bring pressure to bear upon those who refused to co-operate. This job fell almost entirely to the strike committees, composed of young men, which organized the demonstrations and enforced the writ of the UNL. In some localities strike forces collected fees from Palestinians who insisted upon working in Israel when they were not supposed to; in other places, young men set up checkpoints, examined vehicles and turned back those that were carrying workers to Israel.[69] An example of the kind of pressure that could be exerted is found in the announcement of the Qalqilya popular committees to the people of that town. Any car transporting goods to local workshops that manufactured products for Israel would be set on fire. Auditors' offices were to close down and stop acting as middlemen between the merchants and the income tax department. The appointed mayor was asked to resign, or else face the 'long arm of the masses'. Collaborators (mentioned by name) were also warned. The aim, of course, was to assert the authority of the Intifada against that of the occupation authorities.

Popular committees strengthened local communities in their struggle against the occupation. In Burqueen village, calls were broadcast from the mosque for people not to assist a well-known collaborator in the harvest of his olives. He was also asked to donate the proceeds of the harvest to the needy. When the collaborator informed the Israelis, the IDF imposed a curfew upon the village, harassed and beat the young men and closed down the olive presses, but the villagers, organized behind their committees, remained steadfast. They refused to help or work for the collaborator.[70] How far such 'organization' could go can be seen in the example of the Ramallah health committee, whose function was to assure rapid treatment of casualties from demonstrations, but which became so well-organized that it actually took control of the hospital there. When a Palestinian flag was hoisted on the roof, Israeli soldiers had to reconquer the building.[71]

Whenever the IDF relaxed its pressure, some villages would declare themselves 'liberated'.[72] Salfit, a town of 6,000, for a time became a model of a 'liberated' community. In April, a local popular committee made up of members of the PCP and al-Fatah replaced the representatives of the Civil Administration in running the town. Graffiti on the walls was painted over, garbage was collected, and the erection of stone barricades prohibited. Cleanliness was maintained, and services continued to be provided to the inhabitants. The aim was to prove that life could be orderly under a Palestinian administration. Fearing that Salfit's example would be emulated, IDF troops entered the town, arrested about 70 suspected committee members, and placed it under curfew.

IDF-initiated operations restored control over such communities, but usually only for a short time. The minute Israeli troops departed, the popular committees resumed their activities. Without them, communities would not have been able to go nearly so far in their resistance to the occupation. The survival and persistence of these committees in the face of strong Israeli measures to eradicate them can be explained by the fact that at the most basic level of society, the leadership had become the mass, and the mass, the leadership. A fusion had occurred. A new popular authority was establishing itself alongside that of the Military Government.[73] The late Moshe Dayan had once described Israel's strategy by the anti-guerrilla principle of distinguishing 'the fish from the water'.[74] By this he meant that Israel should endeavour to separate the population from the activists in order to ensure that the bulk of the people remained neutral, if not actually on Israel's side. Only then could Israel defeat the PLO guerrillas. Once the population assisted them, they would be able to move as freely as fish in water. By the summer of 1988, all the fish were in the water. In Beit Sahour, Palestinians wanted by Israeli authorities walked freely in the streets. 'You would not have seen this before,' a local resident exclaimed. 'There are fewer collaborators now; that is one reason. Yet Israeli troops are stationed in Beit Sahour and still such men go totally free, uncaptured.'[75]

The Intifada had thus become institutionalized, a way of life for the entire society. And this could be seen not just in the structures of popular committees, but in individual and collective behaviour, even in the popular consciousness.

The important thing in all of this [observed Dr Abu-Amr] is the sense of unity that has been inspired. Eighty people work on the same small plot. You don't need 80 persons but community spirit is important. People are willing to pay any price in the struggle for emancipation. Their willingness and commitment to sacrifice is the key.[76]

This was evident from such simple actions as the people of Taibeh taking food by donkey back over the mountains at night to the villagers of Kafr Malek who were under curfew; or the residents of the town of Tulkarm putting out electrical lights and blacking out their windows at night to help the shabab who came out into the dark streets to confront Israeli troops; or the relief given by food committees in Ramallah to the refugee camps of Jalazone, Qalandia and al-Amari.[77]

The strength that such co-operation could generate can be most clearly seen in the way people survived and resisted Israeli-imposed curfews. The village of Husan was subjected to three curfews. During the first one, which lasted twelve days, 'soldiers would fire rubber bullets at you if they saw you standing near a window,' a local resident related.[78] 'There were more than one hundred soldiers in the village, walking around with binoculars, trampling through gardens.' How did the community face this?

All houses keep food for these times, like flour and milk. But the village is poor and people have food saved only for a few days. In the village are underground springs, and around them beans, peas and eggplant were planted. At night, the women would go outside quietly and watch to know when the soldiers left. They would tell their sons that it was safe to come out, and they would collect the tomatoes, beans and eggplants from their gardens, and [some would gather] the vegetables growing near the springs and take some for themselves and give the rest to those in need. Neighbouring villages also got together milk – children's milk – canned food and things that Husan could not produce itself. The soldiers refused to let them bring it into the village, but at night the shabab sneaked out and brought it in. The second curfew [which lasted seventeen days] was really tough. The Israelis cut off our water, electricity and telephones. UNRWA brought in sixteen tons of food like rice, sugar, milk and flour, and put it in the mosque. The food stayed there. The soldiers would not let it be distributed. But we survived until the curfew was lifted. [The Israeli Commander] Mitzna told our notables: 'more than 200 persons from your village are in prison. Our soldiers have thrown gas bombs, done everything. Yet the Intifada continues strong. We do not know how we can finish the Intifada in this village.'

What was the secret? 'The village is one big family; that is the thing.'

In Beit Sahour, which was under curfew for 21 days in July with only a day's let-up, and where the Israelis refused to let food enter, the inhabitants resisted by going to their gardens and distributing the fruits and vegetables which they had gathered to needy families. They also engaged in defiant behaviour. Residents infuriated Israeli soldiers by asking for more arak and whiskey (pretending that they were enjoying the curfew) and by barbecuing chickens (one soldier stole a chicken and barbecued it himself). Throughout, the residents managed to feed themselves and even saw to it that newspapers were delivered daily.[79]

In Gaza, where the pressure upon the population was generally much greater than on the West Bank, advance planning was crucial. 'At first,' said one Gazan,

we were not organized to face Israeli curfews, to have our telephones and electricity cut. But we began to [organize ourselves to] anticipate curfews. We learned that whenever the UNL declared a full strike, the Israelis would impose a curfew. So we studied our needs, for milk, medicine, etc., and arranged to store things, just the essentials. Because people are in the habit of giving to people in need, storing large amounts was not always essential. The people responsible [for distributing food] knew which families were most in need. After two or three days of curfew, the authorities would give [some people] permission to go out for an hour or two to buy things. So the women went out. People on the outside were waiting for this hour, and were ready to give fruits and vegetables to the women. When Israelis did not grant this hour or two, people moved in a secret way from one place to another, carrying food and supplies.[80]

The attitude of many Palestinians who had to face these measures is exemplified in the words of an elderly man seen standing on the road in front of Qalqilya just after it had been released from the grip of a long curfew. 'If it had been 40 years, it would not have mattered to us,' he told a passerby.

Such words embody the invisible factor, which lies in the consciousness of Palestinians. 'You do not capture the institutionalization [of the Intifada] only by talking about structures,' noted Dr al-Jarbawi, 'but by moulding this with the emotional and psychological. The Intifada has become institutionalized because it is embodied in the psyche of people.'[81] An illustration of this is the games children played and the language they used. Youngsters flew kites with Palestinian colours and drew watercolours of Palestinian flags at school. At a boys' orphanage in Tulkarm, children acted out the drama they saw unfolding daily.[82] Some tried to dress as soldiers, identifying with the most powerful. 'I am a soldier,' one child said to another. 'You are a Palestinian. I am coming to seek you out. I will find you. You cannot hide from me.' Others imitated the voices they heard when soldiers entered their homes at night or in the early morning hours. '*Iftah-al-bab* (Open the door),' one shouted. '*Feen ibnik* (where is your son)?' '*Feen jozik* (where is your husband)?' Sometimes a child would come to school the morning after the IDF raided his home and paint over, in sombre black and grey colours, a drawing that he had done the day before, cancelling out all of the original bright, vivid colours.[83] In Beit Sahour sat a little boy, about six years old. To all Israeli patrols that passed by, he said: 'Get out of Beit Sahour; this is my country.' Once a patrol stopped and a soldier asked him why he said this. 'You came to my house twice and took my brother away,' he replied. 'I hate you. And I don't want to see you.'

Although the Intifada had come a long way, the analyst must resist the temptation to exaggerate its accomplishments. 'Popular committees,' Dr Abu-Amr cautioned,

have not become a coherent system. Their most important feature is the strike. With respect to health, agriculture, education, it is off and on. In some places, they are strong; elsewhere they are weak. So when you write about the institutionalization of the Intifada, be careful.[84]

Even in places where popular committees were well-organized, their control was not constant. By staging raids and stationing themselves in or near places of unrest, IDF troops interrupted and interfered with their activities. In fact, little is really known about their day-to-day work. To what extent, for example, were popular committees actually adjudicating disputes, displacing the clans and local mayors? Answers to questions like this are currently unobtainable. Palestinians tend to magnify the importance of the popular committees because they were such powerful symbols of the Intifada. The same caution must be observed in generalizing about the home economy. 'Victory Gardens are exaggerated,' noted Dr Abu-Amr. 'They do not produce enough [for people] to survive.'[85] This statement is contested by Dr Jad Issac of Beit Sahour:

Victory Gardens were important both politically and economically. They were a good social activity which brought people together and helped them realize their strength. They may not have been profitable economically, especially in cases where there was no follow-up or extension, but they helped people in a major way to survive curfews.

Without Victory Gardens, the residents of Qalqilya would have starved.[86]

In Gaza, backyard gardens hardly existed, since space was enclosed, water scarce and one-third of the total population lived in refugee camps. 'A lot of people breed chickens in their homes,' an UNRWA spokesman said, 'but there is little chance for co-operatives here.'[87] Vegetable growers did donate part of their produce to camps that were under curfew. In general, Gazans could obtain fruits and vegetables in the local market for relatively low prices. Eighteen per cent of the total workforce was wholly or partially employed in agriculture on the Strip, which could not market its fruits and vegetables in the West Bank or Israel. Yet it is true that to survive, Gazans had to co-operate more and make do with less than West Bank Palestinians. For many Gazans, Duqqa provided a basic meal for the day. Made from wheat which was ground up, roasted and then flavoured with spices, Duqqa was placed upon a piece of bread and eaten. With wry humour, Gazans called this 'eating dust', because that was what Duqqa looked like.

With respect to infrastructure in general, Palestinians were just getting started. They had a long way to go. In rural areas, no central body existed to co-ordinate prices, provide transport fees and help people move their produce from one place to another. UNL leaflets called for the establishment of a modern health clinic in every village, but in one West Bank village a clinic established in late summer, 1988, may well have been typical. There a physician, who came from another village, sat each morning, remaining until mid-afternoon. One day a week a pediatrician paid a call. The physician took no money from the poor. Those with a little money paid the costs of their medicine. Those with more money paid the doctor a fee. There were two small rooms, one a waiting-room. In the other was a medicine cabinet, containing a limited supply of the most elementary materials; a desk for the doctor; and an examining table for the patients. The clinic had no running water, not even a toilet. The doctor's face wore an expression that combined sadness with despair. 'I was trained to be a physician,' he said. 'Now, here I am in a clinic where I cannot even wash my hands unless I go somewhere else. And I cannot help people very much with the kinds of medicine I have.' An elderly woman was waiting to see him. She was suffering from tear gas inhalation. Her head, she said, felt like it was exploding. 'What can I do?' the doctor sighed, and shrugging, motioned her in.[88] This, at least, was better than nothing at all.

One obstacle to the development of Palestinian self-sufficiency was Israeli counter-measures designed to stifle Palestinian initiative and reattach the population to the Civil Administration, which, though crippled, continued to function. Among them were marketing prohibitions, monetary restrictions, agricultural sanctions, fuel bans, closures of organizations and institutions, continued large-scale arrests, the isolation of communities for long periods of time and the enforced payment of taxes.[89] In order to increase Palestinian dependence upon the Civil Administration, Israeli authorities changed the licence plates of all cars, made the granting of permits contingent upon the payment of taxes, forced Gaza residents to obtain new identity cards, initiated tax raids against local communities, introduced new taxes and issued a host of new regulations. Home owners, for example, were made responsible for the removal of Palestinian flags and anti-Israeli graffiti from their property.[90]

In one sense, this aided the Palestinian cause. By further impoverishing the people, the Israelis helped ensure that there would be less money¨n the Palestinian economy with which to buy Israeli products. 'The Israelis have contributed to our new way of life,' observed Dr al-Jarbawi:

For example, the Israeli Civil Administration refuses to give Palestinians [direct] access to money. Professors' salaries come from abroad. These are deposited in a bank in Jordan, and people draw cheques on a bank here. After the Intifada started the Israelis [in mid-March] said that we could not write cheques for more than 400 Jordanian dinars a month. This has reduced the Palestinian ability to buy and has hurt the Israeli economy.[91]

These Israeli measures did hamper the development of Palestinian economic and political-administrative structures. Mass arrests and the restriction of funds that came into the occupied territories hindered the effectiveness of the popular committees. In March the Shabiba organization was outlawed, followed in August by the banning of all popular committees. Between 200 and 300 people thought to be activists were detained.[92] Members of these groups were thus driven further underground and co-ordination between them became even more difficult. Yet the committees could not be eradicated. Younger and perhaps more radical men arose from the bottom as quickly as those at the top were arrested.

With respect to the home economy, raids and other measures limited the extent of self-sufficiency.[93] In June the population of five villages that had been placed under curfew were denied access to their fields (fruits and vegetables rotted on the ground). In a number of other West Bank localities, the Israeli army uprooted olive and fruit trees. Some villages were prevented from marketing their crops. Selective bans were also imposed upon herding livestock and against feeding lambs and goats. In some cases shepherds were prevented from grazing their flocks. Such sanctions impeded co-operation between communities and made co-ordination in the transport and marketing of produce ever more difficult. These measures ensured that the development of the Palestinian infrastructure would not only be severely limited, but based upon small communities.

* * * * * * * * * *

If Israel's policies greatly restricted Palestinian efforts to achieve self-sufficiency, '50 per cent civil disobedience' was enough to destroy the profits which Israel had made from the occupation. By April Israeli sales to the West Bank and Gaza had dropped dramatically.[94] Total industrial production was down by 3 per cent, of which 70 per cent was due to the fall in sales to the occupied territories and to Palestinian worker absenteeism. The construction industry, which employed about 46 per cent of Israel's Palestinian workforce, saw a 20 per cent decline in its activities. Textile factories were also hard hit, and had to be promised compensation from the government. In May most of Israel's industries were registering a drop in sales, some by 15–25 per cent. There were also other costs. Police expenditure for additional law enforcement had risen $130 million; security costs had increased by $400 million; tourism revenue was down 15–20 per cent, not to mention lost income from the cancellation of Israel's participation in international trade fairs, the EEC's failure to ratify the trade agreement, and so on. By June the total cost of the Intifada to Israel's economy was estimated at 2 per cent of its Gross National Product, or $600 million. This represented half of its projected economic growth in 1988. Comparative statistics for 1987 and 1988 round off the picture. In 1988, the number of Palestinians employed in Israeli industries had dropped by 33 per cent. Sales of Israeli agricultural goods to the occupied territories had fallen by 60 per cent; the production of Israeli textiles sold there had declined by 18 per cent; rubber and plastic by 11 per cent; clothes by 8 per cent; quarry stone by 8 per cent; non-metallic minerals by 10 per cent.

'From the beginning of the Intifada,' observed Dr Bishara,

the Palestinians had had two goals: to organize the population and to make the occupation as expensive to Israel as possible. Now Israel isn't profiting. Israel must sustain a large army in the West Bank and Gaza and this is costly. Before, there were 2,000–3,000 soldiers; now there are 20–30,000 soldiers. The occupation is already unprofitable.[95]

A wider point could also be made. A dramatic decrease in traffic of all kinds between Israel and the occupied territories was occurring. The high absenteeism of Palestinian workers in Israel had its counterpart in the disappearance of Israeli shoppers from the markets of Jenin and Tulkarm.[96] Jewish drivers refused to take products into the West Bank and Gaza. The Egged bus company had to dismiss hundreds of its employees owing to such developments. Jewish settlement projects were considerably slowed. The process of economic integration – a major feature of Israel's 'creeping annexation' – had been checked. A return to the Green Line – Israel's original pre-1967 border – was now becoming more of a physical reality.

6

The 'Outside' responds

Israel was not the only country to be affected by the Intifada. It captured and held the attention of millions of people around the world. In Europe, the US, Japan and the Middle East, newsmen broadcast nightly the latest story from Gaza and the West Bank. Television pictures of children using slingshots and hurling rocks at fully armed Israeli soldiers generated sympathy for the Palestinians, reversing the old image of Israel as David fighting the Arab Goliath, and greatly improving the moral standing of the Palestinian cause worldwide.

The Intifada also shattered the complacency which surrounded a 'peace process' that had been blocked for almost ten years, since the signing in 1979 of the Camp David Accords between Egypt and Israel. It revealed the illusoriness of the notion that peace could be made between Arabs and Israelis without the consent and participation of the people most directly involved – the Palestinians themselves. In the US, Europe, Israel and elsewhere, policy makers began to realize that a major change was occurring and that the Intifada would have to enter into the future calculations of their governments.

In the US, there was a revulsion at the violent methods employed by Israel to crush the revolt. People who had previously shown no concern about this problem now knew that something was wrong. Sentiment grew that the US government should do something to bring about peace in the area. In February 1988, Secretary of State George Shultz visited Israel, bringing with him a hastily-drafted peace plan largely based upon the Camp David Accords, but departing from them in some respects.[1] According to it, a brief international conference would be held to launch talks between Israel and Jordan (whose delegation was to include some Palestinians) and a quick agreement reached between them on an intermediate period of autonomy for the people of the West Bank and Gaza. During this interim period, a Palestinian authority, chosen by elections, would manage local affairs (e.g., police, water). Immediately after reaching agreement upon an intermediate stage, Israel and Jordan would begin talks on the ultimate status of the occupied territories. The final settlement was to be based upon UN Resolution 242, which laid down the principle of the exchange of land for peace. This plan was fatally flawed by its concentration upon Jordan as principal negotiator for the Palestinians and the inclusion of the 'land for peace' formula, which was unacceptable to Shamir and the Likud. Palestinians and the Israeli government both rejected it. None the less, Shultz continued to push his plan, and returned twice to the area in hopes of convincing people on both sides to accept it. After a long period of inaction on the Middle East diplomatic front, the US was once again focussing upon a negotiated solution of the Arab–Israeli dispute. The Palestinian problem could no longer be sidestepped. It had once again acquired a place on America's global crisis agenda.

The Intifada had a much greater impact upon the PLO. Not only did the Intifada rescue the PLO from the relative obscurity into which it had fallen, but also, and far more importantly, it resolved a long-standing political struggle within it between those who clung to the old idea of replacing Israel by a secular democratic state in the whole of Palestine through armed struggle, and those who supported the negotiating tactics that had been developed by Arafat since the mid-1970s.

As we have seen, the PNC in 1974 declared its support for the establishment of a Palestinian 'national authority' in any part of Palestine that was 'liberated' – the first time that the PLO leadership had accepted an intermediate goal short of the 'liberation of Palestine'.[2] This latter phrase, which was part of the PLO's National Charter, had been replaced in the 1974 PNC resolution by the words 'liberation of Palestinian land'. Such ambiguous wording was naturally interpreted in different ways by the various PLO factions. One interpretation of the new 'national authority' formula was that the PLO would accept a state in the West Bank and Gaza, and thus be willing to co-exist with Israel. However, this view was not adopted by the PLO leadership. The main point is that after 1974 contradictions within the PLO became ever more clear.

After 1974, Arafat was able to use the new position adopted by the PNC to develop his negotiating strategy, which he hoped would lead to a place for the PLO in the peace process. He made diplomatic gains for his organization and even opened a discussion with Zionist groups. Arafat's task became more difficult after 1982, when the PLO was driven from Lebanon – its last base of operations against Israel and the source of a large measure of political independence. To keep his strategy alive, Arafat took his organization into an alliance with Jordan rather than Syria, which maintained a hardline position with respect to a settlement. This led to a split in the PLO when its most radical factions left to join forces with the Syrians. The result was a setback for Arafat. His efforts to establish a dialogue with the US via the mediation of King Hussein were unproductive, and he himself chafed at having to submit more and more to the King's wishes. But Arafat had learnt a valuable lesson: he could not go it alone. Without a solid Palestinian front behind him, he would achieve nothing. At the 18th session of the PNC in 1987, Arafat had to make concessions to both the DFLP and the PFLP by abrogating the 1985 Accord that he had concluded with King Hussein. Palestinian unity was thus restored. However, without a physical base for the organization to regroup, the PLO could not re-establish itself. Its fortunes continued to ebb. At the summit meeting of Arab states in Amman in November 1987, Arafat was snubbed by King Hussein, who refused to meet him at the airport, and the PLO itself came close to losing its position, recognized at previous Arab summit conferences, as the sole legitimate representative of the Palestinian people.[3] Dominated by concern of the Iran–Iraq War, the delegates placed the Palestinian question on the diplomatic back burner.

The Intifada catapulted the PLO into prominence once again. Throughout the occupied territories, Palestinians made it clear that the PLO – not King Hussein or anyone else – was *their* representative. The indisputable leadership of the PLO in the occupied territories was thus legitimized. Having lost one territorial base in 1982, the PLO saw its influence consolidated and raised to new heights in the West Bank and Gaza.

Regionally, too, the PLO attained a new standing. A measure

of the change could be seen in January 1988, when Arab foreign ministers meeting in Tunis declared the PLO to be responsible for Palestinians living under occupation.[4] In June, an Arab summit conference meeting in Algiers voted over the objections of King Hussein to support the establishment of an independent Palestinian state under the PLO. From the Amman summit conference in November to the Algiers meeting in June, the PLO had come a long way. The Palestinian issue was once again at the top of the Arab states' political agenda, and Arafat could now work for unified Arab action on the diplomatic front instead of pursuing a bilateral policy, as he had done in his earlier (now abrogated) agreement with Jordan. The big loser, of course, was King Hussein, whose claims to represent the Palestinians in the occupied territories (for example, through the establishment of a joint Palestinian–Jordanian delegation) were dealt a fatal blow. To preserve Jordan's position among the Arab states, King Hussein had little alternative but to move closer to the PLO. In January, the Jordanian Prime Minister, who had previously refused even to meet with PLO officials, headed a Jordanian delegation to talks with the PLO.

How was the PLO to translate the sacrifices being made by Palestinians in the West Bank and Gaza into concrete political gains for their movement? People in the occupied territories expected it to produce something that would lead to a political settlement. This could not be achieved by means of armed struggle or by reliance upon old formulas which had produced no positive results and which in any case had become impossible of achievement once the PLO lost its Lebanese base. The new climate of détente and the peaceful resolution of disputes also militated against extreme solutions. The Soviet Union under Gorbachev was now nudging the PLO toward recognition of Israel, and letting it be known that the Soviet Union would no longer support radical Palestinian demands.[5] (This position must have had a particularly direct impact upon the PFLP, which had long-standing ties with the Soviet Union.) At the same time, sentiment was growing inside and outside the PLO that no settlement was possible without the intervention of the US. All signs were pointing toward the consolidation of Arafat's negotiation strategy and the weakening of the hardline position.

It was the Intifada, however, that brought Arafat's strategy to fruition. Without the impetus provided by the revolt, the PLO could not have moved so fast or travelled so far toward a political settlement. The Intifada encouraged a policy of compromise and negotiation in two ways. First, while Palestinians were fighting against the occupation, they were not rejecting the state of Israel itself. In its leaflets the UNL did not call for the establishment of a secular, democratic state in the whole of Palestine, but rather for statehood for Gazans and West Bankers. In other words, it wanted a two-state solution. The preferred method for achieving this was declared to be an international conference, sponsored by the members of the UN Security Council, and including Israel and the PLO as the 'sole legitimate representative of the Palestinian people'. Armed struggle was also rejected as a tactic. People in the occupied territories wanted a political solution and knew that this could only come about through strong international pressure upon the Israeli government.

The Intifada could also encourage the moderate tendency within the PLO leadership because political opinion in the occupied territories now had more weight in PLO decision-making. The PLO leadership abroad had to take into account the sentiments and desires of Gazans and West Bankers because they, and not the PLO fighters outside, were bearing the brunt of the struggle, creating their own martyrs, and achieving more for the Palestinian cause than at any other time during the occupation.

Just as important was the unity projected by the Intifada. For the first time, the four groups comprising the PLO in the occupied territories had formed a unified leadership, and this leadership had direct links and ties with the PLO factions and decision-making authorities abroad. Since the PLO was one organization, all were connected. The Intifada thus helped unify Palestinian factions outside the territories. Every Palestinian could take pride in the revolt, and no group would consider breaking away from the PLO. This sentiment of unity was expressed by George Habash, leader of the PFLP, who declared that his group would struggle from within the organization. 'We will differ,' he said, 'but we will not split.'[6] PLO leaders abroad began turning to Palestinians inside the territories for advice, ideas and support. Gazans and West Bank figures thus became more forceful in expressing their opinions. As the result of all these factors, West Bankers and Gazans, who had always had a major impact in determining the policy of the leaders outside with respect to local affairs, came to have a major influence in overall strategy.

At a certain point, a dialogue began spontaneously among Palestinians about the ways and means of achieving independence. These discussions, as characterized by Dr Abu-Amr, soon assumed the proportions of a national debate[7] – not only between Palestinians inside the occupied territories and those living outside, but also within factions (and their affiliated groups) and between factions. During the summer of 1988, this debate greatly intensified, because political developments were rapidly moving to a conclusion.

The Islamic camp was also involved in this debate indirectly, through pamphlets and leaflets. While the Islamic forces did not accept the national camp's goal of a secular Palestinian state, or the means (i.e., an international conference) for achieving it, or even the leadership of the PLO, their desire for legitimacy among the mass of the Palestinian population led them to soften their position on some of these points. As summer wore on, however, tension increased between the uprising's leadership and Hamas, whose influence, whilst still limited, was growing daily.

One major question was the kind of programme which the PLO should adopt. One trend, supported by the PCP, the DFLP and many in al-Fatah, favoured a plan centred upon the establishment of an independent state in the West Bank and Gaza, with East Jerusalem as its capital. The refugee problem, its advocates argued, could be solved through the right of return or in accordance with UN resolutions. Supporters of this trend believed that the PLO should reject all extremist positions and adopt an explicit programme, rather than satisfying itself with a mere statement of goals, because this would not win the requisite international support. This trend was opposed by another group in al-Fatah, which, though agreeing in principle with the idea of establishing a Palestinian state next to Israel, believed that its borders should be negotiated rather than defined in advance. Finally, a third group, led by the PFLP – which took a sceptical attitude throughout this debate – saw no urgent need for a new political programme since the PNC in previous sessions had already called for the establishment of a Palestinian state. It did not believe that the formation of a Palestinian state automatically entailed recognition of Israel, and it also held that the establishment of a Palestinian state in a part of the land would merely be an interim solution pending the institution of a democratic secular state in all of Palestine in place of Israel. Dr Abu-Amr has noted, however, that proponents of this viewpoint also advocated an international conference as a means to a settlement, and knew that documents would be signed which recognized Israel. Would they be willing to adapt their position once a settlement approached?

Another question was tactical. What practical steps could be taken to support the Intifada and accelerate movement on the diplomatic front? One trend favoured the idea that the PLO should make a daring and dramatic move without prior conditions, even at the risk of creating a split among Palestinians. The argument was that this would prove Palestinian good intentions, produce favourable reaction internationally and create pressure upon Israel. Supported by certain public personalities in the occupied territories and by some members of al-Fatah, this position did not have a majority support within the national camp. Many Palestinians, while agreeing upon the need for an initiative, required some evidence that it would be beneficial, and believed that, in any case, nothing should be done that would divide the Palestinian movement.

What should the Palestinian initiative be? One idea was to seek UN custodianship for the occupied territories. From the beginning of the revolt, the PLO had sought to gain some kind of international protection for Palestinians in the West Bank and Gaza, but, aside from producing UN resolutions that condemned Israeli practices as violations of international law, these efforts had yielded little. By the summer of 1988, however, the idea of obtaining a UN resolution that would establish de jure UN custody over Palestinians in the occupied territories was being discussed. Most Palestinians could support this, even though they knew that an actual UN administration would not be established. Would this 'reward' for the sacrifices made by Palestinians be sufficient to propel the revolt forward and gain more international support for the movement? Another idea debated was a declaration of independence or statehood. Some Palestinians enthusiastically endorsed this on the assumption that it would spur the revolt and expand international support for their cause. Others, especially the PFLP and some within al-Fatah, while not excluding the idea, questioned its practical utility in the current situation. A declaration of independence, they feared, would raise Palestinian expectations too high and create confusion. Upon what would a declaration of independence rest? The formation of a government-in-exile and the establishment of a provisional government were both discussed, but many people raised objections as to their practicality or desirability. As a legal basis for the state-to-be some Palestinians suggested the 1947 UN Partition Resolution (181) which divided Palestine into a Jewish and an Arab state. But this raised the question of borders. Should the UN resolution be accepted for tactical negotiating reasons, or regarded as final?

As the debate continued, developments occurred which stimulated it further. One was the publication on 7 June of an article by Bassam Abu Sharif, an adviser to Arafat, in which he advocated direct negotiations with Israel at an international conference that would bring into existence a Palestinian state alongside Israel.[8] Abu Sharif reasssured Israelis that Palestinians sought peace, not Israel's destruction, and said that its security concerns would be properly addressed. According to Sari Nuseibeh, this statement by a PLO leader abroad was a product of the encouragement being given by Gazans and West Bankers to a negotiated, two-state solution:

All the talk in the occupied territories [at that time] was about the two states, about independence. Palestinians asked the PLO [leadership] to translate this. Abu Sharif's statement was a positive sign within the PLO towards this.[9]

At the end of July, the Israelis uncovered in the East Jerusalem office of Faisal Husseini, a prominent supporter of al-Fatah, a draft declaration of independence which seemed to have been circulated and discussed only among a small circle of pro-Fatah supporters.[10] A Palestinian state was to be unilaterally proclaimed within the boundaries established by the 1947 UN partition plan, and negotiations would then take place between it and Israel to determine the final borders between them. The publication of this document, merely one of many papers and proposals that had been circulating in secret, weakened support for the idea of UN custodianship and enhanced the prospect that the PLO would declare an independent Palestinian state.

Another development which helped to bring matters closer to resolution was the announcement by King Hussein on 31 July that he was severing all administrative and legal ties between Jordan and the West Bank. He also acknowledged the PLO as the sole legitimate representative of the Palestinian people, and called for the establishment of an independent Palestinian state in the occupied territories. As Quandt has observed, Hussein's decision disposed of the idea of Jordan as the main negotiator for the Palestinians and put the focus squarely upon the two parties most directly involved in the conflict: the Israelis and the Palestinians.[11] The PLO no longer had a competitor for the right to represent Palestinians. On the other hand, it would now have to find a way to fill the gap created by Jordan's disengagement. This made it more likely that the PLO would advance a claim to the land, in the form of Palestinian statehood or independence.

By the end of summer, a unified Palestinian position had yet to crystallize, but Arafat was finding it easier to make his views prevail within al-Fatah, and seems to have won the backing of a group within the DFLP.[12] Support from the occupied territories also strengthened his hand against the opposition of other Palestinian factions (e.g., those of Abu Musa and Ahmad Jibril), and helped mute criticism from Syria, whose regional influence was not strong. In late summer, two leaflets (24, 25) issued by the UNL expressed its appreciation of the PLO leadership's efforts to support the uprising, and encouraged the PNC (now scheduled to meet in an emergency session in the autumn) to

adopt a clear and comprehensive political programme which would ensure the greatest international support for Palestinian national rights and . . . undertake practical steps which would support and escalate the uprising.

Arafat's strategy was at last prevailing and the PLO was working towards a new consensus that would include a readiness to negotiate peace with Israel.

The new Palestinian programme was presented in detail and approved at the 19th session of the PNC which met in Algiers on 12–15 November 1988. Its centrepiece was the proclamation of an independent Palestinian state, with Jerusalem as its capital, based upon UN Resolution 181, which was adopted in order to establish its legality or legitimacy.[13] This state was to be a parliamentary democracy with a constitution that would ensure rule of law and provide for an independent judiciary. Freedom of worship, freedom of expression and other rights were guaranteed. The Palestinian state was to be the patrimony of all Palestinians, wherever they lived. The question of refugees would be settled in accordance with UN resolutions. The PNC requested that the PLO Executive Committee act as a temporary government, until a provisional government could be established. It asked the UN to place the occupied territories, including Arab East Jerusalem, temporarily under international supervision in order to protect the Palestinian civilian population and prepare for the convening of an international conference. The PNC also called for an Israeli withdrawal from the lands occupied in 1967. The territory of the new Palestinian state was thus defined as Gaza and the West Bank (including East Jerusalem).

The other component of the Palestinian programme was a peace offensive. To resolve the conflict with Israel, the PNC requested the convening of an international conference with the participation of the permanent members of the Security Council and all parties to the conflict, including the PLO. This much, of course, had been said before, but the PNC went further. It rejected terrorism in all its forms (though it also affirmed the right of people to resist foreign occupation) and recognized the state of Israel. This was done not only by identifying the land from which Israel should withdraw as the West Bank, Gaza and East Jerusalem, but by accepting UN Resolutions 242 and 338, which recognized the right of all parties and states in the region to live in peace and security. While it is true that the passage accepting 242 and 338 also spoke of the attainment of the Palestinian right of self-determination and the need to act in accordance with the 'relevant United Nations resolutions on the question of Palestine', their endorsement was itself a significant step forward, since in 1987 the PNC had explicitly rejected 242. The PNC was proposing a two-state solution, thus recognizing Israel and indicating its willingness to make peace with it.

The Palestinian programme was designed not only to appeal to Israel, but also to the US, whose further involvement in the peace process was deemed crucial to the initiative's success. 'The PLO only had one eye on the uprising when it drafted the PNC declaration,' noted Dr Abu-Amr. 'Arafat's other aim was to open a dialogue with the United States.'[14] A comment by the PLO Chairman at a press conference after the PNC session seems to bear out this observation: the ball is now in America's court, Arafat told reporters.

The position of the US administration was also beginning to change. King Hussein's disengagement from the West Bank had been a rude awakening. After the King's speech of 31 July, it became clear that the peace process could only remain alive if it sprang from Palestinian–Israeli discussions. Yet both the Labour Party and the Likud bloc were firmly set against talks of any kind with the PLO. A dialogue between the US and the PLO, however, would enable Israelis to talk with the PLO indirectly without having to alter their official posture. The US knew that Arafat was seeking a dialogue with it, not just to gain further legitimacy for his organization but also in hopes of securing a PLO role in future peace negotiations. The US too stood to gain. It would acquire new leverage over the PLO, and both Israel and the PLO would have to rely upon it. The US could control and shape the process. If real progress were ever achieved, the US administration could take full credit for it, without having to share accolades with the UN or any other world power.

There was one obstacle to the opening of a US–PLO dialogue. According to a 1975 commitment to Israel, the US would not recognize or negotiate with the PLO unless it (1) recognized Israel's right to exist; (2) accepted UN Resolutions 242 and 338; and (3) renounced terrorism. The Reagan administration could have announced that the PNC declaration at Algiers had met these three conditions, but it chose not to. Instead, it called upon the PLO for clarification, insisting, as Quandt has put it, that the PLO say certain words.[15] Was this not being excessively legalistic? Could not any remaining ambiguities have been cleared up in the course of American–PLO negotiations? Why did the US insist that precise words be spoken? Some have speculated that the US may have been trying to moderate the PLO even further, to induce it to reduce its demands to a minimum. After all, Arafat needed the US more than the US needed Arafat. The Intifada had not created a crisis for

America's Middle East policy. 'Arafat knew and was explicitly told what he had to do in order to open a dialogue,' observed Dr Abu-Amr. 'This dialogue was his aim. The US said "the PNC declaration is not enough. You must do more."'[16]

Arafat thus began the work of 'clarification'. Addressing a news conference in Stockholm on 7 December, he declared the PLO's acceptance of Israel as a state in the area, rejected and condemned terrorism in all its forms, and said that the basis for an international conference was UN Resolutions 242 and 338 and the right of Palestinian self-determination, thereby excluding mention of other UN resolutions which the PNC declaration had stated should also serve as a basis.[17] The US demanded more. On 13 December, after being denied an entry visa that prevented him from addressing a UN session on Palestine in New York City, Arafat delivered his speech to a special UN session in Geneva. In it, he accepted the existence of two states, based upon the 1947 UN partition resolution, and repeated his earlier acceptance of UN Resolutions 242 and 338 within the framework of an international conference in order

to guarantee equality and the balance of interests, especially over people's rights, in freedom, national independence, and respect [sic] the right to exist in peace and security for all.

He also condemned terrorism in all its forms, while saluting those in the audience who had fought for their country's freedom and been called terrorists. This was still not quite enough. The next day, Arafat held a press conference. UN Resolutions 242 and 338 would be the basis for negotiations at an international conference, he said. Individual, group and state terrorism were rejected. Israel was mentioned as a state having the right to exist in peace and security. The West Bank and Gaza would comprise the territory of the Palestinian state. At last, he had done it. At a press conference held shortly afterwards, the US administration announced its decision to open a dialogue with the PLO.

Arafat could stretch the PNC declarations because he had behind him the unity inspired by the Intifada and a new Palestinian consensus over a policy of moderation and negotiation. 'The significance of the PNC decision is revolutionary,' said Sari Nuseibeh:

They [its framers] have transported positions which have been on the periphery of national thinking and put them at the centre so that they have become the core strategy of the PLO. No one now makes a statement on his own and is denounced by others.[18]

Arafat and the PLO had achieved their objective: an enhanced negotiating position and greater legitimacy. As a result, al-Fatah, or rather Arafat, had become the 'ultimate broker', possessing links with virtually every important group and party. (By contrast, the PFLP, al-Fatah's closest rival, had ties almost exclusively with the Soviet Union.)

Palestinian politics had come a long way since the mid-1970s. A fundamental change had occurred on the very question of Palestine. The central focus of the national movement had shifted, coming to rest upon the West Bank and Gaza. Palestinians had finally been willing to say they recognized that Israel was there to stay. They did not like doing this, as Quandt has observed, because it implied recognition of the legitimacy of establishing Israel on what had been Palestinian soil and Palestinians felt that a terrible injustice had been done to them. But they were now prepared to make peace with Israel, and this willingness had legitimized their movement to such a degree that it would henceforth be difficult indeed for Israelis to argue that the Palestinian goal remained the destruction of the Jewish state. The PLO had been changed substantially, and the Palestinian peace offensive had captured the moral high ground from the Israelis.

* * * * * * * * *

For political observers, a historic reversal seemed to have occurred. It was the Palestinians who were making proposals, offering compromises, showing a willingness to negotiate, saying 'yes'. The Israelis, on the other hand, were resisting, dragging their heels, saying 'no'. Shamir had rejected the plan put forward by Shultz at the beginning of the Intifada. His government did not even acknowledge the Fourteen Points issued by the Palestinians in mid-January. Sari Nuseibeh has commented that a positive Israeli response to these demands might have brought the Intifada to an end.[19] While this is probably an exaggeration –

the Fourteen Points were not accepted by the uprising's leadership until after January – it is true that had Israel met some of these early demands, the focus might have shifted from confrontation toward political issues at a crucial time, before the revolt had spread to the whole society. In the event, the Israelis were left only with the application of force, which spread and deepened the revolt until it went way beyond the Fourteen Points. 'Later,' commented Dr al-Jarbawi,

no one asked for the release of prisoners as a condition for stopping the Intifada. No one asked for the evacuation of troops from towns as a condition. People said 'we want our independence, our state.' The consensus of the people changed with the development of the Intifada.[20]

During the entire first year, despite mounting international criticism and the IDF's inability to stop the revolt, the Israeli government advanced not a single plan or policy for dealing with the Intifada politically.[21] There were three reasons for this. First, the Israeli Cabinet was deadlocked on the question of the occupied territories, and any political initiative risked destroying the government and forcing new elections. Second, Shamir and his Likud bloc did not want a negotiated settlement with the Palestinians. Third, the Israeli electorate was not sufficiently exercised or united to push the government toward a political resolution of the dispute. This stood in contrast with its reaction to Israel's 1982 invasion of Lebanon, when a large segment of society demanded the withdrawal of Israeli troops. Israel's government did, of course, eventually make a political proposal, but this came during the second year of the revolt, in 1989, after Israeli elections and after the US administration had begun talks with the PLO. Even then, as we shall see, the Israeli initiative hardly succeeded in moving the 'peace process' forward. The question thus remains: what made it so difficult for Israel to take political action? More particularly, why was Israeli society not pushing its government harder during the first year of the Intifada? What lay behind the opposition of Shamir and his party to a political settlement? Why was the government so deadlocked that action was virtually impossible?

Israelis, Meron Benvenisti has said, could not accept another independent nationality which had claims to the same land, since this would imply renouncing their own exclusive claims.[22] Even Shimon Peres, for all his pragmatism, Benvenisti observed, could not relinquish the Zionist ethos of reclaiming the ancestral land.[23] The ideological value assigned to regaining and holding onto the land of Israel (*Eretz Yisrael* in Hebrew) is, of course, basic to an understanding of the Zionist movement. But finding answers to our questions is a much more complicated matter than this. Changes were underway in Israeli society that were not directly related to the occupation but which affected attitudes towards it and the political structure that had to deal with it. Moreover, is it the case that in order to fulfill Zionism, Israeli Jews needed an exclusive claim to the West Bank and Gaza? According to an opinion poll taken in March 1988, 39 per cent of Israelis desired the immediate opening of negotiations and 58 per cent believed that their government should make a positive response to the Shultz plan, which was based upon the exchange of land for peace.[24] Many Israelis did not define *Eretz Yisrael* as encompassing the entirety of the West Bank and Gaza.

In considering the reasons for governmental inaction on the question of the occupied territories, we must keep in mind both the general – two peoples locked in a struggle for the same territory – and the particular – the immediate and specific reasons for obduracy on the political front. This requires an examination of the constraints, material and ideological, that complicated the undertaking of a political initiative by the Israeli government.

The first constraint was the existence of a government in which power was divided between two rival political blocs, the Likud and the Alignment (dominated by the Labour Party), representing different constituencies and holding divergent views on how to deal with the occupied territories. Within the Cabinet a rule of parity also existed, which meant that the government could act only when a consensus obtained. One side, then, could block the other. Deadlock on the Palestinian question was guaranteed.

While this was not the first time that Israel's two main parliamentary blocs had sat together in one government, the more usual situation had been for Likud or the Alignment to form a government with some of the smaller religious parties and thereby exclude its principal rival. (Israel's proportional representation system meant that no party could win a majority and thus ensured coalition government.) However, the 1984 election had produced a situation in which neither bloc could form a coalition without the other. A government of 'national unity', as such cabinets were called, was formed that included six other small coalition partners drawn from the political left, the right and the ultra-orthodox religious bloc. The 1984 coalition agreement also provided for a rotation of the office of prime minister. Peres, head of the Labour Party, served the first two years, with Shamir, leader of the Herut party in the Likud, succeeding him.

On the Palestinian question, the Labour Party stood for territorial compromise. Its programme called for Israel's retention of a portion of Gaza and the West Bank on security grounds, and the ceding of the rest to Jordan's King Hussein – the so-called 'Jordanian option'. To this end, Labour was willing to enter peace negotiations on the basis of UN Security Council Resolutions 242 and 338. Labour Party members, who held many different opinions, were greatly concerned about the long-term impact of maintaining permanent control of a hostile Palestinian population that soon after the turn of the century would outnumber the Jewish population of Israel. The Likud, by contrast, was opposed to any territorial concessions in the West Bank and Gaza. These areas, it believed, belonged to Israel by historic right. Likudniks saw the conflict with the Palestinians as a life-and-death struggle between two peoples, and were absolutely convinced of the moral superiority of the Jewish claim and of eventual victory. It should be noted that both Labour and Likud desired to limit and restrict Palestinian nationalism. Hence their common position of rejecting all talks with the PLO, the embodiment of Palestinian national aspirations. Neither party wished to see a Palestinian state in the West Bank and Gaza. Differences between them on this point were tactical, not strategic. It should also be emphasized that Labour's programme called for Israel to retain a large amount of land. Half of the total area of the West Bank and three-quarters of the Gaza Strip were to be kept by the Jewish state.[25]

Despite this, the difference of principle between the social-democratic Labour Party and the right-wing Likud were important, and after the government's formation in 1984 each side worked to get its way. Labour's half of the Cabinet tried to initiate peace talks, while Likud's half sought to block these efforts. In 1987,

Shamir succeeded in thwarting the implementation of an accord between Peres and Jordan's King Hussein which aimed at negotiating a comprehensive peace at an international conference based upon UN Resolutions 242 and 338.[26]

Another source of division within the Cabinet was personal rather than ideological. In the Labour Party, an old rivalry existed between Rabin and Peres, though this was not nearly so serious as it had previously been. Of much greater intensity was the competition inside the Likud betwen Shamir and Sharon, the former military commander and architect of Israel's invasion of Lebanon. An opportunist of vaulting ambitions, who was supported by hard-line nationalists and extremists in the religious parties, Sharon had carved out a position in the Likud to the right of Shamir. Leader of the Likud opposition to Shamir, Sharon was poised to take advantage of any failing or weakness displayed by the Prime Minister. Shamir in turn sought to block Sharon from becoming Defence Minister (a prize he openly coveted) by relying upon Labour's Rabin. A government thus divided could hardly be expected to reach a decision on so intractable a problem as that of the occupied territories.

Why were Israel's two main parties sitting in the same government together? There were two reasons for this. First, the National Unity Government had been brought into existence in 1984 with a mandate to solve two short-term but pressing problems: rampant inflation and the withdrawal of Israeli troops from Lebanon. These, it was thought, could be better achieved by Labour and Likud governing jointly. Israeli society also desired some respite from the intense struggles and bickering that had marked the preceding period of Likud domination. For many Israelis, a unity government implied national reconciliation – a desirable objective. The second and more basic reason was a badly fragmented political system. Beginning in the 1970s, a shift occurred within the political order, manifested in the decline of the Labour Party, the rise of the Likud (which replaced the Labour government in 1977) and, in the 1980s, the proliferation of small parties of all kinds on the right and left of the political spectrum. These parties gained influence at the expense of the major blocs, and this eventually produced a stalemated political situation in which Labour and Likud had little alternative but to join together.

This development was largely the result of a mutation in the basic structure of society, which became much less European and more Oriental in composition and culture. This, added to already existing tensions and divisions, brought the society to a point where no basic agreement was possible on solutions to the fundamental problems facing the country (e.g., the restructuring of the economy). The stalemated political system was thus the result of a divided electorate.

The roots of the problem were planted in the 1950s when a large influx of Oriental or Sephardic Jews into Israel took place. To their chagrin, these newcomers had to face not only job and educational discrimination, but also cultural ridicule by the then-dominant European (Ashkenazi) Jews. Since they originated mostly from Middle East countries, Oriental Jews brought with them values and attitudes quite different from the secular ideals of Ashkenazi society, on which the state of Israel had been founded. Zionism, for example, was based upon the principle that Jews were a culture and a civilization, a pluralistic people; hence, the religion of Judaism had an important but not central or dominant role in the state. By contrast, Oriental Jews, whose culture contained many popular religious practices (e.g., saint worship), tended to believe that the state should possess a religious basis. Through sheer force of numbers – Oriental Jews tended to have much larger families than European Jews – these newcomers began to make an impact upon the electoral system and gradually impose their culture and habits upon society. By the 1980s, more than half of Israeli Jews were Oriental or considered themselves equally Oriental and Ashkenazi.[27]

As a result of their early experiences, Oriental Jews tended to develop resentful and bitter attitudes toward European Jews and Western culture – attitudes they retained long after they themselves had attained middle-class status. The growing pressure of Oriental Jews also helped fuel a revival of Judaism, centred especially on ultra-orthodox parties, led by Rabbis, which acquired ever greater material resources and power. These doctrinaire groups rejected modern science and education, denied the legitimacy of all other Jewish movements (e.g., Reform, Conservative), and dedicated themselves to the replacement of the secular Zionist state by one based solely upon Jewish law. Finally, the Oriental Jewish presence contributed to the growth of intolerant and anti-Arab sentiments already present in Israeli society.

Such developments naturally provoked a reaction from certain segments of Israel's important but relatively declining population of European Jews. These people resented the diversion of more state funds to support religious schools and other projects. They complained about the exemptions from military service granted orthodox students, and lamented the loss of toleration, as revealed in surveys and opinion polls. In short, society was falling into bitter and deep disagreements. Conflict was occurring between Ashkenazi and Oriental Jews, between secular and religious, and over the question of basic values.

This is not to suggest that Oriental Jews 'caused' the revival of Orthodox Judaism, or were responsible for the relative lack of toleration and the anti-Arab sentiments in Israeli society, or brought into existence and constituted the right wing. Nothing could be further from the truth. The leaders and activists of most of the extreme right-wing groups were overwhelmingly Ashkenazi. The Zionist labour movement itself had always contained a strong element with a hard-line attitude towards the Palestinians. In the West Bank and Gaza, the most uncompromising of the Jewish settlers were often former Americans. The picture is obviously a complicated one. The point is that the Oriental Jewish presence added to problems and divisions already in existence, making them worse, not better.

These changes in the structure of society were bound to affect the political system. In 1977, the Likud came to power on the backs of an Oriental Jewish constituency among which its tough talk and anti-Ashkenazi establishment rhetoric found a receptive audience. Small religious and nationalist parties also established themselves to the right of the Likud, which found them natural coalition partners. Secular European Jews, on the other hand, tended more and more to support parties on the left, not just the Labour Party, but groups such as Shinui and the Civil Rights Movement. The Labour Party also did itself no favours. Early scandals involving charges of corruption and the mismanagement of its economic empire (the Histadruth health insurance programme, the Koor industrial complex and the Kibbutzes) helped discredit it and the social-democratic values for which it supposedly stood. 'Remember,' cautioned Danny Rubenstein,

the left wing here is considered as the establishment – Histadruth owns
one-half of the country, the entire health system – and the establishment
has been corrupted. When people vote against Labour, it is not for
political reasons necessarily, but because Labour's values are not
relevant to the new society, which is Oriental.[28]

From 1981 onwards, the transfer of voters to the extremes of
the political system increased. Both Labour and the Likud bloc
started losing seats in the Knesset to smaller parties on the right
or the left.[29] Elections became drawn games. In 1981, Likud
gained just a few thousand votes more than Labour; in the 1984
election, Labour had not many more votes than Likud. This
reflected a badly divided society, the result largely of its changing
social composition.

Despite this, the 1984 National Unity Government was able to
reduce inflation and bring about the withdrawal of Israeli troops
from Lebanon. This was accomplished by each side (Labour and
Likud) separately running its part of the show. Matters needing a
collective decision were resolved by a triumvirate of Shamir,
Rabin and Peres. Aside from these two problems, however, little
else was accomplished.

'National Unity' was not good for Israel. Supported by 97 of
120 Knesset members, the coalition government left an opposition
that totalled only 23 members.[30] 'Israel needs an opposition party
and this is good for democracy,' Tom Segev, correspondent for
the Hebrew-language daily *Haaretz*, explained. 'We need someone
to tell the rulers that they are doing a bad job.'[31] Cabinet
ministers could publicly criticize the government's policy without
being forced to resign. The real weakness of national unity,
though, was that it maintained the status quo. No change of
policy or prevailing patterns could occur when one side had the
power to block the other. Deadlock left untouched the central
issues of peace and the disposition of the occupied territories.

The second constraint upon a political initiative was ideology,
in particular, the beliefs of one man – Prime Minister Shamir –
and their concrete expression in the policies and programme of
the Likud bloc which he headed. Shamir was a true believer in
the doctrine of Greater Israel, for which he had fought his entire
life. Born in Poland in 1915, Shamir arrived in Palestine in 1935
where he became a Zionist guerrilla fighter and resistance leader.
First a member of the Irgun, an underground direct-action

organization led by Begin, Shamir became one of the leaders of
Lehi, another military group, following the killing of its founder,
Abraham Stern.[32] Until the establishment of Israel in 1948,
Shamir planned and helped carry out attacks and political
assassinations against Palestinians, the British and others who, he
believed, stood in the way of the Zionist dream of statehood.
After Israel's establishment, Shamir joined the Herut Party,
whose leadership was drawn almost entirely from former Irgun
and Lehi fighters. He had a long career in Israeli intelligence
where he rose to become head of European operations.
Following Begin's resignation as Prime Minister in October 1983,
Shamir assumed this office for the first time.

Like Begin and many other Likud 'veterans', Shamir's ideas
derived from the principles of the Revisionist Movement, a
Zionist political party founded in 1925 by Zeev Jabotinsky. Its
core belief was that the Jewish state-to-be should encompass the
areas both east and west of the Jordan river, and that armed
struggle be conducted if necessary, in order to achieve this goal.
This doctrine was adopted by the Herut Party; after 1965,
however, calls by its members for Israel to incorporate what was
essentially the Kingdom of Jordan were dropped, and this part of
its programme more or less abandoned. The Gaza and West
Bank areas were another matter entirely. 'Judaea and Samaria',
as Zionists called them, formed an integral part of historic Israel.

Shamir possessed far more political talent than appeared at
first sight. Diligent, even meticulous, he did his homework. He
knew what to say, when to say it, and, more importantly, what to
withhold. He appreciated the limits of a small state like Israel,
which had to depend upon the outside for support, but he also
knew how to stretch these limits to the utmost. Perfected during
his days in the underground, his political trademarks were
elusiveness, cunning and patience. During a long public career,
he developed into a clever tactician and became known as a
master of political tightrope walking. On the question of Israel's
conflict with the Arabs, Shamir held one position. Israel would
not cede any land for peace. Peace could only come when the
Arabs accepted the fact that Israel was the strongest power in the
region. The Palestinians living in the West Bank and Gaza were
'outsiders'. They should be resettled in one or more of their
'fellow' Arab states. On the Palestinian issue Shamir was no

pragmatic politician. Under pressure, he would manoeuvre and might even compromise, but only as a tactic.

It was the Likud that translated the ideology of Greater Israel into a practical programme, and which built a huge constituency to support it. In Israel a hard-line position on the Palestinian question was one way to win votes, especially from Oriental Jews who, because of their inferior status and desire for acceptance in Israeli society, held strong patriotic sentiments and tended to oppose attempts to make peace with Arabs. In the occupied territories, the Likud threw its weight behind the settlement movement, which, as we have seen, expanded greatly after 1977. The settlers were presented to the Israeli public as pioneers, and the occupied territories as a new frontier – an appeal attractive to Israeli youths in search of a new direction. While not a religious party itself, the Likud benefited from the growing desire among some Israelis for the retention of the West Bank and Gaza as a sacred, religious duty. The spiritual redemption of the Jewish people, these people argued, depended upon continued possession of the land. The Likud also created a huge network of support services. Inside Israel the settlement movement became a sacred cow, receiving disproportionate favour in budgetary allocations and enjoying priority in almost every sector. A portion of the religious public was mobilized to support it through educational institutions, youth groups and in other ways. In the Knesset a powerful pro-settler coalition emerged, based upon the Likud but going beyond it to include ultra-nationalist and some religious parties.

From the foregoing, two conclusions can be drawn. First, the retention of the occupied territories and their incorporation into Israel had become the Likud's raison d'être. Under Begin, and then Shamir, a great amount of time and effort was spent in financing, maintaining, advancing and developing Israeli control of Gaza and the West Bank.[33] The Likud had no real economic programme (aside from promoting private enterprise and reducing the state sector), let alone an economic doctrine, and no well-defined social policy. Its programme was almost entirely political. The West Bank and Gaza were not Sinai (ceded to Egypt by the Camp David Accords). These areas could not be discarded, as the East bank of the Jordan River had been after 1965. They were an integral part of *Eretz Yisrael*. It is not too great an exaggeration to say that without the occupied territories, the Likud would not have been the Likud.

The second conclusion is that the occupation was shaping Israeli politics and, what is more, adding its weight to existing social divisions. 'In Israel, the left and the right are divided first and foremost by their attitude towards the Arab–Israeli conflict,' explained Tom Segev.

It is almost equal to hawks and doves. In addition to this, and in recent years the left and the right can be defined in terms of support for democracy, attitudes towards religion, and attitudes towards nationalism. This is a recent development. Ask an Israeli if he is for withdrawal from the territories. If he says yes, does this make him non-religious? Probably, but not always. A man is for the expulsion of the Arabs. Does this mean that he is religious? Perhaps, but not necessarily. Where do the ultra-orthodox parties fit in? There are some religious people who on religious grounds prefer the sanctity of land and others who on religious grounds say that preserving human life is more important [than holding onto territory].

According to Segev, the occupation was also helping push society to the right:

The criterion of patriotism today is to keep the territories – a general mood. Israeli patriotism equals something basically in contrast to democracy, and here is the danger. The occupation increases the general mood of nationalism, of Israel closing itself off from things in the outside world, the vision of the settlements, religious fanaticism, and the willingness of people to give up democratic values.[34]

Israeli society could not escape the effects of the occupation.

If the Likud did not want a negotiated settlement and had constructed a political combination to prevent it, there was yet another reason why the government did not rush to advance any political proposals during the first year of the Intifada. This was the general acceptance of the revolt by Israeli society, which became resigned to it. After the initial months of excitement, debate and increased polarization, Israelis learned to live with the Intifada. The absence of strong pressure upon the government was thus a significant negative factor.

The most important impact of the Intifada upon society was psychological:

The revolt took away the justification of the occupation which Israelis had given to themselves, that it was improving the standard of life of the Palestinians [noted Danny Rubenstein]. Israelis now do not believe that their government has any positive role to play there. The occupation cannot be justified.[35]

The second effect was political. The Intifada stimulated a tremendous amount of discussion among all sections of the general population, and helped polarize society even more.

Prior to the Intifada, the Palestinian question had objectively been the most important political issue, but the majority of Israelis had succeeded in blocking it out of their daily lives. Now Israelis had to talk about the Palestinians. Should the government recognize and negotiate with the PLO? Should part of or all of the occupied territories be given up, and, if so, under what conditions? The right questions had finally emerged and were being discussed as part of ordinary political discourse. The Intifada also gave a stimulus to the Israeli left, especially the Peace Now movement, moribund since Peres had brought the Labour Party into coalition with Likud.[36] The conscience of the Israeli left was pricked by the government's beatings' policy and some widely publicized instances of IDF brutality – the burial alive of four Palestinian youths; the beating to death of a 41-year-old Palestinian in his home, even though he had not resisted arrest; and some deaths of Palestinian infants following their exposure to tear gas.[37] The Israeli right was also prompted to take action, for the Intifada posed a grave threat to the realization of its programme. The right thus became more right, the left more left.

As time passed, however, society began moving ever so slightly to the right. As late as November 1987, opinion polls showed Labour with a 10 per cent lead over Likud; by the following June, there was parity.[38] The 'transfer' idea also began to gain acceptance. In a poll conducted in June 1988, almost half of the Israelis questioned supported the mass expulsion of Palestinians from the West Bank and Gaza.[39] Yet in the same poll, 50 per cent of people supported a redivision of the occupied territories between Israelis and Palestinians even before negotiations had begun. Curiously, many polls exhibited conflicting or contradictory results. In explaining this, Bar-On has argued that public opinion was harder on questions of short-term policy (e.g., most Israelis supported the use of greater force by the IDF to curb the revolt) than on long-term issues (e.g., many Israelis favoured negotiations).[40] A more basic explanation, however, is that Israelis were confused and held contradictory views on the same subject.

By early autumn 1988, many Israelis had begun to tire of the steady stream of news, none of it good, emanating from the territories. People continued to talk about the problem, but most discussions led nowhere, only to more arguments, greater tension and the confirmation of entrenched positions. The tendency to blame the press also grew. 'Down with the hostile press' read bumper stickers on cars in Jerusalem and elsewhere. Some Israelis grew more defensive, taking refuge in a 'fortress Israel' mentality. Most, though, learned to live with the Intifada by blocking it out. 'Most Israelis don't want to know,' Segev observed. 'Israelis do not know the names of the refugee camps. The press publishes more than the reader wants to know.'[41] Yehuda Litani, veteran reporter for the *Jerusalem Post* on the occupied territories, agreed. 'People are talking about the problem,' he said, 'but they are consciously preventing themselves from confronting this situation.'[42]

Why did society react in this way? How is one to explain the acceptance of the Intifada as routine? Why were Israelis not sufficiently aroused to pressure the government to act? Segev responded to this question by referring to the phenomenon of escapism, which developed after the Israeli invasion of Lebanon.

Today a tremendous amount of escapism from politics exists. This is recent and bad, and comes from the Lebanon war and the establishment of the National Unity Government, which killed all real debate. People are escaping the collective. Even the press deals less with politics than before. Individual success stories are featured, not a discussion of collective problems, yet you have problems that must be faced.[43]

A more important part of the explanation is that most Israelis regarded the Intifada as a dangerous development, at least potentially. Like the youthful Palestinian demonstrators who had known nothing but the occupation, an entire generation of Israelis, now of military age, had grown up to think of the West Bank and Gaza as part of Israel – a perception insufficiently challenged by teachers in the classrooms where maps of Israel often did not even show the Green Line (the pre-1967 border of Israel). Moreover, Israelis who heard interviews with Palestinians and watched television footage of demonstrators clashing with IDF troops saw the pent-up bitterness and hatred of twenty years being released. Under such circumstances, Israelis were not likely to make fine distinctions between rejection of an occupation and repudiation of the state of Israel itself. The publication of a poem written by Mahmud Darwish (a PLO official) angered and upset many Israelis, who interpreted it as rejecting all conciliation.[44] Deep down, however, Israelis mistrusted and feared the Palestinians.

Palestinian national feelings are regarded as a threat to the existence of Israel [explained Segev]. There is no reason for this. Israeli thinking is irrational and based upon fear. There is a tremendous fear and anxiety towards Arabs, the feeling that you can't trust them.[45]

In a sense, Israelis saw and heard what they wanted to see and hear. Attending a workshop at the Hebrew University on the psychological affects of the Intifada, Dr Mahdi Abdul-Hadi spoke about the revolt to the Israeli participants.[46] 'The Intifada is a peace message,' he told them. 'It is not to undo Israel but to co-exist with Israel. It is to change the status quo, to end the occupation. It is a White Intifada, which means not bloody, an unarmed resistance movement.' An Israeli scholar responded. 'This is the first time I have heard the message from the people concerned,' he said. 'The Israeli media is filtering all the information.' Tom Segev would disagree. 'The Israeli public has enough information to understand the Intifada,' he emphasized. 'Most Israelis don't want to know.'[47]

For ordinary Israelis the Intifada was a future threat, not a direct or immediate one. Most were not really affected by the revolt. 'The reservists are the only ones who carry the burden among the Israeli population,' commented Yehuda Litani. 'Only two–three per cent of the total population is actually involved in the territories. The rest of the population enjoys life and doesn't feel the effects of it.'[48] Israelis did not demand that their government find a political solution because they felt that there was no pressing need to. 'Israelis will only get excited if [other] Israelis are hurt or killed,' observed Segev. 'This is a problem for the Intifada, which hasn't gotten them [the Palestinians] anywhere because Israelis are not getting hurt.'[49] (After ten months, only five Israelis had died as a result of it.) The liberal-left discussed the conflict, but its members rarely visited the West Bank or Gaza. For Israelis the Intifada was not a major issue. Until it became one, most people would continue to support the status quo in the occupied territories.

Thus time passed, without the Israeli government advancing a proposal of its own. Ironically, however, it was precisely the political establishment which had been most affected by the Intifada. Israel's leaders had to plan and conduct the 'war', face the frustration of seeing the revolt spiral out of control, deal with settlers' accusations of lack of governmental protection, parry international criticism and combat attacks in the press. An important distinction, however, must be made between the period from 9 December 1987 (the start of the Intifada) to 15 November 1988, on the one hand, and the period following the mid-November 1988 PNC declaration, on the other. The proclamation of Palestine statehood, the PLO's recognition of Israel, and Arafat's speech and Geneva press conference had marked a major propaganda victory for the Palestinians internationally. In Europe and elsewhere, governments opened official dialogues with the PLO, issued formal invitations to Arafat to visit and generally upgraded the Palestinian issue. In addition the US administration's decision to begin talks with the PLO suggested a shift in policy that had grave implications for US–Israeli relations. In late December 1988, some Israeli political analysts were estimating that their government had not more than ten weeks to state a policy, before the US government (and perhaps the Soviet Union) began submitting proposals.[50] Under these new circumstances, no Israeli government could ignore the kind of pressure that was building up. Something would at last have to be done.

To a certain extent, the formation on 22 December of a new National Unity Government was a response to this situation. Elections held on 1 November had confirmed the earlier trend toward political polarization and the weakening of the centre.[51] The Likud received 40 Knesset seats (30.8 per cent of the vote) and Labour 39 seats (30 per cent), but the real gains were made by parties on the left and the right and especially those in the ultra-orthodox religious bloc.

At first, it seemed as if Shamir would be forming a coalition government with the ultra-orthodox parties; however, attention soon shifted to negotiations between Shamir and Labour Party representatives. It was argued that another National Unity Government, however weak, would at least be stronger than a narrow right-wing government of Likud and the religious parties, which most pundits gave little chance of surviving a full four-year term. With Labour sitting in the Cabinet, the US would find it more difficult to pressurize Israel. Labour's presence would also make Israel's relations with the new US administration easier, and, it was hoped, enable the Israeli government to find ways of offsetting the US decision to talk with the PLO. However, the reconstitution of the National Unity Government re-established the same basic constraints which had previously existed. In the inner Cabinet, divided equally between Labour and Likud, a tied vote automatically defeated any proposal under consideration. Any initiative would have to be supported by both halves of the coalition.

As a result of the election, the Likud's position in the Cabinet became strengthened. Shamir would now be Prime Minister for a full four-year term, and the Likud also acquired control of the Foreign Ministry. Rabin returned to his former post at Defence and Peres became Minister of Finance. Labour extracted an agreement from the Likud to accept a limit upon the number of new settlements in the occupied territories. Another change was the elevation to Cabinet rank of a trio of pragmatic young protégés of Shamir, thus giving the Likud an appearance of flexibility, since these men were known to be restless with the status quo and desirous of finding some new policy.

The political positions of Likud and Labour seemed to be coalescing. During the election campaign, Labour's position of territorial compromise had become less clearly defined. In addition, a small group of Likud politicians had proposed 'unilateral autonomy', to be achieved after the holding of elections. These men also rejected formal annexation and proposed to leave open the question of sovereignty. Peres and Rabin proposed a temporary settlement: negotiations with a joint Jordanian–Palestinian delegation at a brief international conference, followed by elections in the occupied territories six months after the uprising had ended. Labour pledged no Israeli withdrawal to the pre-1967 borders and no removal of the settlements. Following the PNC Declaration, Peres and Shamir declared in almost identical language that it had not changed the PLO's hostility to Israel. There would be no Palestinian state and no negotiations with the PLO. This, however, did not imply an identity of policies. Peres and Labour still stood for territorial compromise, while Shamir was adamantly opposed to an international conference, to talks with Hussein or, for that matter, with Palestinians. Labour, on the other hand, saw an advantage in making contacts with Palestinian public personalities in East Jerusalem who, its leaders believed, were moderate and flexible. Thus it was that the Labour Party became the first to open talks with Palestinians in the occupied territories.

In January, Rabin proposed that elections be held to choose Palestinians who would administer the occupied territories for an interim period of 'autonomy'. He and other Labour Party officials also began meeting with Palestinian journalists, academics and other personalities from East Jerusalem and Ramallah.[52] By appealing to the most moderate elements, Rabin may have hoped to divide Palestinians and thereby weaken the Intifada, but the Labour Party was also trying to assert itself politically. Its 'peace' message no longer being heard in Israel's Foreign Ministry, the Labour Party was trying to pre-empt the Likud by advancing a modest proposal of its own. Fearful that he and his party would be outmanoeuvred, Shamir also began to consider the idea of undertaking an initiative.

The Prime Minister was personally uncomfortable with the notion of a peace proposal, but pressure was mounting. Shamir was aware that loud voices were being raised by certain elements in the US Jewish community about the need for a dialogue with the PLO,[53] and he was concerned that the new Bush administration, more pragmatic than its predecessor, might have a change of heart. In its annual report on world human rights practices, the US criticized the IDF policy of opening fire upon Palestinian civilians. This, it said, had caused many avoidable deaths and injuries.[54] Clearly, the US administration was uneasy about events in the occupied territories. Following his inauguration, Bush invited Shamir to Washington, but he accompanied this by direct signals that the Prime Minister should bring with him a definite proposal. Shamir was thus placed in a situation where he had to produce something.

That 'something' was Rabin's idea of elections, tailored to Likud specifications. The real question was how to satisfy the US without jeopardizing the Likud's long-standing position of not ceding an inch of land to the Palestinians. In late February, the US informed Shamir of its desire that he advance a serious offer of autonomy that could appeal to West Bankers and Gazans. The US would then use the offer as the basis for its dialogue with the PLO.[55] Accordingly, Shamir and his men drew up a proposal which provided for the election by Palestinians in the occupied territories of representatives who would negotiate with Israel for a five-year period of autonomy.[56] During this period, Israel would be responsible for foreign affairs, security and all matters concerning Israeli settlers. At some point, but no later than three years after the beginning of the period of autonomy, negotiations would begin for a permanent solution. Each side could then introduce whatever proposals it wished. Shamir's election-cum-autonomy plan was explicitly based upon the Camp David Accords, rejected ten years earlier by Palestinians and opposed until the onset of the Intifada by Shamir himself. The most important departure from Camp David was the new emphasis placed upon the Palestinians in the occupied territories. Israel would talk to them, not with Jordan, Egypt, or any other party. It should also be noted that UN Resolutions 242 and 338 were to be the basis of this plan, as they had been of the Camp David Accords.

At the same time, however, the Likud's basic position was reaffirmed. A section of the document entitled 'Basic Premises' stated that Israel would not talk with the PLO, would not accept the establishment of a Palestinian state in the West Bank and Gaza, and would not agree to any change in the status of the occupied territories.

This initiative was presented to Americans as an election plan, which it was only in part. The public relations job was handled by prominent members of the US Jewish community and promoted on television through interviews with younger, good-looking Likud politicians, like Ehud Olmert, who became a leading spokesman for the initiative. Shamir also helped himself with statements (e.g., 'For peace, risks can and should be taken') that made him sound like a moderate. During a visit to the US in early April 1989, Shamir officially presented the general details of his plan to President Bush, who accepted it, though cautiously.[57] The US administration, Bush said, would also like to see Israel advancing ideas for ending its occupation of the West Bank and Gaza. However, the Bush administration was pleased that a link had been established between autonomy and final status negotiations. The net result was that the Shamir plan became the basis of US Middle East diplomacy.

One problem was that too many questions remained unanswered. The nature of the final settlement was left entirely open, discussion of it being postponed until later. Would the inhabitants of East Jerusalem, where a large proportion of the nationalist leaders lived, be able to vote? As for the elections, would the Intifada have to come to an end before they could be held? Washington pressed for answers, and asked Shamir to produce an acceptable formula for how the elections would be held.[58]

In a sense the Bush–Baker team had allowed itself to be trapped by Shamir. It had asked for a plan and, once the Prime Minister provided one, was stuck with it. Since the US had already ruled out the idea of a high-profile international conference and had resolved to adopt a low-key approach, Shamir's peace plan became its only real choice. For Shamir, ambiguity was an advantage, a key to short-term success. The postponement of discussion of the terms of the final settlement had averted a clash between Labour and Likud (not to mention within the Likud), enabling the two to unite in support of the plan. By not dealing with issues on which there was disagreement, the Israeli government could exploit the potentialities of the initiative and improve its international standing.

Unamended, this plan stood little chance of being accepted by Palestinians. After more than a year of Intifada sacrifices, after having recognized Israel and accepted a two-state solution, Palestinians were being asked to postpone consideration of the most important issues for several years. Nor was there any real promise that the one thing they insisted upon – statehood – would ever be realized. Shamir was fond of saying that during final status talks all options would be open, that any subject could be raised, but the document itself, not to mention statements by Israel's leaders, made it clear that a Palestinian state was not an acceptable option. Palestinians also feared that at some point the plan might be stopped or aborted, leaving them with only limited autonomy. The US hoped that it could entice Palestinians at least to begin some kind of negotiating process, but this was made difficult by Shamir himself, whose statement in early April that he was searching for Palestinians who would stand for election without the PLO's blessing suggested an effort to build a fence between Palestinians in the occupied territories and the PLO leadership outside.[59] The Israelis, many Palestinians believed, wanted to deal only with the most moderate people, since their demands would be minimal.

Directed more toward the Americans than the Palestinians, Shamir's plan was not a serious attempt to engage Gazans and West Bankers in negotiations. Its basic assumption was that Israel would have to talk to the leadership in the occupied territories. If this was true, why were elections needed? Israel could talk to the leaders of its choice without elections. Elections were not needed to identify leaders because the Israelis already knew who they were and had indeed been talking to them (talks initiated in January by Labour were continued by the Likud). The Shamir plan was an attempt to buy time and to undermine the PLO's public relations successes. Shamir's belief that it would take nine–twelve months just to prepare for elections (Rabin had estimated six) lent credence to this view.[60] The outside observer can only regret that Israel's leadership chose to dig in and play for time, that no one at the top said 'here is a chance for peace, let's seize it.' In March, in a state-of-the-nation assessment presented to senior ministers, authorized analysts stated that the PLO had undergone a substantial change toward finding a realistic political solution; the intelligence community's annual review declared that the PLO sought a negotiated resolution of the dispute and that there was no alternative to the PLO as a partner in peace talks.[61] These findings, however, went unheeded.

In the short term, Shamir succeeded. The Bush–Baker team reportedly gave him six to twelve months to find Palestinian interlocutors.[62] By May, his government had already embarked upon a broad international campaign to generate support for the election idea. In the US the plan was officially promoted and ballyhooed in the press as the 'only game in town'. Many Americans thought it a great idea. The word 'elections' had a nice ring to it. At a Likud Central Committee meeting in July, Shamir asked the delegates to compare Israel's relations with the

US, and its position in Congress and the media, with what it had been prior to his initiative.[63] The implication was clear. Israel's government had already achieved its main aim. Shamir had regained the initiative where it mattered most, in the US. Approved by the entire Cabinet on 14 May, Shamir's plan became the official policy of the state of Israel. It was now up to the Palestinians, and especially the PLO, to deal with this new situation.

7

Losing the initiative

During its first year, as we have seen, the Intifada was the dynamic producing all change. A historical event, it had engaged the emotions of millions of people and affected the policies of outside powers. In its second year, however, a dramatic shift ensued. Now the Intifada had to respond to external changes – in Israel, the US and the PLO leadership abroad. Dealing with these proved to be as daunting a task as had been the initial confrontation with Israel. Two problems arose. On the political level, feuds erupted among Palestinians over (1) Arafat's concessions; (2) meetings between Palestinian public figures and Israeli authorities; (3) the Shamir plan; and (4) the dialogue with the US. Increased political strife not only occurred between factions, but could also be found within them. This 'problem of unity', as it has been called, was mostly confined to the political groups, including those of the Islamic camp. The second problem involved practically everyone. Palestinians found it more and more difficult to wage their struggle against the occupation authorities, develop their home economy, and build structures that would reduce their dependence upon Israel. The basic cause was a series of economic developments (e.g., the fall of the Jordanian dinar and the effects of Israel's new economic policies) and an intensification of Israeli pressure at levels. None the less, the Intifada continued through a full second year, showing little sign of let-up. Youths confronted the occupation forces, casualties mounted, commercial strikes were called and observed, and the economic boycott was maintained. The survival of the Intifada is as much in need of explanation as the new problems confronting it.

The first problem – disunity among the political groups – was predictable. The independence declaration had aroused high hopes among Palestinians. Many people, especially those from the upper and middle classes, had come to believe that the Intifada could produce almost anything. 'That was the problem,' a prominent resident of Beit Sahour said. 'Hopes were too high. People started believing their mythology and romance.'[1] These high hopes, he added, pertained mostly to the upper and middle classes. Following Arafat's concessions to obtain the dialogue with the Americans, dissenting voices arose.

Some people here said Arafat should have done this in a more calculating manner [observed Dr Abu-Amr].[2] 'Compromises cannot be one-sided,' they said. 'We have recognized Israel. Why won't Israel recognize us?' A lot of people felt that it [these concessions] was a kind of capitulation, a bad way to start.

'You recognize Israel at the negotiating table, not before,' another Palestinian and former political prisoner said. 'Why? because once you do it, the American administration will say: "OK, now you must do something more." I am afraid there will be too many concessions piece by piece until we are left with nothing.'[3] Leaflets by Islamic groups attacked Arafat's strategy: How could Palestinians congratulate each other, they asked, after all the concessions that had been made?[4]

From the beginning, the PFLP had objected to Arafat's efforts to gain US approval. After the PLO Executive Committee had given its full backing to Arafat's statements at Geneva, the PFLP and the DFLP declared that in their opinion Arafat's moves did not represent official PLO policy and that his remarks at Geneva contradicted PNC resolutions.[5] Yet these two factions accepted the decision of the majority. They did not pull out of the PLO. 'There will now be inevitable dissension between the PFLP and Fatah,' Dr al-Jarbawi predicted during an interview in December 1988. 'If Arafat's moves [later] come to be taken for granted,' he added, 'and new demands are made, the Intifada might suffer.'[6] Arafat's concessions thus made some trouble inevitable.

But dissension is not quite the same thing as strife. Had not other difficulties arisen, the problems created by Arafat's concessions would have been minimal. The Israeli government's decision to open talks with local communal leaders, especially

with the public personalities or political brokers – men like Faisal
Husseini, Sari Nuseibeh and others – soon created new problems
for Palestinian political unity. Begun when Shmuel Goren, co-
ordinator of government activities in the occupied territories, met
with Faisal Husseini, these talks covered a wide range of topics,
including the idea of elections. Palestinians were summoned to
military headquarters or administration offices to meet with
military commanders, civil administration officials, politicians
and government officials who posed questions on a variety of
matters. By March, such meetings, highly publicized by the
Israelis, were being held throughout the occupied territories, and
had been expanded to include a wide range of people from
parties and factions in both the Islamic and nationalist camps.[7]
Emphasis, however, was placed upon meetings with older
Palestinians, figures of wealth and standing in their communities.
At one session, a participant told Shay Erez (head of the Civil
Administration in the West Bank) that the Israelis should really
be talking with the Intifada generation rather than the aging
leadership, whose advice was no longer heeded anyway.[8] The
Israelis, of course, had their own ideas. Decided preference was
given to those 'moderate' nationalist figures, most of whom were
followers but not members of al-Fatah. In March, four of these –
Sari Nuseibeh, Fayez Abu Rahme, Hanna Siniora and Elias Freij
(who had Jordanian sympathies) – met with Shamir.[9]

   The UNL had grave reservations about these meetings. In
early January, it declared that the uprising was not up for
bartering or bargaining, and asked Palestinians to pay no
attention to rumours being circulated about talks between
Palestinians and Israeli leaders.[10] On 27 February, the UNL
stated that it was alright for Palestinians to meet with Israelis who
acknowledged Palestinian rights and opposed the continuation of
the occupation, thus implying that these were the only Israelis
with whom Palestinians should be in contact.[11] On 15 March it
accused Shamir of trying to destroy the Intifada with politics.[12]
The PFLP also got into the act, warning Palestinians against
meeting with Israelis.[13] The main reason for the UNL's
discomfiture was the fear that the Israelis were trying to split
Palestinians from each other and undermine the Intifada. In
particular, Palestinian activists and others believed that the
Israelis aimed at separating Palestinians inside the occupied

territories from those outside. This was confirmed by statements
from Israeli Cabinet members about driving a wedge between
PLO supporters in the West Bank and Gaza and the PLO
leadership abroad; and by Shamir's intention of finding and
talking to Palestinians who did not actually belong to the PLO.[14]
(Shamir subsequently admitted that his peace plan had been
intended to remove the PLO from the stage.)

The other Israeli objective, many believed, was to sow
divisions in the Palestinian movement inside the occupied
territories. In meetings with communal leaders, Israeli authorities
put the focus on 'quality of life' issues. Arye Ramot, head of the
Gaza Civil Administration, discussed with Palestinian physicians
ways of improving the local health system. He promised to
redress the grievances of Muslim leaders and, in meetings with
journalists, to attend to any problems that might arise among
them.[15] Thus encouraged to speak up, local notables began to
express their dissatisfaction. Some wanted more lenient taxes,
others the release of detainees, still others the reunification of
families. When leaders of communities met with the Israelis, they
complained. They urged that the schools be reopened. They did
not say: 'leave the schools shut; the Intifada is more important.'
In messages to Shamir, Erez and others said that the people were
talking about the standard of living, that they were tired.[16] In
early March, the UNL warned Palestinians against meetings in
which the Israelis were concentrating upon standard of living
demands, as if Palestinians had lived in peace before the
occupation. These meetings, it declared, gave a negative
impression and harmed the Intifada. Palestinians were to end
their participation in them. Yet the UNL did not entirely close
the door on dialogue between Israelis and Palestinians.[17] The
Israelis released some political prisoners, restored loudspeakers
in mosques and lifted curfews here and there. They also
announced a new policy of permitting Palestinian notables to
travel abroad.[18] 'The Israelis were differentiating among the
people,' explained Dr al-Jarbawi. 'They were hitting the activists
hard but leaving the [political] brokers to move freely.'[19]

The real source of concern for Palestinian activists was Israeli
efforts to promote the political brokers and a consequent fear
that negotiations might be getting underway focussed upon
elections, which many Palestinians believed were really aimed at

ending the Intifada.[20] The brokers were not popular with the mass of Palestinians. They rarely visited refugee camps or villages; they hardly ever explained the results of their meetings with Israelis to their people.[21] They themselves had little confidence in Palestinian capabilities and, as we have seen, had been surprised (and alarmed) by the outbreak of the Intifada. Dr al-Jarbawi has written that for them the revolt was a random event which would soon exhaust itself. Hence the need to exploit the opportunity to reach a settlement. Hence too their belief that the really important actors were the US, the Europeans and the Israelis. 'How can we be represented by such leaders,' an elderly man from a West Bank village exclaimed.[22] Without a popular following, let alone a structure from within which to assert leadership, these men could not possibly have been the leaders of the uprising, as some Israelis were trying to claim. Real leadership resided with the UNL, the 'PLO's arm and organic extension', and in the popular committees. Unlike the UNL, which was composed of all four PLO factions, the political brokers (dubbed the pro-PLO élite in the Israeli press) were connected only with al-Fatah. When Hanna Siniora said something, his words did not represent the sentiments of the PFLP, the DFLP, or the PCP.

In February and March, discussions between Israelis and the political brokers focussed upon the idea of elections:

By holding an election [explained Dr al-Jarbawi] you [the Israelis] might be able to bring in the most moderate elements possible. Talking about it might lead to an alternative leadership. You will also divide the Palestinian camp between those who are for it and those who are against it, and maybe the Intifada will crumble. A feud could arise over whether we should go into this process or not.[23]

The main problem which the UNL had in dealing with this was that meetings had been quietly authorized by Arafat himself.[24] This is why the UNL could not denounce all talks, and it also explains the ambiguities in some of its leaflets. 'The General Command said: If you are summoned, you can go, but you have to be careful to represent our programme,' said Dr al-Jarbawi. 'All those who went said they had been summoned, but some who were summoned did not go.'[25] Here was one of the problems of unity. The Palestinian struggle was against the Israeli occupation, and this gave the public figures who met with Israelis a certain immunity. Arafat's purpose in permitting these meetings was to probe Israeli intentions, and journalists could hardly be blamed for calling them indirect Israeli–PLO talks. With respect to the idea of elections, it is doubtful that the PLO leadership wanted an election to take place, since this could lead to increased factionalism (the PFLP, for example, might harass voters and stop them from going to the polls). Moreover, Arafat may not have felt entirely comfortable with the idea of legitimizing the public personalities through an election process. These al-Fatah supporters would never publicly take a position that contradicted what the PLO had said or done, though in private they could and did try to influence the PLO leadership outside. However, once elected, there was a slim possibility that they would claim to represent the Palestinians and that Israel would confirm them in this.

The PFLP, of course, roundly attacked these election talks, as did Hamas. Elections were aimed at aborting the Intifada, one Hamas leaflet declared; they should not be held until the occupation had ended.[26] The PFLP also spoke of the negative effects of the meetings, and warned that through them Israel hoped to bring an end to the Intifada.[27] By late March, with arrangements for Shamir's trip to the US completed, voices were raised from many sides for the talks to stop. One reason was that Rabin and others had begun to assert widespread Palestinian support for the election idea.[28] In addition, Palestinians did not want to help Shamir obtain American support for his plan by permitting him to claim that he had identified an alternative Palestinian leadership. Through its leaflets and supporters the PFLP threatened Palestinians who continued to participate in the meetings; in late March, a leaflet issued in the name of the 'national institutions' called for an immediate halt to Palestinian–Israeli talks.[29] Following the PLO's rejection (on 10 April) of the Shamir plan, the public personalities followed suit. Later that month, 80 leading Palestinians, including the most promin-ent political brokers, signed a memorandum rejecting the Shamir plan, which, it said, aimed at ending the uprising.[30] Talks between Palestinians and Israelis ceased, at least for a while.

US acceptance of the Shamir plan in early April marked

the beginning of a new diplomatic process, one of indirect negotiations between the PLO and the Israelis through the mediation of outsiders. Attention would henceforth be focussed upon this plan. While Palestinians in the occupied territories did have some input into this negotiating process, the principal players and action were elsewhere, in Tunis, Washington, DC, and Jerusalem. None the less, the US–PLO dialogue and the talks which ensued became yet another source of division among Palestinian political groups. How and why this occurred can be revealed by examining the course and evolution of these talks, and especially the modification of the PLO's original opposition.

Following its initial rejection of the Shamir plan, the PLO came under renewed pressure from the US, which regarded the plan as the starting-point for any subsequent talks.[31] Another requirement had thus been added to those already fulfilled by the PLO. The PLO really had nowhere to turn when faced with the new US demand. Arafat believed that without US efforts no agreement with Israel was possible. For years, he had been moving in the direction of a negotiated settlement. He valued the dialogue with the US highly, and wanted to pursue it. Thus, he could not remain indifferent to American importunings that the PLO accept the plan as a starting-point. US officials suggested that it could be manipulated or tinkered with in the future, but the PLO must first accept it in its entirety.

Like the US, Palestinian public figures in the West Bank and Gaza (who, Faisal Husseini indicated, could serve as a bridge between Israel and the PLO) did not want to see the 'peace process' come to an end.[32] In their communications with the PLO leadership, they urged acceptance of the election idea but not of the Shamir plan as it stood. Total rejection, they argued, threatened to wipe out public relations gains achieved during the first year of the Intifada. Arafat was pressed to indicate a qualified acceptance of the plan. A faction inside the PLO (e.g., Bassam Abu Sharif), which wanted to keep up the momentum, also argued for this position. Members of the Labour Party added their views. 'Grab it,' they told the nationalist figures. Labour, they suggested, would help them later on. As a result of US pressure and the internal dialogue, the PLO changed its position. It sent signals that it was prepared to accept the plan subject to conditions, the most important of which were (1) that it be linked to the realization of Palestinian national goals; (2) that Palestinians from outside the occupied territories be represented in the delegation to negotiate a permanent solution; (3) that East Jerusalem residents be allowed to participate in the elections; (4) that there be international supervision of the elections; and (5) that Israeli troops be withdrawn from the West Bank and Gaza prior to elections. Following this, the US, other Western countries and some Eastern bloc nations began to examine the PLO's position and the Israeli plan in order to find some common ground. Through these international intermediaries, talks occurred between the PLO and Israel. Israel's Labour Party also continued to press the Palestinian side to accept the plan.

At this point, the right-wing opposition to Shamir in the Likud began to assert itself. Having opposed the plan from the outset for fear that Shamir had conceded too much, and believing that the US and the Labour Party were going to divert the plan, three Likud ministers (Yitzhak Modai, David Levy and Ariel Sharon) succeeded in imposing four conditions which reduced Shamir's plan to a minimum.[33] The Likud Central Committee meeting held on 5 July 1989 adopted the following constraints: no participation of East Jerusalem Arabs in the election; no negotiations as long as violence continued; no foreign sovereignty in any part of the land of Israel; and no cessation of new settlements. With this the positive public image of the Shamir plan began to evaporate. The PLO and its supporters quickly capitalized upon their opportunity. 'The plan is dead,' they said. 'Sharon killed it.' Having gone all-out to support the original plan, the Bush–Baker administration was not only embarrassed but under pressure to react. Some prominent American Jewish leaders leaned hard on the Israelis, telling Shamir that he simply could not go back on his proposals. The Labour Party also indicated that it would leave the government. Shamir thus had no choice but to return to the proposal. He came back to the government for a vote reaffirming the original plan, and on 23 July he got it.

The failed attempt by the Likud right-wingers to impose their restrictions only made the plan more attractive. Talk centred not upon the PLO's conditions but the 'victory' that had been won. The plan, almost dead, had been revived. Shamir's image as a 'centrist' was strengthened. He now had the best of both worlds: the renewed backing of the US and, within the Likud, a formal

statement which was right-wing, and which would gain him
support from the settlers and others. The plan was presented to
the Palestinians as a gain. The time had come, American officials
said, for the PLO to soften its position still further. 'Seize the
opportunity while you have the chance,' was the message. Inside
the occupied territories some Palestinian personalities also began to
speak more positively about it. Shamir's plan had been 'legitimized'.

As a result, some officials within the PLO started intimating
that it would lower its demands. Now acceptance would be based
upon two main conditions: (1) that there be a clear link between
the plan and the final outcome; (2) that Palestinians outside the
West Bank and Gaza be part of the final delegation. The other
conditions were shunted aside to be worked out later.

At some point, talks began moving toward the idea of forming
an internal and external Palestinian delegation as a first step in
talking to Israelis *about* elections. Presumably, this occurred
because Shamir was unwilling to modify or 'open up' his own
plan, and Palestinians could not accept it as it stood. The
intermediaries were the Soviet Union, the US, Egypt and, to a
lesser extent, Rumania. The aim of the US and the other
intermediaries seems to have been to begin negotiations for
elections which would themselves be the end result – in other
words, to have real negotiations but under the cover of
preparation for elections. For the Israelis this would obviate the
need for Labour and Likud to resolve their differences (e.g.,
Labour wanted the East Jerusalemites to be included in the
elections in order to counter the strength of the PLO organizational structures; Shamir opposed their participation). For the
PLO this would avoid the danger of an internal feud arising
between radicals and moderates over the elections. The PLO
therefore moderated its position once again. An understanding
was even reached as to which Palestinians from the occupied
territories would be members of the delegation.[34] The only
question left open was the matter of its 'outside' composition.[35]
Shamir was now under pressure. His plan had been designed to
buy time. He did not want to enter into serious negotiations with
Palestinians. Consequently, he opposed the participation of
'outsiders' in the Palestinian delegation. On 28 July IDF troops
kidnapped Hizbullah leader Sheikh Obeid in southern Lebanon,
and days later US Marine Lt. Col. William Higgins was murdered

by his Shiite Muslim kidnappers. The hostage crisis was reignited. Attention was distracted from the Shamir plan at a critical juncture and focussed elsewhere. The visit to Israel of US Assistant Secretary John Kelly, sent to discuss the modalities of elections, was completely overshadowed by the new crisis, which occupied much of the rest of the summer. The 'peace process' had been stalled again, and was going nowhere.

By summer a tremendous deflation of hopes and expectations had occurred among Palestinians in the occupied territories. 'Hopes were dashed when Arafat made all these concessions and the US produced nothing,' said a prominent resident of Beit Sahour.[36] Many Palestinians had assumed that the US administration would exert pressure upon the Israeli government, and they had expected to see some progress towards the realization of Palestinian national goals. The vast majority had been willing to give Arafat's negotiating strategy a chance, but not without a time limit. Arafat's decision to make unilateral and unreciprocated concessions to the US caused some Palestinians to wonder if the dialogue itself was worth pursuing. Early fears that Shamir had no intention of entering serious negotiations seemed to be confirmed. Within the national camp the PFLP was the chief beneficiary. This faction had from the outset disagreed with the course chosen by Arafat, but had declared that it would go along with the will of the majority. Many Palestinians now believed that what the PFLP had said all along was correct. The PFLP, informed Palestinians acknowledged, was growing stronger.

Political opinion in the occupied territories became organized around two poles of thought. On one side were those, led by the PFLP, who rejected the idea of elections, had no faith in the Shamir plan, desired to intensify the Intifada and insisted that the dialogue with the US show progress. (The PFLP supported this dialogue, but said that it must be based upon progress.) On the other side were those, mostly from al-Fatah, who supported Arafat's political moves, and insisted that his negotiating strategy be pursued to a conclusion with the US and the Israelis.[37] The point is that this basic division existed not only between factions, but within them. In al-Fatah, for example, some people supported Arafat, others the PFLP; the same split could be discerned in the DFLP.

Factional strife thus continued, mainly expressed in differences over meetings between pro-Fatah national figures and Israeli authorities. (These meetings, however, occurred on a much smaller scale than previously.) Palestinian participants came under greater pressure than ever not to attend. In mid-July, Hamas issued a leaflet rejecting Shamir's plan and calling upon the PLO to end the dialogue with the US.[38] At the same time, the PFLP was waging an all-out campaign to discourage Palestinians from meeting with Israelis. In leaflets it denounced the government's initiative and urged Palestinians to intensify their struggle against the occupation.[39] The UNL also continued to declare its opposition to meetings between Palestinians and Israeli government officials and even denied that meetings were taking place; yet it indirectly acknowledged their existence by demanding the publication of their contents.[40] Partly in order to counter such pressures, Arafat announced his support for the meetings which had occurred between some Palestinians and Shamir.[41] (Arafat also did this in order to assert PLO authority over the talks and to prevent Shamir from claiming that he had found non-PLO Palestinians to negotiate with.) Jamil Tarifi, a West Bank al-Fatah supporter who had met with the Israeli Prime Minister, became the subject of death threats in graffiti signed by the PFLP.[42] Members of al-Fatah countered with graffiti in support of Tarifi's meeting.[43]

By summer's end, divisions were growing.

Strife can be seen mostly through graffiti, something very important [noted Dr al-Jarbawi], because you can sense a division between the lower cadres and the upper leadership. [Faisal] Husseini of Fatah says something but graffiti from Fatah in the occupied territories says something different.[44]

A leaflet signed by the 'Popular Army-Fatah' warned the pro-Fatah political brokers against meeting with Israelis.[45] These struggles, however, were occurring only at the political level. 'No one has yet been killed because of this,' Dr al-Jarbawi emphasized.

In al-Fatah Arafat was in trouble, not as its leader, but as a man who had made too many concessions and received too little in return. Over the summer, an internal conflict had been brewing. At its General Congress meeting held in Tunis in early August, al-Fatah's ageing leadership faced a real challenge from a more radical second generation of middle-level officials, who came to the conference angry at Arafat. Arafat, though, emerged the winner by giving the radicals much of what they wanted: a hard-line platform which called for intensified military action to end the occupation and which ruled out the holding of elections in the occupied territories until the Israeli army had withdrawn.[46] In the elections for the allocation of seats that followed, a compromise was reached, and the radicals did not emerge in the strength that some Palestinians had been predicting. 'Arafat permitted this to occur,' explained Dr al-Jarbawi:

Now he has a more radical position within Fatah and a more moderate position within the PLO generally [based upon the concessions of November–December 1988]. You have Bassam Abu Sharif talking about a diplomatic solution, and Arafat can go back to Fatah when he wants and base himself upon this radical statement, and say 'I agree with you.' There is now a consensus inside Fatah because of what Arafat gave the radicals. This doesn't restrict the PLO because Fatah is only a faction of the PLO. Arafat has the best of both worlds now. He saved his neck and bought time. This move gave him six to nine months to deliver something.[47]

* * * * * * * * * *

In addition to the problem of political unity, Palestinians faced new economic hardships and increased pressure from Israel that made it more difficult for them to confront the IDF, build up their own local infrastructures and reduce dependence upon the Jewish state. The source of the new economic difficulties lay outside the West Bank and Gaza, and thus highlighted the vulnerability of a society with an economy bound to Israel and a monetary system tied to a great extent to Jordan. (Only the West Bank, however, had strong monetary links with Jordan.) 'The Palestinian economy is not a traditional but a complex system linked with the international monetary system,' remarked Dr Ifrah Zilberman, an Israeli anthropologist who is conducting a study of the Hebron area. 'Some Palestinians are now saying that those people who thought they could rely upon vegetable gardens made an error.'[48]

From the start of the new year, Palestinians were hard hit by the collapse of the Jordanian dinar, a sharp decline in the purchasing power of the shekel, and the steeply rising prices of essential commodities.[49] The Jordanian dinar was the primary medium of exchange in the West Bank: Palestinians had their savings in dinars and many people (e.g., teachers and employees of Islamic institutions) continued to receive salaries in this currency. In January 1989, the dinar plummeted, losing about half its value. As Jordan's economic crisis deepened, matters only became worse. By July, the dinar had reached an all-time low, occasioned in part by the mass selling of the currency in the West Bank. About the same time, the Israeli government, facing serious economic problems of its own, devalued the shekel and began implementing a new austerity programme. It cut subsidies for elementary foodstuffs, a measure that fell particularly hard upon the Palestinians, for whom basic commodities comprised about 50 per cent of their daily food basket and who did not benefit from the allowances granted Israeli citizens to compensate for some of the cutbacks. As a result, the price of flour, sugar, rice and other foodstuffs rose by fifteen to twenty per cent in the occupied territories.[50] The currency squeeze was made still tighter by intensified Israeli efforts to collect taxes and the imposition of new fines and fees aimed at destroying Palestinian attempts to achieve self-sufficiency. Tax officials, accompanied by armed escorts, set up checkpoints on the major roads and at entrances to towns and villages, and made surprise raids on shops and stores. Merchants, travellers and others found in tax arrears had to pay their taxes immediately or face the confiscation of their cars, goods and other property. At the Erez exit and entry point in Gaza, vehicles were required to pass through a computerized tax check: those who had fallen behind in their tax payments saw their cars impounded. New and higher fees were required for the renewing of automobile licence plates, and fines were imposed upon merchants and others whose papers and tax records were incomplete. Taxes were demanded from fruit and vegetable shopkeepers regardless of the declared income of their stores.

Palestinian agriculture also suffered from renewed Israeli harassment. IDF units raided West Bank co-operatives and confiscated produce. They cut the water off from some villages on the grounds that they had not paid their bills. Greenhouses, goat and chicken farms were demolished on the grounds that they were not licensed. Tree uprootings also continued. One estimate, compiled by the Jerusalem Media and Communications Centre, placed total losses from almond, olive and citrus trees destroyed by the IDF at $3,800,000.[51] If this was not enough, 1989 brought a very cold winter, with several frosts that damaged and destroyed crops from the fertile Jordan Valley to the Gaza Strip.

The economic damage caused by these convergent developments was incalculable.[52] The fall of the Jordanian dinar eroded savings, pushed up the prices of milk, chickens and eggs, and reduced sales and business activity. Lay offs by Israeli companies of their Palestinian employees, owing to worker absenteeism, meant that money, already in short supply, became scarcer still. Unable to purchase chemicals, greenhouses and other items, many farmers in the Jordan Valley and elsewhere let their fields lie fallow or shifted from fruits and vegetables to fodder and grains. The worsening situation was reflected in UNL leaflets which asked property owners to reduce rents, raise their employees' salaries, and avoid dismissing their workers. The recession that had begun during the first year of the Intifada thus became broader and deeper. By summer 1989, Palestinian incomes had fallen to between one-half and one-third of what they had been prior to the Intifada.[53] According to one Palestinian economist, per capita income had declined to $800 in the West Bank and $500 in Gaza, owing to strikes, curfews, currency devaluations, and the taxes and fines imposed by the Israeli government.[54]

Increased tax collection and pressure upon the agricultural sector were one component of a wider Israeli policy designed to place maximum stress upon the Palestinian population without causing a disaster that would provoke a new outburst of the revolt, more international criticism and renewed pressure upon Israel.[55] As we have seen, the Israelis had been differentiating among the population by appealing to the upper and middle classes. On 22 July 1989, Israeli authorities permitted the reopening of all West Bank elementary schools, closed since January 1988. (Schools in Gaza had remained open, save for curfews and strike days.) This, of course, had been one of the requests made by Palestinian notables. On the other hand, beginning in May, Israel stepped up its military pressure in an effort to destroy the organizational structures of the revolt – the popular committees and the factions of the national and Islamic camps. If successful, this would have enhanced the influence of the visible leadership, the political brokers, giving them greater freedom of manoeuvre than they otherwise enjoyed. Special operations, carefully planned in advance, were carried out against local bands of fugitive youths, faction members and individual inciters who were followed, arrested and, in some cases, murdered.[56] Rules were changed permitting the IDF to take tougher and more violent measures. Open fire regulations were relaxed: Palestinians who went into the streets masked could now be shot after ignoring an order to halt.[57] Houses belonging to the families of fugitive suspects were demolished, whereas this had previously been done only after the apprehension of suspected persons.[58] By making the families of wanted youths homeless, the IDF hoped to induce these runaways to give themselves up. Administrative detention was extended to one year, up from the previous term of three or six months, with the option of renewal for a second year.[59] Stiffer sentences were also meted out. For throwing stones, one youth received five years in prison, of which he had to serve 28 months; two others were sentenced to three-and-a-half years, serving twenty months each.[60]

The increased aggressiveness of IDF troops is reflected in the casualty statistics. In Gaza total casualties for the first 24 days of May were 2,184 against 1,688 for the month of April. 'In May, casualties were higher than any other month of the Intifada,' an UNRWA spokesman said.[61] While allowance must be made for the Muslim holy month of Ramadan (a time of fasting), which began in early April, total casualties for April were still considerably above Gaza's monthly average of about 1,132.[62] Overall, 35 Palestinians died in May; only in March and April of 1988 had more Palestinians been killed. In July, Palestinian deaths in Gaza and the West Bank reached 32, another high monthly toll.[63] In September, 392 Gazans were shot and injured by live ammunition, an increase of 100 over the previous month and the highest since May.[64] According to the Israeli press, one reason for this was the army's tendency to rely more upon its own fire-power. Soldiers were also better prepared to deal with the situation. Previously, they would sometimes pause to decide what to do. Now they immediately went after people. In June troops shot and killed a Palestinian who had been throwing stones at cars carrying workers to Israel; in August soldiers opened fire at masked Palestinians writing graffiti on walls.[65]

These escalating casualties occurred at a time when Israelis were making massive attacks on known activists and other Palestinians. In May the Israelis cracked down hard on Hamas, arresting between 200 and 250 activists, including their reported leader, Sheikh Ahmad Yassin.[66] 'Taking out 200 activists was a real blow,' commented Dr Zilberman. 'One-quarter of their men are gone. Today they are less powerful.'[67] This was followed by large-scale arrests of suspected members of the organized nationalist factions. Hundreds of Palestinians were seized in carefully planned operations.[68]

Today there are 9,000 Palestinians being held in jail for Intifada offences, plus 4,500 who were in jail before the Intifada [the UNRWA spokesmen commented]. The Israelis are planning to increase the capacity of the detainment centres so they can hold 15,000 by 1990.[69]

These operations, which were among the largest of their kind since the beginning of the Intifada, did bring a measure of temporary 'calm' to certain areas. 'Israel has weakened the organizational infrastructure,' acknowledged Dr al-Jarbawi. 'Jenin and Tulkarm are relatively quiet these days. But this does not mean that they can stop the Intifada. They cannot.'[70]

The problem was that the war was not solely against the activists. The Israelis were fighting on two fronts: against the organizations; and against ordinary Palestinian men, women and children who were busily working in their localities to free themselves from the occupation. As they stepped up their campaign against the organizations, so too the Israelis extended collective punishment measures against the wider population. This can be demonstrated statistically by curfews. In, Gaza, curfews were increasingly used as a weapon by the occupation authorities. Beginning in March, Gazans living in refugee camps spent one-third or more of their time under curfew (see table). During May – the peak month – they were confined to their homes for half of the time. On 15 May Rabin announced new restrictions on the movement of Palestinian workers from the occupied territories into Israel. Shortly afterwards, three days of total curfew were imposed upon Gazans, who were told that only holders of special permits would be allowed to enter Israel.[71] Banning Palestinians and harming their livelihood in this way, observed Danny Rubenstein, would only fuel the Intifada. ' . . . the more Rabin tries to lock up the Arabs of the territories as he did last week in Gaza,' he wrote, 'the quicker the deterioration will be.'[72] In addition to curfews, a new form of collective punishment was imposed. Gazans who worked in Israel were required to exchange their old identity cards for new magnetic cards at a cost of twenty shekels each.[73] Only Palestinians who held these new cards would be granted entry into Israel. The purpose behind this move was not only to reassert Israeli control and force Gazans into greater dependence upon the Civil Administration, but also to police workers. 'To get these cards,' said the UNRWA spokesman, 'you must have paid all your bills and not have any close family members in jail or with a record. The objective was to disqualify a lot of workers.'[74] Israel was trying to wear out the Palestinian population in the hope that the Intifada could be brought to an end.

Danny Rubenstein was right. The harder the Israelis pressed the population, the more determined Palestinians became to carry on their struggle. Violence, he had predicted, would increase, and find new outlets.[75] The Intifada simply could not be ended. It had become too deeply rooted in the behaviour and consciousness of the population. People had become accustomed to strikes and to following the instructions given in the leaflets. And they were also becoming accustomed to beatings, arrests, house demolitions and shootings.

If you follow a radical policy – a harsh policy – too long [explained Dr al-Jarbawi], it loses its effectiveness. People throw stones without wearing masks now – they just don't care. Going to prison is not so bad. Israel has lost its capacity to intimidate.[76]

This view was shared by others.

Now if you throw a stone or are a member of a popular committee, your house is demolished [the UNRWA spokesman said]. Before you had virtually to have shot at someone or, at the beginning of the Intifada, thrown a petrol bomb for this to happen. So people figure 'if we are shot

CURFEWS IMPOSED IN THE GAZA STRIP

	DEC 87	JAN 88	FEB	MAR	APR	MAY	JUN	JUL	AUG	SEP	OCT	NOV	DEC	JAN	FEB	MAR	APR	MAY	JUN
		88												89					

Values shown: 10, 101, 29, 82, 57, 34, 47, 36, 103, 44, 74, 141, 113, 98, 94, 89, 125, 143, 151, 101

30 DAYS/MONTH × 11 CAMPS/AREAS = 330
PARTIAL CURFEW AND GENERAL CURFEW EVERY DAY
2000–0300 HRS NOT INCLUDED

Courtesy of UNRWA

STRIKE DAYS

1987	DEC	– 1
1988	JAN	– 1
	FEB	– 5
	MAR	– 4
	APR	– 2
	MAY	– 8
	JUN	– 8
	JUL	– 6
	AUG	– 11
	SEP	– 4
	OCT	– 8
	NOV	– 10
	DEC	– 11
1989	JAN	– 6
	FEB	– 6
	MAR	– 6
	APR	– 10
	MAY	– 7
	JUN	– 7

for throwing stones, we might as well throw grenades. The Israelis are losing deterrence by these measures.

Psychologically speaking, an activist from a West Bank village declared, those who threw stones were ready to throw something else.

By creating new martyrs for the Intifada, the Israelis helped keep it going. In August, the shooting death of a six-year-old boy in Shati refugee camp sparked the worst demonstrations in months. Hundreds, perhaps thousands, of people took to the streets.[77] Funerals served as occasions for new demonstrations. Vigils were held at the family homes of the deceased, where plans were laid for renewed activity. In one West Bank village, the father of its first martyr became the founder of the first popular committee. Streets were renamed after martyred youths, and small piles of stones erected on the sites of their deaths. In this way, legends were made out of stone throwers. The arrest of a young man was often a sufficient training for politics and entry into the national movement.

Renewed Israeli pressure also helped keep the Intifada going by increasing hatred of the occupation. 'The Israelis are tightening the noose,' said an activist from the village of Husan, 'but the people are stronger because the hate is more.'[78] Despite Israeli efforts to appeal to them, the upper and middle classes continued to suffer. 'Israel's actions make people angry,' explained Dr al-Jarbawi. 'The upper and middle classes can't even have a breather.'[79] Their cars were likewise pulled over at roadblocks, impounded, or held for days even though they had paid all their taxes.

The upper and middle classes are tired [al-Jarbawi continued]. But they know that there is no way out. They have invested too much in the Intifada. A new way of thinking and living has been established for all social classes, so complaining can't break it up.

Israeli attempts to differentiate among the population were thus bound to fail. Deep down, Palestinian society was slowly being radicalized. 'It is not only the young people,' Dr al-Jarbawi said, 'but the whole society. Underneath, this has occurred.' IDF behaviour, a member of the Israeli general staff declared, had sown hatred deeper even than had the Palestinians lost another war. He expressed profound sorrow over the killing of women and children. 'I believe,' he said, 'that the confrontation could have been given a less extreme character.'[80]

The harder the Israelis tried, the worse things became for everyone. 'The Israelis cannot relax,' said one Palestinian. 'If they could, the Intifada would slow down. But they keep pushing more and more.'[81] Israelis could not relax because they themselves claimed a right to the land on which the Palestinians lived. Their occupation implied possession, ownership. Israelis therefore had to uproot, to remove every Palestinian flag, to bring down every kite flying the Palestinian colours, and to make a 'hostile' act out of every 'V' sign flashed by Palestinian youngsters.[82]

Having long since become a movement of the entire society, the Intifada continued at its own pace. In the streets, groups of youths confronted Israeli troops and attacked other symbols of the occupation. Stone-throwing – the principal form of confrontation – changed somewhat. Instead of large numbers of people, little groups were formed, ranging from five to ten people, who would watch the soldiers, making them nervous. Quick attacks by small groups of stone-throwers became the rule. 'You can't sustain high mass participation with the level of repression used by the Israelis,' explained Dr al-Jarbawi. 'You don't want people to be killed in the hundreds.'[83] Stone-throwing was important in keeping the revolt going at the base of society. A stone-throwing attack required organization, planning and the careful recruitment by the group of new members. It was also a visible sign that the fight was continuing, and encouraged other Palestinians to struggle in their own ways against the occupation. Because soldiers reacted immediately to stone-throwing attacks, innocent Palestinians were often hurt. A farmer might have a grove of trees uprooted by IDF troops because youths had launched an attack from there. Palestinians were frequently arrested because they happened to be near the scene of an incident. In this way, the pot was kept boiling.

Palestinians also began resorting to more violent methods, using handguns and grenades, and throwing more molotov cocktails. And there was also a tendency for individuals to carry out acts of personal revenge. In Ramallah four Israeli tax collectors were injured when a molotov cocktail was hurled into their car; in Gaza's Khan Yunis a hand grenade was thrown into the main street, wounding three border policemen.[84] The most dramatic incident occurred on 6 July, when a young Palestinian ran an Israeli passenger bus into a ravine on the Tel Aviv–Jerusalem highway, killing 14 people on the spot.[85] This tragic incident launched a wave of violence and revenge attacks by Israelis against Palestinians.[86] Later, it was revealed that the young man had a brother and a nephew who were in jail, a close friend who had been paralysed as result of a gunshot wound, and that he and his wife had been beaten by Israeli soldiers on their wedding day.[87] Increased violence by Palestinians had been predicted. It was the direct result of Israel's own harsh measures.

One new expression of resistance was marches by popular 'armies' through the main streets of towns and villages.[88] Such military parades had been occurring ever since the PNC meeting in November 1988. The PLO had called for the formation of popular armies, and in January a 'Palestinian popular army' (*jaysh shaabi filistini*) had issued its first leaflet. Popular armies were very much like the Strike Forces, whose job had been to organize demonstrations and enforce strikes. Marches were staged to show the population that the people, and not the Israelis, possessed the real authority. An announcement would be made that at 10:00 a.m. a march was to occur in Nablus. If the Israelis could not prevent it, that proved something. Villagers watched with pride these marches by local youths dressed in military uniforms that bore the colours of the Palestinian flag. Some of the young men carried clubs, others had real weapons. 'Our youths make marches,' said a lady from the village of Husan, 'to show the people that we are continuing.'[89] Unmoved by economic hardships, the younger generation was determined to carry on the Intifada.

Another development was the increased killing of collaborators. The killing of Palestinians who worked for Israel as agents and informants was not new. In the early days of the revolt, collaborators had been asked to repent and join the Intifada. The shabab talked with many of them, told them that their actions were wrong, warned and threatened them. As time passed, pressure upon these people intensified. In January 1989 the UNL requested that popular courts be formed to try 'thieves, agents and brokers'.[90] Underground tribunals were set up to gather evidence, conduct trials and issue sentences. Soon reports began surfacing of Palestinians being knifed, bludgeoned or hacked to death. Murders (including shooting deaths) began to take place in broad daylight in town squares. Eyewitnesses gave gruesome accounts of beatings.[91] The Israelis kept score. Thirty-five Palestinians were murdered between April and mid-July, according to one account, whereas only ten had died in the three months preceding April.[92]

Many Palestinians excused these murders by saying that the victims had had trials, or that all revolutions have collaborators, or that the dead had received plenty of warnings and time to 'repent'. Other Palestinians were less apologetic. The Intifada, they argued, was not a neat tidy revolution that could produce results overnight. No central commanding authority existed to control the popular committees that were the only real authorities in their areas. Under such circumstances things like this were bound to happen.

Why did this occur? The increased killing of collaborators was a separate matter from the problem of political unity. Palestinians who died were not members of rival factions fighting each other over the Shamir plan or the dialogue with the US. In the main, these killings were a way of striking back at the occupation authorities, a form of resistance to Israel. After Arafat went to Geneva in mid-December 1988, popular committees began putting more pressure upon collaborators so as to indicate to the Israelis that Palestinians were serious about having a state, and that they would strike at them where they could in order to weaken their hold. The first reason for the increased killing of collaborators, then, was to disrupt Israel's communications and weaken its intelligence-gathering system. The second reason was that collaborators were becoming more of a problem. As we have seen, thousands of young Palestinians, many of them without a strong political consciousness, had been arrested. Many were beaten. As a result, some agreed to gather information for the Israelis. On this understanding, they were released. Their families knew nothing of what had happened. Prior to and in the first months of the Intifada, Palestinians had known or at least had had a good idea of who most of the collaborators were. But by late 1988, no one could be sure who was or was not an Israeli agent.[93] As part of its effort to sow dissension, Israel began using its collaborators as inciters or instigators of trouble. The goal was to foment strife within communities. One night, a car belonging to a popular committee member from al-Fatah would be torched; the next night the same thing would happen to the car of a PFLP member. Fights broke out and mediation committees were formed to deal with such problems. Palestinians eventually realized what was happening. Collaborators were making trouble. Some threw petrol bombs into people's homes at night; a few even threw grenades at fellow Palestinians. In one of its leaflets, the UNL attacked Israeli agents for creating confusion and spreading sedition within the Palestinian community.[94] This, then, became the second reason to pursue them. The third reason was the success of Israel's own counter-measures, which had somewhat reduced the effectiveness of the resistance. As we have seen, it had become impossible for Palestinians to move to real local autonomy. The Intifada thus shifted its focus a little, and the killing of collaborators increased as an expression of resistance.[95]

The problem was that this got out of hand. People who were not informers or Israeli agents were killed. 'Some mistakes were made,' a popular committee leader acknowledged in August 1989.

People were killed just for doubts; [charges were] not proven against them. Some people were killed who had close ties with Israel or the Israeli army but were not really collaborators. Also, many more were killed than announced in the papers.[96]

The people to whom he referred came from the stratum of middlemen – people upon whom Palestinians had depended before the Intifada for obtaining permits and licences. Now all of these people were suspect.[97]

As time passed, another kind of Palestinian came under pressure – the narcotic addicts, drug dealers, thieves and, occasionally, prostitutes. Many of these people were threatened. Their homes and cars were attacked. Some were even killed. This was carried out by members of the Islamic groups, mostly Hamas but also Islamic Jihad. Graffiti and leaflets by Hamas threatened drug dealers and criminals, warning them to stop their activities.[98] A leaflet dated 20 July 1989 by the Islamic Jihad called for

Palestinians to conduct a holy war (jihad) against thieves, to oppose persons who sold drugs, and to fight against the agents of Israel.[99] The campaign against thieves and 'immoral persons' was not directly related to the struggle against the occupation. Such people were innocent of any collaboration. They were the fallen, hence presumably redeemable, members of the community. Hamas' previous emphasis upon reform of the individual person was being tragically superseded by an enforced 'purification' of society.

By this time, the Islamic forces had been accepted as a legitimate movement by the mass of Palestinians. This acceptance found expression in the attitudes of many people in the national camp. In response to a question about the killing of drug dealers and others by members of Islamic groups, one secular Palestinian replied: 'The Islamic Jihad is trying to purify society. Hamas is trying to purify society, and confront the occupation. The UNL is confronting the occupation. This is good. They all add to each other in a nice way.' Because the Islamic Jihad was only slowly rebuilding itself and had just begun to renew its activities, Hamas was the only significant religious organization in the occupied territories. As we have seen, most Palestinians had previously considered Hamas more interested in gaining support for itself than in helping the national cause. By the autumn of 1988, and especially after the opening of the new year, this attitude no longer prevailed.

The most important thing is that Hamas has won the battle for legitimacy [declared Dr al-Jarbawi]. Today you will see a slogan by Hamas on a wall, and if you are a Palestinian, you won't clean it off. Hamas and the Islamic Jihad have become a fact of life.[100]

Many Palestinians, including the merchants of East Jerusalem, began to heed strike calls made in Hamas' leaflets. This did not mean, of course, that the nationalists were receding. If Hamas increased its membership, so did the factions of the national camp, which continued to enjoy the support of most Gazans and West Bankers.[101] Many Palestinians who supported Hamas, as opposed to being active members of it, favoured a Palestinian rather than Islamic state. These same people followed the instructions in the UNL leaflets. The legitimation of Hamas was not at the PLO's expense.

Three reasons account for the widespread acceptance of Hamas. First, its members had gained the support of the people by sacrificing themselves for the Intifada; by forcing things on the ground, they had won respect. Second, shopkeepers and merchants in East Jerusalem and elsewhere who supported Hamas did so not simply because it helped to continue the struggle. The strike had become a way of life. They were accustomed to following UNL calls for it, and also did not want to have their stores attacked or stoned (Hamas' enforcers were very aggressive). Third, Palestinians were returning to their traditional ways and Islam was a central part of their culture.

When some people began to shout 'Allah Akhbar' [God is the greatest] during a demonstration [said an activist from the village of Husan] this made the shabab feel better. There was also some trouble in our village between the PFLP and the DFLP. People felt that they needed a stronger base so they turned to Islam. Support shifted from al-Fatah to Islamic Jihad. But there is no trouble between Islamic Jihad and Fatah.[102]

The same people who supported Islamic Jihad, he added, wanted a Palestinian, not an Islamic, state.

The Islamic movement was a positive rather than a negative factor in the overall confrontation of Palestinians with the Israeli occupation forces. The strike, of course, was a primary weapon and powerful symbol of resistance. Calls in Hamas leaflets for the boycott of Israeli products and for the establishment of a home economy dovetailed with similar requests from the UNL. By augmenting the number of its activists and spreading its influence to areas where it had been weak, Hamas helped produce a more intense Intifada. 'Hamas is strong on the West Bank,' declared Dr al-Jarbawi in August 1989.

There is support for it at all levels and among all classes, though religious tendencies are stronger when you go down the ladder. In the West Bank, its strength is in the periphery, in Tulkarm, Jenin and Qalqilya and not in the centre.[103]

It was no coincidence that the most active area of fighting in the West Bank was the north, where the population was conservative and close-knit, and where Hamas and the Islamic Jihad were strong. Nearly 30 per cent of all Palestinian shooting deaths occurred in the region of Nablus, where 5 per cent of the total population (9,740 out of 200,000) had been hospitalized for wounds.[104] After the Ramadan fast had ended in early May, Hamas members carried the attack to the Israelis and even kidnapped Israeli soldiers.[105] Israel could not tolerate a new force throwing stones. The massive attack against Hamas by the IDF proved that it had become a force to be reckoned with. In the West Bank as well as Gaza, Hamas activists helped keep the struggle going.

The legitimation of Hamas among Palestinians ultimately led to its acceptance by the nationalist leadership, which in the autumn of 1988 had been denouncing Hamas strike calls and efforts to 'impose' itself upon the people.[106] (One reason for its attitude was that Hamas had rejected the PNC Resolution, including a two-state solution and acceptance of UN Resolutions 242 and 338.) '[George] Habash himself called upon Palestinians to unite and work together with Hamas,' observed Dr al-Jarbawi.

He said that Hamas could be included in the General Command [UNL]. This was conciliatory talk, and very important. The lines were open to co-ordination, and they [Hamas and the UNL] did co-ordinate, not on strike days – Hamas wanted to keep its strike days separate to show its legitimacy – but in the planning of demonstrations. Co-ordination meant that each side recognized the other.[107]

Although Hamas called upon Palestinians 'to co-ordinate and unify efforts and to brush aside disunity and differences',[108] it refused to join the UNL, where it would have been only one group out of five and where the nationalist organizations might have been able to circumscribe or neutralize it. Differences between it and the UNL persisted. After the reopening of the West Bank schools, Hamas declared that schools should remain open on most strike days, whereas the UNL said to close them on strike days. The UNL remained unhappy with the idea of separate strikes by Hamas. In the spring a fight broke out when nationalists tried to abort a Hamas strike in the West Bank. (The two sides later made up.)

Differences between Hamas and the UNL did not mean that Palestinian society was polarized, or that there were two separate

Intifadas, as some Israelis claimed.[109] 'The problem will only come,' said Dr al-Jarbawi, 'if Hamas and Islamic Jihad leaflets say "don't listen to the UNL, don't follow its leaflets, don't face the occupation as the number one goal."'[110] The Islamic and nationalist camps, noted Dr Abu-Amr, were both working to gain Palestinian national rights.

And they agree on what these are: self-determination and the right of return. Each claims it is the one to define the direction of society and lead it, based upon different perceptions. The Muslims say 'We will have a Muslim society' and the nationalists want to do it from the PLO platform. But Hamas doesn't try to make things seem too fragmented. Hamas says 'We are [all] nationalists. We are in the same boat but we are not the same.' Consensus now means commitment to fight against the occupation. The majority of the population respects the wishes of both camps because they are doing something for the struggle.[111]

If one reason for the continuation of the Intifada through a full second year lay in the policies of the Israelis, the success of Hamas also played an important role.

Hamas' legitimacy had come from stones, but public confrontation with the occupation forces was not the principal form of resistance. What had given the Intifada staying-power was the determination of Palestinians of all ages and at all social levels to disengage from Israel and make themselves as self-sufficient as possible. Facing far more difficulties than they had during the first year of their revolt, Palestinians none the less continued to struggle and work together, especially in the rural areas.

People know human needs are increasing, so they are going to income-generating projects more and more [observed Nora Kort in July 1989]. People are initiating on their own. They are looking for a return on their investment, for things that will help them in the long run.[112]

In the northern West Bank regions, people pooled their resources, organizing co-operatives or 'investment companies'. One group of young men packaged and sold almonds in the local market.[113] Men and women's co-operatives discussed ways of integrating local specializations. Tulkarm, for example, had a lot of small businesses as well as expertise in citrus-growing and marketing; Nablus had small workshops and leather and food-processing industries. How could these be organized to benefit people in the area? In the Jenin district, some Palestinians were searching for ways of producing jewellery (previously made for Israeli factories). Elsewhere, businessmen were considering ways of starting medical health insurance for the people. In the Ramallah district of the central West Bank, where larger businesses (e.g., dairy companies) could be found, an agricultural relief committee, with its headquarters in East Jerusalem, worked with farmers to help fund and market their crops. Palestinian vans with yellow (Israeli) licence plates collected the produce and brought it into the cities. (East Jerusalem legally was part of Israel proper.) Female members of another agricultural committee talked with farmers, arranged for the purchase of their tomato crops, helped women make tomato paste in their homes, and marketed it in the urban areas. In Gaza women made products in their homes and brought their goods to a central depot, which marketed them and gave the women a little more than cost price. Transport work was also done mostly by women, since female drivers were less frequently stopped by IDF troops than men.

Palestinians did not operate in a vacuum. 'Structures' existed to sustain and augment local efforts to survive and continue the resistance. Without such help, Palestinians probably could not have survived the new hardships for a full second year. Many international and church-affiliated organizations operated in the West Bank and Gaza. The activities of these groups ranged from relief work (for example, UNRWA) to developmental aid (for example, Catholic Relief Services, and Save the Children). In Gaza especially, UNRWA's clinics, schools and food relief projects had become ever more important for the population. On 23 July 1989 UNRWA gave a food distribution of 50 kilogrammes of flour to every Gazan family, even non-refugees.[114] In the West Bank, one private aid organization helped purchase a mobile mill for a women's co-operative and trained its members in bookkeeping and managerial skills so that they could run the project. These women hired a man to drive their tractor from one farm to another, grinding lentils, barley and wheat, and ran the entire project, managing the books, making appointments with villagers for the tractor, and the like. In this way, they brought in more income for their families and also helped their community.[115]

Development organizations assisted in other ways, too.

There is a man, 22 years old, who has contacts with a relief agency [said an activist from a central West Bank village]. He goes to this agency with a list of families who need help, and receives money. The agency trusts him. If soldiers enter and vandalize a home, money comes in to repair it. This man's work – getting aid for needy Palestinians – covers about seven villages.[116]

Another source of support came from the popular committees which, as we have seen, fulfilled many functions. Popular committees and the factions which lay behind them had some funds, direct and indirect, that were a modest source of community aid and development. Monetary support was given to the families of arrested persons and to needy families.

When I was arrested [a youth from the Old City of Jerusalem recounted] my father got a lawyer for me. He went to a tourist agency [associated with a particular faction] and told them about this. They put my name on a list and paid all my lawyer's fees.[117]

Palestinians who had been injured or whose property had been damaged by Israeli raids could put in claims and receive some reimbursement.[118] Some claims, however, had to be made at PLO offices in Jordan, not easily reachable for most people.

In localities where popular committees were weak or non-existent, communities could fall back upon traditional practices to sustain them. 'Customary law is the backbone of Palestinian society,' observed Dr Zilberman.[119]

This is becoming stronger in the south [of the West Bank], not by popular committees, but by local people. More policemen remained in their posts in the south than in the north. Civil courts remain in function, more or less, with a lower profile. Sharia (Islamic) courts are still functioning. People cannot create their own courts, so customary law is the regulatory mechanism. Even the civil courts sometimes appoint someone as arbitrator [a way of solving disputes according to customary law]. There is not a wall between the civil courts and arbitration.

Mediation was used to deal with the problems arising from the killing of collaborators. In the north, a collaborator was killed by a fellow villager. Shots were fired and petrol bombs thrown into the home of the murderer's family, presumably by the family of the murdered person. It turned out that the perpetrators were other collaborators living in the village who were trying to pit the two families against each other. To solve the dispute, trusted persons from outside the village were asked to intervene. They talked to the families, and brought the dispute to an end. According to custom, if one person was hurt, the entire clan was injured. This was the danger posed to Palestinian society by Israel's use of collaborators as inciters. Since collaborators, being fellow villagers, also had clan affiliations, it was possible that a community might dissolve in internecine violence. One way of dealing with this was for the families of collaborators to denounce them, allowing their blood to be shed.[120]

How much progress had Palestinians made toward self-sufficiency and disengagement from Israel? 'Today we can produce all our own needs in meat, eggs and dairy products,' commented Dr Jad Isaac of Beit Sahour.[121] 'We are producing finished fabrics. The threads come from Israel but we do it ourselves: design, sewing, labelling, and selling Palestinian.' Palestinian entrepreneurship, he added, covered most of society's needs. According to Nora Kort, Tnuva products (especially powdered milk) were still being purchased, though not in large quantities, and mostly in the cities or in situations where the population had to buy them.[122]

Vegetables, sweets, juices and candies are all Palestinian produced. People still buy textile fabrics from Israel but we are also producing jackets, underwear and so on in our workshops. Medicine is coming more and more from Palestinian companies. People are going back to the old things: there are now dressmakers, and Palestinians are rolling their own cigarettes.

A village lady from Husan was asked what she still purchased from Israel: 'Flour, milk and clothes,' was her reply.[123]

In August 1989, a return trip to a central West Bank village first visited in October 1988 revealed that rudimentary progress had been made. The village had a new popular committee for teaching children, a new first-aid course taught regularly by visiting physicians, and a second clinic, built in the village mosque.[124] Its original clinic now possessed a wash-basin with running water, but no toilet. Medical supplies were the same as before. The local physician rated conditions between 'good' and 'not very good'. The clinic no longer had as much business, he said, not just because the new one siphoned off potential customers, but because people had less money with which to pay for treatment.

A worker used to work 24 days a month. Now he works 14 days. Earlier, if a boy got sick, the father took him to the doctor; now the father goes to the pharmacy and buys an antibiotic. If the father is sick, he just stays home until he is well.

Occasionally, signs of real progress could be seen. Beit Sahour, for example, had a clinic which started with one empty room. 'Now it is equipped with a diagnostic lab, endoscopy, ultra-sound and other facilities,' said Dr Jad Issac.[125] 'A person can see a doctor, or general practitioner, or specialist at a price of $2.50. It receives 1,500 patients a day from the Bethlehem area.'

However, a certain slippage had also occurred. 'People did not pay taxes for a while during the first year,' observed one West Bank Palestinian political analyst. 'They didn't go to the Civil Administration for a while. Today, most people are paying their taxes.'[126] A Palestinian journalist disputed this statement, but there could be little doubt that through their harsh measures, the Israelis were regaining at least a proportion of the revenue losses which they had earlier suffered. (The occupation was still running at a loss, however.) People did return to the offices of the Civil Administration, though not at the same rate as before.[127] This did not mean that civil disobedience had been crushed, as some Israeli officials were trying to pretend. The vast majority of Palestinian policemen who had resigned their posts did not return to work; nor did most other officials who had left. The Civil Administration, whose services had been cut back sharply, had become little more than a punitive arm of the Israeli security forces. Palestinians continued to demand more local products and found ingenious ways of developing their infrastructure. An Israeli supplier, for example, was given the business of providing equipment to Palestinian clinics on the condition that he import ambulances and use his contacts with the authorities to get permits so that Palestinians, who could not get permits on their own, could use them. (This man also received a healthy bribe.) The greatest progress towards economic independence was made in the northern West Bank, which was less dependent upon the Israeli economy and outside aid than the central and southern areas. In the Hebron region, villagers were drawn into the settlement labour force, and so relied more upon wage labour.

The conclusion? During the second year, the Intifada reinforced itself. 'Fifty per cent' civil disobedience was maintained, with the losses and gains balancing each other out. If Palestinians were unable to effect a total boycott of Israel, they had achieved a measure of self-reliance and had significantly reduced their dependence upon Israeli products.

One new problem to emerge was tension between popular committees and villagers in certain localities. In the Hebron area, some people complained that measures taken by the committees were unco-ordinated and disorganized.[128] 'After August [1988], popular committees became more factionalized,' said one prominent West Bank Palestinian.[129]

Why? We were getting close to the proclamation of statehood and each faction wanted to increase its influence. Also, the Israelis had banned them so committees could not operate openly. The factions had the structure for underground activity.

Was this good or bad for the Intifada? Some Palestinians believed that the increased participation of faction members in the popular committees helped the struggle because each group wanted to be seen as the most active in support of it, whether that involved organizing street demonstrations, building clinics, or whatever. Others expressed a contrary opinion. 'In some villages there is more than one clinic with poor facilities, each supported by a faction,' continued the West Banker. 'If the two [groups] pooled their resources, they would have one good clinic.'

There were three sources of tension between villagers and popular committees. In the first place, instructions issued in UNL leaflets tended to be very broad and general. 'The UNL,' commented Dr al-Jarbawi,

called upon Palestinan property owners to reduce rents by 25 per cent across the board. In implementing this, one popular committee would tell owners to cut rents if they were over 250 dinars, another would ask that rents be cut for shops that were leased, but not for home rented property, and so on. One village would see this command being interpreted in a less restrictive way in another village, so people complained.[130]

The second source of tension derived from the existence in a village of a committee for al-Fatah (or another faction of the national camp) and one for Hamas. Sometimes these would clash, as in the dispute over whether students should attend schools on strike days. Third, some people used these committees for their own advantage. 'A member of a committee might canvas a neighbourhood asking people to donate money,' continued Dr al-Jarbawi, 'even though the UNL in its leaflets asked people not to donate money to anyone.' People feared that if they did not give, something might happen. The phenomenon of people taking advantage could be seen practically everywhere, from the street vendors who sold goods all day long while shopkeepers had to close their doors at noon, to those who filed false claims for injuries or property damages. This was the result of attrition. The Intifada had been going on a long time. Popular committees and village elders, however, had ways of handling these problems. Some difficulties were settled by informal mediation, or the committees just worked them out. Committees were not only able to issue leaflets, but they also possessed loudspeakers, and these were used at night to explain to the people what had gone on. Committees sometimes issued apologies for things they had done.[131]

The real question was whether the UNL could handle the advent of new conditions, which included the increased killing of collaborators. In mid-August the UNL issued Leaflet 44, which tried to deal with some of these problems.[132] Individual factions, the leaflet said, could continue to write slogans on walls, but they were asked to use the name of the UNL as a signature rather than their own. This, it was hoped, would generate more unity among the groups. Before collaborators could be put to death, permission had to be sought from a high authority. By mid-August Palestinians making claims for injuries or damages were required to obtain the stamp of a local committee as certification. Such problems did not pose an immediate danger to the revolt.

However, if they were not brought under control, they could kill the Intifada in the long run. Following this leaflet, the number of reported murders of collaborators declined.

By the end of 1989, the Intifada had stabilized at its own level. Politically, its main achievement during the second year had been to produce indirect talks between Israel and the PLO, which had become established de facto. The idea of forming a Palestinian delegation to begin talks with Israel about elections would, if realized; be a continuation of these indirect talks, not something new. In early September 1989, Egyptian President Husni Mubarak, supported by the US administration, had begun pushing his so-called 'Ten Points', which aimed at moderating the Israeli election plan in order to arrive at a compromise so that a Palestinian delegation could be formed and talks started. On 6 October, the Israeli government rejected Mubarak's plan. US Secretary of State Baker then put forward a five-point plan, which had essentially the same objective – Palestinian–Israeli talks about elections. At first, the Israeli government strongly criticized Baker's plan, but after it was modified slightly to meet Israeli objections, Israel's Cabinet accepted it on 6 November, subject to conditions. (The PLO also accepted the Baker Plan.) By the year's end, no progress had been made towards Palestinian–Israeli talks. Three-way discussions between Israel, Egypt and the US were expected to begin after the start of the new year on the composition of an eventual Palestinian delegation. Negotiations, then, were not around the corner, and both the Palestinians and Israelis were left with a more violent Intifada.

After two years, at least 626 Palestinians had been killed by the Israelis.[133] Out of an estimated population of 1,701,435, this loss was proportionately much higher than the 57,000 battle deaths suffered by the US during the Vietnam War.[134] Forty-three Israelis had also died, a sharp increase from the five Israeli deaths reported during the Intifada's first ten months. Out of a 1988 population estimate of 4,400,000 million, Israeli death losses were one per 100,000 persons as against 37 per 100,000 for the Palestinians. In addition, between 35,000 and 40,000 Palestinians had been arrested, and, according to UNRWA, 37,439 had been wounded. In these proportions, Palestinian losses can only be regarded as staggering, all the more so as the victims were civilians fighting mostly with stones.

Despite this, and in some ways because of it, the Intifada continued without any significant diminution. Considering the myriad of problems – political, economic and communal – that people had had to face, this was a major accomplishment, to say the least. The question of whether the Intifada should continue was not a matter of discussion among Palestinians. Many said that this was the way it should always have been. Discussions focussed upon political subjects and tactics. The Palestinian people had found a way of maintaining and renewing their struggle until it had become a permanent part of their lives and consciousness. The key, as we have seen, was human input – the commitment of Palestinians to help each other and to make continual sacrifices. These qualities had enabled Palestinians to counter every Israeli move, and to shift the focus if need be. 'We discovered that there is no limit to our ability to adapt ourselves to new circumstances,' said one Gazan.[135] In the countryside, the Intifada was becoming a matter of honour (sharaf). Some people spoke of it like that. It was against honour to buy Israeli products. People knew that the Intifada was still in stage one, and that it might be years before a final resolution of the conflict. But they also knew that the outcome would be decided by what West Bankers and Gazans did, not by the manoeuvres of people outside. For the mass of society, the Intifada had come to be perceived as the vehicle of national liberation.

Epilogue

The outstanding question is whither the Intifada? What does the future hold for this protracted struggle, waged by an entire society, for self-determination and statehood? Three answers are possible. First, the revolt might be halted. This could occur in one of two ways: (1) by Israel's introduction of overwhelming conventional firepower; or (2) through a power struggle within the Palestinian leadership. Given the political stalemate between Labour and Likud, and the possibility of international intervention should the Israelis resort to overwhelming force, this first option is not likely. Israel has in any case lost its capacity to intimidate the Palestinians; so a military solution could be imposed only with the greatest of difficulty and at the cost of many more lives. A power struggle within the PLO would almost certainly put an end to the revolt (when factional rivalry is great, village and other local communities simply cannot function.) But this, too, is unlikely. No Palestinian leader or faction wants to incur the odium of having ended an uprising that the Israelis themselves could not suppress. The real danger is that unless the PLO leadership decides to alter or shift the focus of the revolt in order to yield greater results, disagreements within the national camp and demands by different groups for exemptions from Intifada 'rules' could cause it gradually to run down until it effectively came to an end of its own accord. This, however is a long-term danger, not an immediate one. In 1989 factional rivalry marked merely the beginnings of real trouble. Of course, Palestinians could simply give up and accept the Shamir plan, but this option exists only for analytical purposes. 'In the psychology of Palestinians,' observed Dr al-Jarbawi, 'there is the notion that we have never surrendered, never, in 70 years of struggle. All

Palestinians agree that the Intifada will continue. The only question is on what level.'[1]

The second possible answer to our question is that the Intifada will remain fixed in its present state, indefinitely. As we have observed, the Intifada has come to constitute a new way of living and thinking for all social classes, and it is difficult indeed to imagine a return to the *status quo ante*. The economic relationship between Israel and the occupied territories, for example, will probably never again be the same. A permanent change has seemingly occurred. In Gaza and the West Bank, the Israeli army cannot go into villages as it used to: soldiers must now prepare themselves before entering. The problem is that at this present level the Intifada can yield no further results. Its two main political achievements have been (1) the destruction of the idea of an alternate leadership to that of the PLO, and (2) the dialogue with the United States, which has led to indirect talks between Israel and the PLO. If meetings between Israeli and Palestinian representatives ever do take place, they will be a continuation of these indirect talks, not something new. So the Intifada has already delivered what it can. Political change can now come only from the brokers outside, the United States, the Soviet Union, and other powers. If the Intifada remains at this level, paralysed, incapable of producing further changes – something it can do for years and to which Israel has adjusted – can we not say that it is dead, even in the absence of a death certificate?

The third possibility is that the Intifada will re-ignite, and become more powerful. In the summer of 1989, some Palestinians were discussing its reactivation by moving to total civil disobedience, or complete, non-violent rejection of the occupation. No taxes would be paid, all identity cards would be turned in, shops would not be open at all. Yet if Palestinians were not prepared to envisage full disobedience earlier, how could they be expected to do so in 1989, when society was in a much weaker condition? And could this tactic really guarantee results? Would the US then be willing to put pressure upon Israel to bring it into talks with the Palestinians? If a mass civil disobedience campaign were launched, the Israelis might close the occupied territories to the press and foreign observers, cut off electricity and water to Palestinian communities, let people starve for six months, and then declare to the world that the Intifada had ended. Dr Abu-Amr has observed that as a tactic, civil disobedience might be most useful at the end of a Palestinian offensive, just before moving to statehood, when people could be sure that starving for six months would achieve something.[2]

If the Intifada is reactivated, it will probably happen as a result of renewed and intensified violence. Should this occur, the mass of society will have decided that the peace initiative has failed and that the Israeli government has no intention of dealing seriously with the problem. The radicals, in other words, will have won. The message, as expressed by one Palestinian, would essentially be:

For two years we have said 'We are using stones not guns, please listen. But you don't want to listen. What you are doing with Arafat is playing around. Arafat is the most moderate you can get. You must at least co-operate with Arafat, help him, put some pressure on Israel. Arafat has given the US all it wants. Pressure is the only language you understand. We need a stronger Intifada.

Preparations for a new round would require time. Logistical problems would need to be solved. The decision to move to greater violence could be made locally, but a political decision would also have to be taken at the highest level of the PLO. A new round of violence might be sparked by a catalytic event, or by a seemingly insignificant development. Many people are carrying out dramatic acts in the occupied territories every day; anything could happen to start it. The population would be asked to continue their strikes, but not to throw stones any more. A shift in focus would take place.

Such violence is likely to be much more effective than it has been in the past, because present conditions are more favourable to it. Owing to the Intifada, Palestinian society is mobilized, educated politically and well-organized. Greater violence would also be linked to feasible political goals: independence for the West Bankers and Gazans rather than the destruction of Israel. On the other hand, a move to armed struggle carries great risks. One of its aims would undoubtedly be to re-focus world attention upon the Palestinian problem and provoke external intervention in order to bring about negotiations between Israelis and

Palestinians. However, if the world community viewed this as a return to PLO 'terrorism', rather than the expression of despair and lost hopes, sympathy for the Palestinian cause would quickly evaporate. The US government might also lose interest in Arafat. Palestinians may reply that international support and the US dialogue have led nowhere, but they would also have to take into account the terrible Israeli retaliation that would certainly follow the use of lethal weapons by Palestinians. Many experts believe that an explosion of violence would give the Israelis the opportunity they have been seeking to terminate the Intifada. *Jerusalem Post* correspondent Yehuda Litani disagrees. Violence by Palestinians inside Israel, he declared, would not make it easier for the government to crush the Intifada because 'the Intifada will [then] be inside us'.

Increased violence could play into the hands of the Islamic organizations and lead to the discrediting of the PLO. Sensing the growing radical mood, the Islamic political groups might themselves begin these attacks. The population would, of course, expect them to deliver, that is, practically demonstrate what they have been saying all along: that struggle through holy war works. If they succeed in carrying out their attacks and in sustaining them, and if in the process they can revive the Islamic identity among Palestinians, they will have undermined the secular national alternative. 'The ultimate point,' noted Dr Abu-Amr,

is whether in the final analysis the Islamic movement can provide the Palestinian people with an alternative frame of reference, meaning, a Palestinian two years from now will say: 'We want an Islamic state in the entire area of Palestine.'[3]

The loss, then, may not just be a peace initiative, but an entire orientation. Armed struggle might also be launched by the national forces as a way of pre-empting the Islamic groups. PLO factions are more capable of it in any case, since they have the tradition, the organization and the links (with one another and with the PLO leadership outside). The future course of the Intifada is by no means certain, not even in the short run.

For all these reasons, one must resist the temptation to conclude that the Intifada has ushered in a new period in the history of the Israeli–Palestinian conflict. It marks a new stage of resistance, no more. Some conclusions, however, can be drawn. Whatever the future may hold, nothing can detract from the Palestinians' achievement in staging this revolt and sustaining it for over two years in the face of great pressure and terrible hardships. Their decision to pursue a *political* solution may also bring an end to a long-standing dispute among them. 'For the past 15 years,' observed one insider,

we Palestinians have been quarrelling over our political stance between moderates and radicals. Some believe that we should pursue a political solution and give into American demands, and others believe – and I am one of them – that whenever you lower your demands, the other side will try to screw you up. We have to put an end to the argument that peace will come if only the PLO or the Palestinians will be moderate and make concessions, that Palestinian extremism also causes them to miss unique opportunities. So we say to the world: 'Here we are. We have met all of your demands. What do you have to give us?' Arafat has said this. If we get nothing in return, we can go back to hijacking airplanes and we will have more unity in the long run. When Arafat is unable to get his way with America, he can come back and say to the Palestinian people 'We tried and it did not work, and we will start again.'

Palestinians are great survivors. They take a long-range view of things. Their nationalist aspirations are too deeply rooted to wither and die. Whether the Intifada slows down, speeds up, or comes to an end, they will continue to struggle in one form or another. Sooner or later, Israel will be forced to confront directly the Palestinians' quest for self-determination.

Postscript
1990: End of stage one

The talks expected to begin in January 1990 never did occur. In fact, negotiations between Palestinians and Israelis did not take place at all. Instead, matters took a dramatic turn. By the end of June 1990, the Intifada had suffered three major setbacks: (1) the coming to power on 11 June of a right-wing Israeli government that rejected all territorial concessions and committed itself to realizing a Greater Israel; (2) the formal rejection by Israel of the Baker plan, which brought an end to the peace progress; and (3) the US decision to terminate its dialogue with the PLO. These developments seemed to confirm the assessment of some analysts, made at the end of 1989, that the Intifada was dead politically. The Palestinian goal of a negotiated, compromise settlement based upon a two-state solution seemed further from realization than ever. Without outside help, without an external catalyst to provide new impetus, the Palestinian revolt could not produce any more political results. The time had come for Palestinians to re-evaluate their tactics and perhaps even reassess their strategy. Palestinians were disillusioned and discouraged. 'We are not at a dead end,' the UNL reassured them in a leaflet issued in early July. Anger ran deep at the US for having produced nothing after all the concessions that the Palestinians had made and after all the time spent in the dialogue. The radicals, of course, were the major winners, while the moderates had lost much standing in the Palestinian community. Yet the divisions within the movement were not being healed. Worse still, the new Israeli government had embarked upon a renewed settlement drive aimed especially at East Jerusalem, where it hoped to create a Jewish majority in several years. By early summer

1990, a dangerous situation had arisen in Gaza and the West Bank, one which seemed to lend itself to more, not less, violence.

The first development – the emergence of a new government led by Yitzhak Shamir and the Likud – was the consequence of US pressure, the Labour Party's decision to break up its coalition with the Likud, and the subsequent failure of Labour leader Shimon Peres to form a minority government that could lead Israel into negotiations with the Palestinians. As early as January 1990, Shamir had begun raising new obstacles to the Baker plan, approved in principle by the Israeli Cabinet in November 1989, and aimed at the convening in Cairo of a meeting between an Israeli and a Palestinian delegation. The real problem was the composition of the Palestinian delegation. Shamir wanted it to include only West Bankers and Gazans and not Diaspora Palestinians (who might raise claims to compensation for properties seized by Israel or even assert a right to return), and he opposed delegates from East Jerusalem, lest this jeopardize Israel's claim to the city as its sovereign and undivided capital. The PLO, without whose approval no Palestinian would have agreed to negotiate with Israel, insisted that Palestinians from outside the occupied territories be represented (Palestinians thought of themselves as one people) and that 'linkage' exist between the proposed talks and the Palestinian goal of statehood. Baker's plan was a compromise. West Bankers and Gazans would be the only participants in the Palestinian delegation, but Shamir was asked to agree to allow at least one participant to be a deportee from the occupied territories (thereby satisfying the PLO's insistence upon an 'outsider') and to permit the inclusion of at least one West Banker who possessed a second address in East Jerusalem, which the Palestinians had declared the capital of their state-to-be. Shamir, however, refused to talk with anyone who had an address in East Jerusalem or to have a deportee represented in the Palestinian delegation.

Having secured the support of the Labour Party as well as the PLO's acceptance of its plan, the US administration began verbally to pressure Shamir. Through Republican Senate leader Robert Dole it threatened cuts in aid. It described East Jerusalem as occupied territory, declaring that the settling of Jews there should be forbidden. And in early March, US Secretary of State Baker made a surprise announcement that the

Bush administration would be unwilling to support a Senate bill providing $400 million in loan guarantees to help Israel absorb new Soviet Jewish emigrants, who were flowing into the country in large numbers, unless the Shamir government gave assurances that these funds would not be used to create new settlements or enlarge existing ones in the occupied territories.

By winter 1990, Soviet Jewish immigration into Israel was becoming a new and important political factor, one loaded with explosive potential and complicating the dispute between Palestinians and Israelis. Many Israeli Jews regarded immigration as the only way of 'rescuing' their state from what was known as the Arab demographic threat. Sometime after the year 2000, experts calculated, the combined Arab population of Gaza, the West Bank and Israel would attain parity with the Jewish population. Jews soon would no longer be a majority in the land. Israelis welcomed the new immigration out of a basic belief that Israel was the rightful home of all the Jewish people, but many also did so because it promised deliverance from their worst fears. Having started in the autumn of 1989, this wave of immigration was the product of a new international environment marked by the end of the Cold War, the collapse of the Soviet economy, the growth of more liberal Soviet policies generally and the rise of democratic regimes in Central Europe, some of which began establishing ties with Israel, reversing the policies of their Communist predecessors which had supported the Palestinian cause. The Soviet Union's growing need for credits and loans from the West also led it to pursue a more liberal policy toward Jewish emigration. To induce Soviet Jews to immigrate to Israel rather than to the US, where the vast majority had gone in the past, the Bush administration restricted its previously liberal immigration policy, making it much more difficult for Soviet Jews to acquire US visas. Israel also played its part in attracting these emigrants, paying their air fares to Tel Aviv, and offering immediate cash subsidies to all Soviet Jews who chose to go to the country. Success exceeded expectations. In 1989, 12,000 Soviet Jews had arrived in Israel; in 1990, 4,700 entered in the month of January alone, with 5,500 being registered in February – the highest figures in years. More than 150,000 were expected by the end of 1990, and some officials were estimating that by around 1995–7 perhaps one million Soviet Jews would have entered Israel, increasing its

Jewish population by well over 20 per cent.

This new immigration was welcomed especially by those on the political right. For years, Labour and the parties on the left had argued that given the Arab demographic 'threat', Israel could preserve its Jewish identity and remain a democratic society only if it ceded territory, that is, gave up part or all of the West Bank and Gaza. Soviet Jewish immigration not only undermined the case for territorial compromise by delaying significantly the threat of the Arab demographic 'time bomb', but it also offered new possibilities for the strengthening of the political right. If the new immigrants could be settled in large numbers in the occupied territories, the balance of political forces inside Israel would shift decisively in favour of the retention of these areas. But would the new immigrants be settled there? In mid-January, Shamir suggested that the answer was 'yes'. A large immigration, he declared, required a correspondingly large Israel. (At this time, few Soviet Jews were being settled in Gaza and the West Bank.) This statement produced a loud cry of protest in the Arab world and in the West, where fears arose of a new explosion of violence, and possibly war. Soviet leader Gorbachev delayed the start of direct airline flights between Moscow and Tel Aviv, and warned that the flow of Jewish immigration might be restricted. Taking advantage of this situation to bring more pressure to bear upon Shamir, the US administration labelled renewed Jewish settlement in the occupied territories a threat to the peace process.

US pressure upon Shamir finally bore fruit, but only because the Labour Party decided to break ranks with the Prime Minister. Believing that the concessions required to resolve the conflict with the Palestinians would be more acceptable to the Israeli public if granted under a coalition between Labour and the Likud, Defence Minister Rabin had hoped to bring Shamir around to accepting the Baker plan. By early March, however, Rabin had become convinced that the Prime Minister was procrastinating, that he did not really intend to open negotiations with Palestinians. So Rabin gave Shimon Peres the signal to bring the government down. Labour insisted upon a positive response by Shamir to the Baker plan; then, not having received one, it announced that it would join the side of the parliamentary opposition in a vote of confidence scheduled for 15 March. In order to gain control of the interim government should his party fail to win parliamentary approval, Shamir fired Shimon Peres, Minister of Finance, and the rest of the Labour ministers had little choice but to hand in their resignations. On 16 March, Shamir failed by a 60 to 55 margin to win the vote of confidence, and, soon afterwards, Peres received the mandate from the President of Israel to begin working to form a new government.

Fully expecting Peres to head a government that would lead Israel into historic talks with the Palestinians, the US administration could scarcely disguise its pleasure at Shamir's downfall. The government's fall, one US official declared, had increased the chances for Israeli–Palestinian negotiations. The new government, he added, would pick up matters right where they had been left off. Some experts demurred, suggesting that the US government should be worried about this turn of events. While a majority of Knesset members reportedly favoured the Baker plan, the 120-member parliament was evenly split between Labour and Likud, and surveys of the Israeli public showed no consensus of opinion. Labour itself had not been able to find a way of regaining power for years. Having become convinced after talks with several small religious parties that he could indeed form a minority government, Peres worked to put together a coalition from a number of small parties to Labour's left and from the ultra-orthodox parties. But just as he was about to succeed, defections of key deputies from the religious side, spurred by statements from two Rabbis critical of Labour, killed Peres' chances of returning to power.

To the chagrin of the Bush administration, the President of Israel then turned to Prime Minister Shamir, and gave him the mandate to form a new government. In order to attract support from the right, Shamir's caretaker government increased tensions, especially on religious matters, creating an atmosphere in which violence became more likely. On 11 April, an armed group of ultra-nationalist Jewish settlers took control of St John's Hospice, a large building owned by the Greek Orthodox Church and located near the Church of the Holy Sephulchre in the Christian quarter of Jerusalem's Old City. These men – members of a group dedicated to expanding the Jewish presence in Palestinian areas – held a lease that had been purchased from the Armenian leaseholder of the property, who had disappeared a week before the takeover and was rumoured to be somewhere in the United

States. The Greek Orthodox Church denounced this 'occupation', declaring that as owner of the property its approval was needed for any change in tenancy. This action, which upset the delicate balance by which the different religious communities had lived together in relative harmony, sparked large-scale demonstrations, including one in which a Greek Orthodox priest removed a Star of David which had been placed upon the building. It also elicited widespread protests by US government leaders and others. On Friday 27 April, all Christian shrines in the Holy Land were closed. Shamir's caretaker government at first denied official involvement, but was found to be lying when it became known that Housing Minister David Levy had secretly provided $1.8 million (through a Panamanian front company) to help the settlers acquire the lease.

Escalating tensions came to a head on 20 May at Rishon Lezion, near Tel Aviv, when an armed Israeli civilian, dressed in army trousers and a black jacket, ordered Palestinian labourers to sit in a line, and then opened fire, killing seven persons and wounding eleven. Throughout Gaza and the West Bank, thousands of Palestinians took to the streets in protest. In 11 days of demonstrations, 17 Palestinians were killed. More than 700 were wounded in one two-day period alone. In all, 33 Palestinians died in May at the hands of Israeli soldiers and settlers. The protests also spread into Israel (demonstrations erupted among Arabs in Nazareth, Jaffa, Lod and elsewhere) and even to Jordan. A chorus of international criticism arose, directed against Shamir. Old fears of the Intifada's spread beyond Gaza and the West Bank were revived in the US, where President Bush expressed sorrow for the Palestinians who had been slain.

Amidst this tension, the Knesset on 11 June approved by a slender 62 to 57 margin the formation of a new right-wing government, led by Yitzhak Shamir. Compromising 30 ministers and deputy-ministers, this was composed of the Likud, two ultra-nationalist parties, three ultra-orthodox parties and a national religious party. Almost every member of it supported the idea of Greater Israel and was totally opposed to making territorial concessions. In its platform, the government rejected negotiations with the PLO, directly or indirectly, opposed the creation of a Palestinian state, and called for the development of settlements in the occupied territories. It also accepted the Shamir plan, with its emphasis upon Palestinian autonomy, but excluded the area of East Jerusalem from it. Some ministers were long-time supporters of Gush Emunim and the settlement movement, which regarded this development as a great victory.

The new Likud-dominated Cabinet reflected the triumph of the 'constraints ministers', those men who in July 1989 had imposed limits upon the Shamir plan: David Levy, who became Minister of Foreign Affairs; Yitzhak Modai, Minister of Finance; and Ariel Sharon, who, having resigned from the government in February 1990, was the real architect of this new government. Sharon received the key post of Minister of Housing in charge of immigration and of settlement construction, and subsequently obtained an appointment to the Ministerial Defence Committee, giving him a role in security matters and making him the most powerful man in the Cabinet, after the Prime Minister Shamir.

From the start, Shamir made it clear that the government's first priority was the reception of Soviet Jewish immigrants, of whom 10,500 had moved to Israel in April with an estimated one million more waiting to depart from the Soviet Union, and whose growing presence was already creating housing and other problems within the country. The Palestinian problem would have to be put on the back burner. To downplay its significance, Shamir declared that peace with the Palestinians would be conditional upon the willingness of the Arab states to make peace with Israel. The Cabinet's formal rejection on 28 June of the Baker plan, which was effectively already dead, was hardly a surprise. A government of this bent could hardly be expected to forge a compromise peace with the Palestinians.

The other blow to Palestinian hopes for a negotiated political settlement was the termination by the Bush administration on 20 June of its 18-month dialogue with the PLO. Inasmuch as this came only nine days after the installation of Israel's new government, and eight days before Shamir's formal rejection of the Baker plan, the question arises as to what, if any, connection existed between these two developments? The US–PLO dialogue was, as we have seen, a modest but necessary step towards bringing Israelis and Palestinians into talks. The Israeli government would not deal directly with the PLO, and Palestinians would accept only the PLO as their representative. Hence a

US–PLO dialogue made sense. Through the US, Israel could (and did) talk with the PLO. As a potential contribution to the peaceful resolution of this dispute, this dialogue served US interests. However, it was not an end in itself. Its continuation depended upon progress in bringing the two sides into negotiations. Baker's plan was based upon the premise of Israeli–Palestinian talks. This was its entire rationale and justification. The coming to power of the right-wing in Israel drove a stake through the heart of the American plan. The 'peace process' was dead, or dying. What reason was there for the dialogue to continue when it no longer had a purpose? This argument, however, only raises new questions. If it is true that the absence of progress toward negotiations would indeed have brought an end to the US–PLO dialogue at some point, this dialogue could none the less have been continued for many more months in the hope that the slender margin of parliamentary support for the new government would erode and a new situation more favourable to negotiations arise, or in order to give support to the moderate Palestinians, or for some other reason. The formation of the new Israeli government did not mean that the US dialogue with the PLO had to end when it did. So why did it? To understand this, we must consider other factors: the failed seaborne raid on 30 May against targets in Israel by guerrilla fighters from the Palestine Liberation Front, the domestic political situation in the US, and, above all, the serious deterioration of relations between the PLO and the US administration.

In entering this dialogue in December 1988, the PLO gave the US an exclusive role as arbiter of Middle East peace. This was justified by the argument that only through US influence could Israel be persuaded to make concessions. The PLO quietly set aside its own political programme (e.g., the idea of an international conference) and the focus was shifted away from earlier Palestinian concerns (e.g., securing protection for the inhabitants of the occupied territories). The US then began 'investing' in Arafat. It tried to convince Israel that the Intifada had created an opening for peace, that Palestinian compromises were real, that this was not the old PLO. And it pressed the PLO to make more concessions, to accept the Israeli election plan, for example, and to allow Palestinian brokers in the occupied territories to negotiate its proposed terms. But owing largely to the clout wielded by the Israeli lobby in a Democratic-controlled Congress, the Bush administration would not go beyond words and threats to take tough action and apply real pressure upon Israel. Here was the fatal flaw in the Palestinian strategy. America could not play a truly neutral negotiating role. Thus it could not 'produce'. The PLO also did itself no favours. It failed to launch an effective public relations campaign that would capitalize upon the more favourable image of Palestinians, especially in the US, and its leaders also failed to demonstrate the kind of political sophistication and skill that many Palestinians expected of them. By the winter of 1990, the PLO was having to conduct its dialogue with the US through the intermediary of Egypt, whose President had earlier inserted himself into the peace process by proposing his Ten Point plan. Following the collapse of Israel's unity government in March, Baker's plan was put on hold. By early May, informed observers were saying that the American plan was dead. Frustrated by these developments and having little to show for its co-operation, the PLO leaders became increasingly pessimistic and embittered.

In late May, two events further chilled relations between the US and the PLO. The first was the Arab League Summit meeting held in Iraq between 28 and 30 May, at which the PLO aligned itself with Iraqi President Saddam Hussein, who sought to marshall Arab support by criticizing US policies and attacking US support for Israel. The PLO–Iraq alignment angered and upset officials in Washington, who criticized the PLO for not co-operating with US policy in the region. The second development – the failed raid by the Palestine Liberation Front against Israeli targets (on 30 May) – undercut US efforts, underway since early March, to threaten and cajole Israel. This action shifted the focus away from problems between the US and Israel to the issue of PLO terrorism. The Bush administration, which had earlier told Congress that the PLO had complied with its commitment to renounce terrorism, became the object of abuse by its domestic critics.

These two events explain the surprising action of the US in vetoing on 31 May a UN Security Council resolution to send a fact-finding team to Gaza and the West Bank, a resolution which the Bush administration had five days earlier suggested it would support, and which had been worked out in consultation with the US government. Widely interpreted as signalling US displeasure over the Palestinian guerrilla raid, the US action was seen by some experts as a response to the Arab Summit meeting's tough anti-US rhetoric. In East Jerusalem, 40 prominent Palestinian moderates who had been on a hunger strike in support of UN involvement in the occupied territories immediately declared an end to their strike, cut off all contacts with US officials, and called for a boycott of US products.

Following the foiled guerrilla raid of 30 May, the US still was not eager to break off its dialogue with the PLO, despite the fact that Arafat, while disavowing any PLO connection with the raid, refused to condemn it. Talks with the PLO continued. The US wanted Arafat to (1) denounce the act publicly; (2) disassociate the PLO from any such activity; and (3) expel Muhammad Abbas, leader of the Palestine Liberation Front, from the PLO's Executive Committee. As was the case in December 1988, the US told Arafat what it expected him to say and do. Arafat was neither able nor willing to accept US demands. Sentiment in the occupied territories, to which he had to be sensitive, had changed radically. Many Palestinians, especially after the Rishon Lezion killings, regretted only that the raid had not succeeded. An apology to the US would have undermined Arafat's position among his people, and within the PLO. In any case, why should Arafat humble himself again when the US had provided nothing that could advance his negotiating strategy or be used to justify the concessions he had made? 'Good riddance' was a sentiment shared widely by Palestinians after 18 months of frustrating talks that had led nowhere. Still, the US continued the dialogue. Arafat, one official said, should be given a chance to produce a more 'forthright' explanation.

The critical factor in determining the timing of the decision to end the dialogue was internal US politics. From the start, Congress had been lukewarm, at best, in its support, of the US–PLO talks. In June, congressional elections were only six months away, a fact to which the Bush administration had to be particularly sensitive. At such times, no US politician wanted to make things hard for Israel. The Senate had earlier passed a resolution declaring Jerusalem to be the undivided capital of Israel, thus contradicting administration policy, which was not to recognize Israel's annexation but to leave the city's status open, to be defined through negotiations. In June, the US political atmosphere was beginning to heat up. Two influential Democratic party candidates made strong, pro-Israeli speeches. In the third week, it was learned that the Congress was preparing legislation that would compel the administration to break the dialogue with the PLO. This forced the President's hand. On 20 June, he ended the dialogue, and with it America's role as the arbiter of the Middle East peace process.

These developments were a great setback to Palestinian hopes for achieving a state of their own in Gaza and the West Bank, with East Jerusalem as its capital. Palestinians would now have to rely even more upon the Intifada as a source of political pressure upon Israel. But could the revolt be strengthened? A hardening of attitudes had most certainly occurred inside the occupied territories. The deep-seated cause of this was the behaviour of Israeli soldiers, the thousands of acts of destruction, violence and humiliation that had taken place during the Intifada. The establishment of the right-wing government in Israel and the failed US peace initiative brought Palestinian feelings of resentment and frustration out into the open. 'We are ready for a radical change of pace,' said one Palestinian. 'The tactic of stones, strikes, and civil disobedience have not worked to bring Israel to the conference table.'

By June 1990, a long-standing debate within the movement had come to an end. The organizational leadership had been vindicated and the influence of the brokers and other moderates weakened. Sari Nuseibeh, Faisal Husseini, Hanna Siniora and others like them had believed in using the Intifada as a vehicle to reach out to the Israeli public in order to demonstrate that the Palestinians posed no threat to Israel's existence and wanted only a state of their own. These men had placed all their bets upon the US. By June, this approach had been discredited. Many Gazans and West Bankers perceived the US not only as unwilling to help the Palestinians but also as their enemy. Within Israel, the political left was being weakened, its argument for territorial compromise undermined by Soviet Jewish immigration. The Labour Party itself was in deep trouble, owing to a split between hard-line supporters of Rabin and the doves who followed Peres. The political right, in coalition with religious elements, was in the ascendant, gaining influence in the electronic and print media, passing legislation favourable to its interests in the Knesset, and so on.

Radicalism was growing on both sides. In the occupied territories, an effort to develop and intensify the Intifada began. Yet the strategic goal of a negotiated political settlement was still supported by the vast majority of the people. In its leaflets, the UNL called for the formation of new popular committees and an intensification of the struggle generally. The reconstituted Islamic Jihad began playing a more active role, calling, in one of its leaflets, for Palestinians to stab Soviet Jews with knives. Some stabbings did occur, and pipe bomb explosions also began, thus raising slightly the level of violence against Israelis.

It would not be easy for the Intifada to re-ignite. Despite the defeat of the moderates, divisions were deep and problems were growing. During the first six months of 1990, confrontational activities in the streets, as measured by Palestinian casualties, fell off significantly. As we have seen, these were important in order to keep the social base going, that is, to increase the number of recruits and maintain a mobilized population. Individuals and groups also continued to take advantage of the situation by exempting themselves from Intifada rules. Sidewalk peddlers selling fruits, vegetables and household wares long after shop-keepers, in conformity with UNL instructions, had closed their doors became an omnipresent phenomenon. Some bakers (bakeries were permitted to remain open during strike days) turned their shops into small general stores, also competing with the local merchants. In March, shopkeepers received UNL permission to remain open five hours a day rather than three hours as previously. The greater degree of factional unity achieved in summer 1989 also broke down. In March, fights erupted between supporters of different factions, and some cars and houses were torched. (The UNL condemned this 'sedition and sabotage' against the Intifada.) More collaborators were killed, and the UNL had to reissue its instruction that death sentences be carried out only with an order from a higher authority. Meanwhile, the PFLP continued its attacks against other groups. It protested against the decision to extend shopkeepers' work hours, calling for the lengthening of strikes and the intensification of the revolt. The Intifada, it seemed, was falling to an even lower level of activity and effectiveness.

There were two basic reasons for this. The first was internal, really a complex of factors, among them attrition, the loss by some middle- and upper-class Palestinians of a sense of priorities (Palestinians could not attend schools *and* have the Intifada), and, most fundamentally, the decision made after the November 1988 Declaration of Independence to follow a negotiating strategy before a strong popular institutional base had been created on the ground. This decision hurt the Intifada by dividing Palestinians between those who wanted to emphasize civil disobedience tactics and build popular committees, and those who wanted to direct all efforts toward negotiations and the finding of a political solution.

The other reason for the deceleration of the Intifada was external. As we have seen, the Israeli policy of confronting Palestinians and using force against them had been a very important factor in the continuation of the revolt through its second year. Had the Israelis backed off, the incidence of violent confrontations would have declined markedly because there would have been fewer soldiers to throw stones at, fewer funerals of martyred Palestinians to be taken advantage of, and so on. In order to avoid providing a catalyst for the re-ignition of the Intifada, and as part of a broader strategy aimed at reducing external pressure upon Israel at a time when it desperately needed international loans and support to gather in the Soviet Jews, Moshe Arens, the new Likud Defence Minister, adopted a policy designed to reduce Palestinian casualties. In certain areas, Israeli troops were reduced in numbers; from others, they were withdrawn entirely. Open fire rules were restricted. Soldiers were ordered to avoid head-to-head confrontations with Palestinians. At some demonstrations, Israeli troops sat back and watched, without intervening. A continuation of measures inaugurated in January 1990 by Rabin, this tactic proved highly effective. In June, eight Palestinians were killed by Israelis – the lowest total since the Intifada began – and in July, this fell to only three. Confrontations thus subsided, and there were fewer demonstrations. Of course the moment that Israeli troops withdrew from a refugee camp or a village Palestinian flags could be seen flying from rooftops, and popular armies paraded down the main streets. For the Israelis, however, this was preferable to the risk of a conflagration that might lead to a deceleration of Jewish immigration or the cutting of outside funds to finance it. Besides, by backing off, the Israelis hoped that Palestinians would turn against one another, that divisions among them would increase.

In early summer, a development occurred which had the prospect of strengthening the Intifada. This was the decision by the new government to accelerate Jewish settlement activity in Gaza and the West Bank, and to implant a Jewish majority in predominantly Arab East Jerusalem as quickly as possible. First, however, the Israelis had to allay great-power fears about the Soviet Jews. Towards the end of June, Ariel Sharon made a surprising announcement. Soviet Jewish immigrants, he said, would be encouraged to settle inside Israel rather than in the West Bank and Gaza. The political situation was delicate. Soviet leader Gorbachev had warned Israel more than once against settling Soviet Jews in the occupied territories. And Israel, as we have seen, was dependent upon outside aid for immigrant absorption. By late June, the Israeli government had opted for reconciliation rather than confrontation with the US. Nothing would be done to jeopardize the reception and absorption of Soviet Jews.

None the less, a decision was made to accelerate Jewish settlement activity. This was to be done not by building new settlements but by expanding those already in existence. An unwritten agreement between the Likud and its coalition partners called for the construction of 5,000 housing units a year in existing Jewish settlements in the West Bank and Gaza. In addition, 18,000 new dwelling units would be constructed and 60,000 Jews settled in East Jerusalem. The time frame for the establishment of a Jewish majority there would thus be reduced to several years. The Hebrew-language daily *Haaretz*, basing itself upon the calculations of 17 Jewish settlement councils, concluded that if only half the number of new building units planned for the West Bank and Gaza were constructed, the Jewish population there would increase by at least 25,000 in two years, bringing the total number of settlers to about 120,000.

The new arrivals in the occupied territories would include not only the ideologically motivated and those propelled by 'quality of life' considerations, but also a new category of Jew: the ultra-orthodox. As for the Soviet Jewish immigrants, if they would not be overtly directed to the West Bank and Gaza, they would be a major factor in the government's plan for East Jerusalem, where thousands of them had already been settled.

If implemented, the new Jewish settlement programme might be the spark to re-ignite the Intifada. As we have seen, Jewish encroachment through land acquisitions and settlements had been the cause of the revolt in the first place. Palestinians would certainly resist, but the form and intensity of their reaction could not be predicted. Would the Palestinian movement turn to mass civil disobedience, or to violence? And if the latter, would the violence be localized, sporadic, or widespread?

The possibility of Israeli success in implementing its settlement drive must also be considered. If the settler population were to increase dramatically, partition would become a less likely solution to the conflict. Palestinians might be forced by circumstances to abandon their strategy of a 'two-state' solution and accommodate themselves to the reality of an annexed West Bank and Gaza. In this case, the focus of Palestinian national ambitions would probably shift to a demand for an equality of rights and privileges within a Greater Israel. Israeli Jews could be expected to resist this with all their might. The struggle might turn into a civil conflict. Should such a situation develop, the idea of 'transfer,' a euphemism for the forcible deportation of Palestinians from the West Bank and Gaza, might be seen as a feasible option by Israeli Jews. This 'solution' to the Palestinian 'problem' already has advocates in the new Israeli government and enjoys considerable support among Israel's Jewish population. In a poll conducted between March and April 1990, 59 per cent of those questioned supported the idea of 'transfer'. To implement this, the Israeli government would have to send its army into Jordan, bring down King Hussein, occupy the country, and establish a Palestinian state. 'Transfer' would then become a population shift, something that could take place over a decade or two, with a gradual movement of people. However, since the US and the major world powers would likely be opposed to this, 'transfer' is a remote possibility only. For Palestinians, there is another kind of transfer that is not so remote: the deportation of an élite or layer of men. Each deportee has a family of at least five or six persons. Deportation is tangible in its political weight because it deprives a population of its key men, of its leadership, and does not have to be large-scale to be effective. As a tactic, deportation has not been used widely during the Intifada, which rendered it less effective in any case. It remains, however, more than a theoretical possibility.

If 'transfer' is the Palestinian fear, many Israeli Jews live in fear that Palestinian national ambitions will someday be realized within the borders of their state. Soviet Jewish immigration has certainly postponed by decades the day of demographic 'reckoning', but it has not changed the basic calculus. The birth-rate among Palestinians is much higher than that of Israel's Jewish population, and Israel cannot rely indefinitely upon immigration for its 'rescue'. Should the West Bank and Gaza be made permanently part of Israel, thus dooming the idea of a two-state solution, and should the transfer option not be realized, the time will come when Palestinians outnumber Jews in a Greater Israel. One of the most controversial proposals ever made by Palestinians was the creation of a secular democratic state encompassing all of 'Palestine'. Advanced by the PLO in the 1960s, this idea was interpreted in different ways by Palestinians, who never reached a consensus as to its meaning. Israel worked hard to discredit the motives of its proponents, equating a non-sectarian state with genocide against Israeli Jews. Some Palestinians, on the other hand, argued that it was the most humane solution possible to the conflict. The idea remained an abstract one for Palestinians since prospects for its realization were nil. It is not inconceivable that, at some future point, conditions will arise making possible the reintroduction and discussion of this old idea, or something similar to it. This, of course, would be an anathema to most Israeli Jews, since it would imply an end to the exclusive Jewish state. Many Gazans and West Bankers, however, believe that even with increased Soviet Jewish immigration, Israel still has to make a choice. 'Palestinians today will accept the idea of two states,' declared one West Bank intellectual. 'Will the Zionist dream be fulfilled in 80 per cent of Palestine and not all of it, or will the Zionists end up in the long run doing what some Palestinians have been wanting to do for a long time – have a democratic state in the whole of "Palestine?"'

Chronology of the Intifada

1987

8 December	Death of four Gazans as a result of collision with Israeli vehicle; demonstrations that follow mark beginning of Uprising.

1988

7 January	Public call by Hanna Siniora for Palestinian boycott of Israeli cigarettes and soft drinks.
8 January	Issuance of first (unnumbered) leaflet by UNL.
14 January	Fourteen Demands (Points) issued by Palestinian public figures.
19 January	Policy of 'force, power and blows' announced by Defence Minister Rabin.
3 February	Communiqué by Islamic Jihad defines its objectives and role.
24 February	Muhammad Ayyed killed by fellow villagers in Qabatya.
6 March	Large-scale resignations by Palestinians from positions in the Civil Administration begin.
7 June	Conciliatory statement by PLO's Bassam Abu Sharif advocates PLO–Israeli talks.
31 July	Draft of Palestinian Declaration of Independence discovered by Israelis.
31 July	King Hussein announces severance of all administrative and legal ties between Jordan and West Bank.
August	Covenant of Hamas is issued.
15 November	PNC proclaims independent Palestinian state.
13 December	At UN session in Geneva Arafat recognizes Israel, renounces terrorism and accepts UN

Resolutions 242 and 338.

15 December	US administration announces opening of dialogue with PLO.
22 December	New National Unity Government is formally approved by Israel's Knesset.

1989

January	Talks between local Palestinians and Israelis begin.
6 April	Prime Minister Shamir presents his plan to US Secretary of State Baker.
7 April	President Bush announces US support for Shamir plan.
14 May	Israeli Cabinet approves Shamir's election plan.
May	Mass arrest of Hamas activists.
5 July	Likud Central Committee places limits on Shamir plan.
6 July	14 people die when a Palestinian runs an Israeli bus into a ravine.
23 July	Israeli Cabinet reaffirms support for Shamir plan.
September	Egyptian President Husni Mubarak proposes a Ten Point plan to bring Palestinians and Israelis into talks.

1990

16 March	Dissolution of Unity Government by Knesset vote of no confidence in Shamir, who refused US terms for starting peace talks.
11 April	Failure of Peres to form a new government.
11 June	Knesset approves new right-wing government led by Shamir.
20 June	US ends dialogue with PLO.
28 June	Shamir formally rejects US proposals for peace talks with Palestinians.

Notes

CHAPTER 1

1. This figure is that of Meron Benvenisti, Director of the West Bank Data Base Project and Israel's 'unofficial' statistician of the West Bank and Gaza. All figures on population size are estimates since no census of the Palestinian population has been taken since 1967. Benvenisti's estimates, routinely cited by journalists, scholars and others, are the most carefully researched of all those that have been provided to date. On this, see Meron Benvenisti and Shlomo Khayat, *The West Bank and Gaza Atlas* (Jerusalem: *West Bank Data Base Project*, 1988), pp. 25–31, 112. Population data used in this and subsequent paragraphs come from this *Atlas*. The other source of information used here is Kamal Abdulfattah, 'The Geographical Distribution of the Palestinians on Both Sides of the 1949 Armistice Line', in Alexander Scholch, ed., *Palestinians Over the Green Line. Studies on the Relations Between Palestinians on Both Sides of the 1949 Armistice Line Since 1967* (London: Ithaca Press, 1983), pp. 102–04.
2. Information on the Gaza Strip and the refugee population generally derives from Abdulfattah, *op. cit.*, p. 104; Benvenisti and Khayat, *op. cit.*, pp. 109, 112; interview with Rolf van Uye, UNRWA official, East Jerusalem, 7 October 1988.
3. Information in this paragraph derives from the following sources: Benvenisti and Khayat, *op. cit.*, pp. 51–2; Meron Benvenisti, *The West Bank Handbook* (Jerusalem: The Jerusalem Post, 1986), pp. 37, 51–2, 201–02; Meron Benvenisti, *1986 Report. Demographic, Economic, Legal, Social and Political Developments in the West Bank* (Jerusalem: West Bank Data Base Project, 1986), p. 38.
4. For this and what follows, see Benvenisti, *1986 Report.*, pp. 15, 39; Benvenisti, *West Bank Handbook*, p. 24.
5. Information contained in this paragraph comes from Benvenisti and Khayat, *West Bank and Gaza Atlas*, p. 109; Meron Benvenisti, *1987 Report: Demographic, Economic, Legal, Social, and Political Developments in the West Bank* (Jerusalem: West Bank Data Base

Project), p. 28; Benvenisti, *1986 Report*, p. 16; Emile Nakhleh, *The West Bank and Gaza. Toward the Making of a Palestinian State* (Washington, D.C.: American Enterprise Institute, 1979), pp. 29–35.

6. Benvenisti, *1986 Report*, p. 42; Benvenisti, *West Bank Handbook*, p. 201.
7. For this, see Benvenisti, *West Bank Handbook*, p. 210. I have also benefited from information on this Council provided by Dr Ali al-Jarbawi in an interview in Ramallah, 13 December 1988.
8. See Sara Roy, *The Gaza Strip: A Demographic, Economic, Social, and Legal Survey* (Jerusalem: West Bank Data Base Project, 1986), p. 98, Benvenisti, *The West Bank Handbook*, p. 209.
9. Benvenisti, *1986 Report*, p. 16.
10. *Ibid.*, p. 16.
11. For this and what follows, Benvenisti and Khayat, *West Bank and Gaza Atlas*, p. 109; Benvenisti, *West Bank Handbook*, p. 68.
12. For this and what follows, Benvenisti, *West Bank Handbook*, p. 162; Benvenisti and Khayat, *West Bank and Gaza Atlas*, pp. 39, 109, interview with Rolf van Uye, 7 October 1988; Nakhleh, *op. cit.*, pp. 37–9.
13. For this and what follows, Nakhleh, *op. cit.*, pp. 26, 29, 35–7; Benvenisti, *West Bank Handbook*, p. 25.
14. Benvenisti, *West Bank Handbook*, p. 162.
15. Interview in East Jerusalem, 5 November 1988.
16. Paul Cossali, 'Gaza's Union Elections', *Middle East International* 308 (1987), p. 14.
17. Nakhleh, *op. cit.*, p. 31.
18. Ms Zuhayra Kamal, interview in East Jerusalem, 5 October 1988.
19. Information in this paragraph is drawn from Emile Sahliyeh, *In Search of Leadership: West Bank Politics Since 1967* (Washington, D.C.: The Brookings Institution, 1988), chapter 4.
20. Interview in East Jerusalem, 21 October 1988.
21. Interview in Ramallah, 6 July 1989.
22. Interview in East Jerusalem, 5 November 1988.
23. This information was provided by a women's committee member whose anonymity I have respected.
24. Roy, *op. cit.*, p. 84.
25. Interview in East Jerusalem, 5 November 1988.
26. 'Ali', interviews in Jenin, West Bank, 1 and 20 October 1988.
27. André Rosenthal, interview in West Jerusalem, 16 October 1988.
28. 'Aziz', former political prisoner, interview in East Jerusalem, 10 November 1988.
29. 'Ahmad', former political prisoner, interview in his central West Bank village, 13 October 1988.
30. Sahliyeh, *op. cit.*, p. 121.
31. Dr Ali al-Jarbawi, interview in Ramallah, 13 December 1988.
32. Ibid.
33. Sahliyeh, *op. cit.*, pp. 103–04.

34. Interview in East Jerusalem, 10 November 1988.
35. Information was provided by a member of this Council, who asked not to be quoted.
36. Ann Mosley Lesch, *Political Perceptions of the Palestinians on the West Bank and the Gaza Strip* (Washington, D.C.: The Middle East Institute, 1980), p. 87.
37. See Sahliyeh, *op. cit.,* chapter 4.
38. Interview in Ramallah, 13 December 1988.
39. For this and what follows, see Lesch, *op. cit.,* pp. 55, 86; Sahliyeh, *op. cit.,* pp. 56–7.
40. Ziad Abu-Amr and Ali al-Jarbawi, 'The Struggle for West Bank Leadership', *Middle East International* 304 (1987), pp. 16–18.
41. Sahliyeh, *op. cit.,* pp. 50–1.
42. *Haaretz,* 8 February 1988, p. 9 in *FBIS,* 10 February 1988, p. 38. For what follows, see Alain Gresh, *The PLO: The Struggle Within* (London: Zed Books, 1988), p. 244.
43. Roy, *op. cit.,* p. 10.
44. Material on the youth movement in this and subsequent paragraphs comes from Sahliyeh, *op. cit.,* chapter 6, especially pp. 121–6. ·
45. My discussion of the Islamic movement, unless otherwise indicated, comes from Ali al-Jarbawi, *The Intifada and the Political Leadership in the West Bank and Gaza* [in Arabic] (Beirut: Dar al-Taliya Press, 1989), pp. 43 ff.; and Sahliyeh, *op. cit.,* chapter 7.
46. Interview in Ramallah, 17 August 1989.
47. For a description of the conditions experienced by Palestinians working in Israel, see David Grossman, *The Yellow Wind* (New York: Farrar, Straus and Giroux, 1988), chapter 15.
48. Interview in Ramallah, 25 July 1989.
49. Interview in East Jerusalem, 9 September 1988. Evidence suggests that Israeli authorities did help finance the Islamic movement; see David K. Shipler, *Arab and Jew: Wounded Spirits in a Promised Land* (New York: Penguin Books, 1987), p. 177.
50. Interview in East Jerusalem, 5 November 1988.
51. On this, and the subsequent rupture in the PLO, see Gresh, *op. cit.,* pp. 225 ff.
52. For developments within Palestinian leadership after 1982, see Sahliyeh, *op. cit.,* chapter eight.
53. Benvenisti, *1987 Report,* p. 41.

CHAPTER 2

1. Ziad Abu-Amr, *The Intifada: Causes and Factors of Continuity* (Jerusalem: Palestinian Academic Society for the Study of International Affairs, 1989), p. 9.
2. Interview with 'Yunis' in the Old City of Jerusalem, 17 August 1989.
3. David Kahan, *Agriculture and Water Resources in the West Bank and*

Gaza, 1967–1987 (Jerusalem: West Bank Data Base Project, 1987), pp. 67–70.
4. *Ibid.*, p. 16.
5. *Ibid.*, p. 13.
6. *Ibid.* The highest rate of growth in Gaza's economy occurred between 1968–73: Sara Roy, *The Gaza Strip: A Demographic, Economic, Social, and Legal Survey* (Jerusalem: West Bank Data Base Project, 1986), p. 24.
7. Kahan, *op. cit.,* p. 26.
8. Interview in West Jerusalem, 14 September 1988.
9. Interview in Ramallah, 1 December 1988.
10. Interview in Beit Sahour, 10 August 1989.
11. Kahan, *op. cit.,* p. 71.
12. *Ibid.*, p. 42.
13. *Ibid.*, p. 16.
14. What follows is based upon Roy, *op. cit.*, pp. 33, 35–7.
15. Interview in West Jerusalem, 14 September 1988.
16. *Davar*, 13 March 1988, p. 7 in *FBIS*, 16 March 1988, p. 49.
17. Meron Benvenisti, *The West Bank Handbook* (Jerusalem: The Jerusalem Post, 1986), p. 85.
18. Meron Benvenisti, *1986 Report: Demographic, Economic, Legal, Social and Political Developments in the West Bank* (Jerusalem: West Bank Data Base Project, 1986), p. 32.
19. Interview in East Jerusalem, 23 November 1988.
20. Interviews in East Jerusalem, 6 September and 5 November 1988.
21. Meron Benvenisti and Shlomo Khayat, *The West Bank and Gaza Atlas* (Jerusalem: West Bank Data Base Project, 1988), pp. 62–3.
22. *Ibid.*, pp. 60–1.
23. For this and what follows, see *ibid.*, pp. 32–3.
24. *Ibid.*, pp. 63–4.
25. *Ibid.*, pp. 34–5.
26. *Ibid.*, p. 32.
27. Interview in East Jerusalem, 5 November 1988.
28. Benvenisti, *West Bank Handbook*, p. 89.
29. *Ibid.*, p. 122.
30. International Committee of the Red Cross, *The Geneva Conventions of August 12 1949* (Geneva), p. 172, art. 49; p. 174, art. 53.
31. For this and what follows, see Benvenisti, *West Bank Handbook*, pp. 122–3.
32. Interview in West Jerusalem, 8 September 1988.
33. For this and what follows, see Benvenisti, *West Bank Handbook*, pp. 77, 88.
34. See *ibid.*, p. 19.
35. For what follows, see *ibid.*, pp. 85–6.
36. *Ibid.*, p. 85; Benvenisti and Khayat, *West Bank and Gaza Atlas*, p. 62.
37. Benvenisti, *West Bank Handbook*, p. 87. I am grateful to Mr André Rosenthal and Mr Moshe Negbi for explaining this practice to me.

38. I am indebted to Moshe Negbi for this information.
39. For these two facts, see Roy, *op. cit.*, p. 5; Benvenisti, *West Bank Handbook*, p. 85.
40. Interview, 16 October 1988. See also Benvenisti, *West Bank Handbook*, p. 34.
41. *Ibid.*, p. 37.
42. Benvenisti and Khayat, *West Bank and Gaza Atlas*, p. 64.
43. *Ibid.*, p. 63.
44. Interview in Ramallah, 17 August 1989.
45. Benvenisti, *1986 Report*, p. 30.
46. I am referring to land registered under the 'Settlement of Disputes Over Land and Water Law'. Raja Shehadeh, *Occupier's Law. Israel and the West Bank* (Washington, D.C.: Institute for Palestine Studies, 1985), pp. 22–6. Until the establishment of Israeli control, landownership could be attested to in several ways, including the payment of taxes.
47. Benvenisti, *1986 Report*, pp. 25–7.
48. Benvenisti and Khayat, *West Bank and Gaza Atlas*, p. 61.
49. *Ibid.*, pp. 61–2.
50. For this and the following, see *ibid.*, p. 60.
51. *Ibid.*, p. 32.
52. *Ibid.*, p. 33.
53. *Ibid.*, pp. 58–9.
54. Benvenisti, *1986 Report*, p. 60; Meron Benvenisti, *1987 Report: Demographic, Economic, Legal, Social and Political Developments in the West Bank* (Jerusalem: West Bank Data Base Project, 1987), p. 41.
55. Benvenisti and Khayat, *West Bank and Gaza Atlas*, pp. 35–6.
56. Kahan, *Agriculture and Water Resources*, p. 112.
57. Benvenisti, *1986 Report*, p. 36.
58. Interview in the West Bank, 8 October 1988.
59. Kahan, *op. cit.*, p. 110.
60. Benvenisti, *1986 Report*, pp. 21–4.
61. Interview in Ramallah, 1 December 1988.
62. This information was provided by André Rosenthal. For what follows, see Benvenisti, *West Bank Handbook*, p. 89. The official settlement plan of the World Zionist Organization stated that there was not to be a shadow of a doubt about Israel's intention to remain in 'Judaea' and 'Samaria'.: Benvenisti and Khayat, *West Bank and Gaza Atlas*, p. 64.
63. Benvenisti, *1986 Report*, p. 6.
64. Kahan, *op. cit.*, p. 85.
65. *Ibid.*, p. 32.
66. *Ibid.*, pp. 47, 69.
67. *Ibid.*, p. 26.
68. *Ibid.*, p. 36.
69. Benvenisti, *1986 Report*, p. 7.
70. Interview in East Jerusalem, 6 September 1988.

71. Benvenisti, *1986 Report*, p. 6.
72. *Ibid.*, p. 9.
73. For this and what follows, see *ibid.*, p. 8.
74. Interview in East Jerusalem, 23 November 1988.
75. *Ash Shira* magazine was closed in 1981; the press offices of *al-Quds* Arabic daily and *al-Manar* were closed in 1982; charges of abuse of censorship rules were brought against many papers and magazines. 'Facts about the Palestinian Press under Occupation (Closures, Arrests, Administrative Detention, Town Arrest and Other Measures)'; document provided by Ibrahim Karaeen. For Israel's restrictive policies, see also Emile Sahliyeh, *In Search of Leadership: West Bank Politics Since 1967* (Washington, D.C.: The Brookings Institution, 1988), pp. 83–6.
76. According to Meron Benvenisti, checklists were a factor in causing the Intifada. Interview of 23 October 1988.
77. Interview of 5 November 1988. I am grateful to Dr Bishara for explaining this to me.
78. Benvenisti, *1986 Report*, pp. 43, 78.
79. *Ibid.*, p. 43.
80. For this and what follows, see *ibid.*, pp. 17, 43–5, 78.
81. What follows derives from *ibid.*, p. 44; Benvenisti, *West Bank Handbook*, p. 86; Benvenisti, *1987 Report: Demographic, Economic, Legal, Social and Political Developments in the West Bank* (Jerusalem: West Bank Data Base Project, 1987), p. 40; and from data collected (mostly from al-Haq) and provided by Dr Hanan Ashrawi in an interview in Ramallah on 12 October 1988.
82. Interview in West Jerusalem, 16 October 1988.
83. A summary of the Landau Commission's findings was published in the *Jerusalem Post*, 1 November 1987, p. 4.
84. Benvenisti, *1986 Report*, p. 39.
85. Benvenisti, *1987 Report*, pp. 34–5.
86. Interview with 'Samir' in the Old City of Jerusalem, September 1988.
87. Interview in Ramallah, 12 October 1988.
88. Benvenisti, *1987 Report*, p. 59.
89. Benvenisti, *1986 Report*, p. 26.
90. *Ibid.*, p. 64; Benvenisti, *1987 Report*, p. 41.

CHAPTER 3

1. *Jerusalem Post*, 12 February 1988, p. 20.
2. Makram Khuri Makhul, 'This Is Not a Revolt – This Is a War', reprinted from *HaIr*, 18 December 1987, in *Journal of Palestine Studies* 17, no. 3 (1988), p. 93.
3. *Ibid.*, p. 94.
4. For this and what follows, see entries from Hebrew-language

newspapers in *FBIS*, 10 December, 1987, pp. 9–10.
5. *Jerusalem Post*, 15 February 1988, p. 5.
6. *Jerusalem Post*, 1 January 1988, p. 6.
7. *Jerusalem Post*, 23 December 1988, pp. 1–3.
8. Makhul, *art. cit.*, p. 93.
9. *Ibid.*, p. 95.
10. *Jerusalem Post*, 1 February 1988, p. 1.
11. *Jerusalem Post*, 20 January 1988, p. 2.
12. Makhul, *art. cit.*, p. 98.
13. Interview in East Jerusalem, 9 September 1988.
14. Interview in East Jerusalem, 6 September 1988.
15. Daoud Kuttab, 'The Uprising', *Middle East International* 320 (1988), p. 9.
16. *Jerusalem Post*, 8 February 1988, p. 4.
17. Makhul, *art. cit.*, p. 96.
18. Interview in East Jerusalem, 6 September 1988.
19. *Davar*, 28 January 1988, p. 1 in *FBIS*, 29 January 1988, p. 41.
20. Interview in East Jerusalem, 5 November 1988.
21. Makhul, *art. cit.*, p. 95.
22. Daoud Kuttab, 'A Profile of the Stone Throwers', *Journal of Palestine Studies* 17, no. 3 (1988), p. 17.
23. Interview in Ramallah, 6 July 1989.
24. *Jerusalem Post*, 18 December 1987, p. 6.
25. Makhul, *art. cit.*, p. 95.
26. *Ibid.*, p. 95. The quotation following this was taken from p. 94.
27. Daoud Kuttab, 'The Palestinians' Unified Command', *Middle East International* 318 (1988), p. 10.
28. Intifada leaders from Husan, a village near Bethlehem, were former prisoners. Interview in Husan, 13 October 1988. On the popular committees, see also *Jerusalem Post*, 3 February 1988, p. 2.
29. Ali al-Jarbawi, *The Intifada and the Political Leadership in the West Bank and Gaza* [in Arabic] (Beirut: Dar al-Taliya Press, 1989), p. 131. See also Ziad Abu-Amr, 'The Palestinian Uprising in the West Bank and Gaza Strip', *Arab Studies Quarterly* 10, no. 4 (1988), p. 389.
30. Kuttab, 'The Palestinians' Unified Command', pp. 10–11.
31. For an analysis of these leaflets, see Abu-Amr, *art. cit.*, pp. 389 ff.
32. *Ibid.*, p. 390.
33. Dr Sari Nuseibeh, interview in East Jerusalem, 17 November 1988.
34. Abu-Amr, *art. cit.*, p. 397.
35. Interview in East Jerusalem, 5 November 1988.
36. For this and what follows, see Abu-Amr, *art. cit.*, p. 390; al-Jarbawi, *op. cit.*, pp. 102–06; interview with Dr al-Jarbawi in Ramallah, 2 July 1989.
37. Interview in Ramallah, 6 July 1989.
38. Ziad Abu-Amr, 'Notes on Palestinian Political Leadership', in *Middle East Report* 154 (September–October 1988), p. 23.

39. For this group, see Sahliyeh, *In Search of Leadership: West Bank Politics Since 1967* (Washington, D.C.: The Brookings Institution, 1988), Chapter 8; Ziad Abu-Asmr and Ali al-Jarbawi, 'The Struggle for West Bank Leadership', *Middle East International* 304 (1987), pp. 16–18.
40. This statement was made by a Palestinian journalist in East Jerusalem who knew Siniora. The preceding comment comes from a Professor at Birzeit.
41. Sahliyeh, *op. cit.*, p. 173.
42. *Ibid.*, p. 172.
43. *Ibid.*, p. 173.
44. Makhul, *art. cit.*, p. 97.
45. For Siniora and his campaign, see *Jerusalem Post*, 6 January 1988, pp. 1, 10; 7 January 1988, p. 2; 8 January 1988, p. 1; 10 January 1988, pp. 1–2.
46. *Jerusalem Post*, 15 January 1988, p. 1.
47. This document is reprinted in the *Journal of Palestine Studies* 17, no. 3 (1988), pp. 63–5. It is also discussed by Walid Khalidi, 'Toward Peace in the Holy Land', in *Foreign Affairs*, spring (1988), pp. 771–89.
48. 'The Uprising Against Israel', reprinted from *The Manchester Guardian* report from the West Bank, 17 January 1988 in *Journal of Palestine Studies* 17, no. 3 (1988), p. 160.
49. Gail Pressberg, 'The Uprising: Causes and Consequences', *Journal of Palestine Studies* 17, no. 3 (1988), p. 46.
50. For the PNC programme, see Alain Gresh, *The PLO: The Struggle Within* (London: Zed Books, 1988), p. 243; for Arafat's interview, *Xinhua* (Beijing) in English, 13 January 1988 in *FBIS*, 14 January 1988, pp. 13–14.
51. On 6 January 1988, the *Jerusalem Post* (pp. 1, 10) reported that a committee of 15 men from the 'pro-PLO elite' was going to announce a campaign of civil disobedience the next day. One reason given was their frustration with the militancy of the youth. However, the organizers disagreed over whether they could draw mass support. Military authorities also warned them not to hold the meeting. Siniora therefore decided to do it himself. See also *Jerusalem Post*, 7 January 1988, p. 2.
52. Hanna Siniora, 'An Analysis of the Current Revolt,' in *Journal of Palestine Studies* 17, no. 3 (1988), p. 8.
53. Interview in East Jerusalem, 17 November 1988.
54. Siniora, *art. cit.*, pp. 5–6.
55. *Hadashot*, 9 January 1988, p. 4, in *FBIS*, 12 January 1988, p. 61.
56. *Jerusalem Post*, 10 January 1988, p. 2.
57. *Ibid.*, p. 2.
58. Commentary by Daoud Kuttab in the *In Jerusalem* section of *Jerusalem Post*, 15 January 1988.
59. Interview in East Jerusalem, 17 November 1988.
60. Interview in East Jerusalem, 5 November 1988.

61. Abu-Amr, 'The Palestinian Uprising', pp. 401–02.
62. For this and what follows on the factions, see *ibid.*, p. 400; Makhul, *art. cit.*, pp. 95–6.
63. Abu-Amr, 'The Palestinian Uprising', pp. 390, 393.
64. For what follows, see *ibid.*, pp. 394–5; al-Jarbawi, *op. cit.*, pp. 104–06; *Haaretz*, 20 January 1988, pp. 1, 4, in *FBIS*, 26 January 1988, pp. 35–6; *al-Fajr*, 30 January 1988, pp. 11, 13; Daoud Kuttab, 'Fundamentalists on the March', in *Middle East International* 311 (1987), pp. 9–10.
65. Interview in Ramallah, 6 July 1989.
66. On the UNL as a national authority, see Abu-Amr, 'The Palestinian Uprising', p. 397.
67. Interview in Ramallah, 6 July 1989.
68. Abu-Amr, 'The Palestinian Uprising', p. 396.
69. Abu-Amr, 'Notes on Palestinian Political Leadership', p. 24.
70. 'The Palestinians' Fourteen Demands', in *Journal of Palestine Studies* 17, no. 3 (1988), p. 65.
71. Ali al-Jarbawi, 'The Palestinian Elites in the Occupied Territories: Stability and Change through the Intifada' in Jamal R. Nassar and Roger Heacock, eds, *Intifada: Palestine at the Crossroads* (New York: Praeger, 1990), p. 297.
72. Interview in Ramallah, 17 August 1989.
73. *Jerusalem Post*, 6 January 1988, p. 1. See also Siniora, *art. cit.*, p. 7.
74. *Ibid.*, p. 7.
75. Interview in East Jerusalem, 17 November 1988.
76. Abu-Amr, 'The Palestinian Uprising', pp. 389–90.
77. Siniora, *art. cit.*, p. 6.
78. Spokesman at al-Maqassed hospital, interviewed on 18 November 1988.
79. *Jerusalem Post*, 6 January 1988, p. 2.
80. *Jerusalem Post*, 28 December 1988, p. 1.
81. IDF Radio in Hebrew, 12 January 1988, in *FBIS*, 13 January 1988, p. 46.
82. *Jerusalem Post*, 7 January 1988, p. 1.
83. IDF Radio in Hebrew, 12 January 1988, in *FBIS*, 13 January 1988, p. 46.
84. Makhul, *art. cit.*, p. 95.
85. Jonathan Kuttab, 'The Children's Revolt', *Journal of Palestine Studies* 17, no. 4 (1988), p. 30.
86. *Jerusalem Post*, 19 January 1988, p. 1.
87. Makhul, *art. cit.*, p. 97.
88. *Jerusalem Post*, 18 December 1987, p. 5.
89. *Jerusalem Post*, 25 December 1987, p. 18.
90. *Jerusalem Post*, 20 December 1987, p. 1.
91. Information on American Jewish reaction is from Arthur Hertzberg, 'The Illusion of Jewish Unity', *New York Review of Books* 35, no. 10 (1988), pp. 6, 8, 10, 11–12; *Jerusalem Post*, 23 and 27

December, 1987, pp. 1–2, 2 respectively.

92. *Jerusalem Post*, 22 December 1987, p. 1.
93. The travel advisory was issued on 21 December 1987. *Jerusalem Post*, 22 December 1987, p. 1.
94. *Jerusalem Post*, 29 December 1987, p. 1.
95. Jules Kagian, 'The United Nations. The Four Resolutions', *Middle East International* 317 (1988), pp. 8–10.
96. The information which follows comes from Shada Islam, 'Germans Take the Lead', *Middle East International* 318 (1988), pp. 8–9; Islam, 'Weighing Their Words', *Middle East International* 319 (1988), p. 10; *Jerusalem Post*, 18 December 1987, p. 18 and 19 January 1988, p. 1.
97. *Jerusalem Post*, 18 December 1987, p. 18.
98. *Jerusalem Post*, 18 December 1987, pp. 7, 20; 23 December 1988, pp. 1–2; 27 December 1988, p. 2.
99. *Jerusalem Post*, 12 January 1988, p. 1.
100. What follows comes from *Jerusalem Post*, 1 January 1988, p. 2; and 6 January 1988, p. 2; 8 January 1988, pp. 1, 18.
101. *Jerusalem Post*, 14 January 1988, pp. 1–2.
102. *Jerusalem Post*, 18 December 1987, p. 9.
103. *Jerusalem Post*, 12 January 1988, p. 2. For Shamir's discovery of autonomy, see *Jerusalem Post*, 15 January 1988, p. 20.
104. *Jerusalem Post*, 23 December 1988, p. 1.
105. *Jerusalem Post*, 11 January 1988, p. 1

CHAPTER 4

1. *Yediot Aharonot*, 15 January 1988, pp. 4, 19, in *FBIS*, 19 January 1988, p. 42.
2. Interview in Ramallah, 1 December 1988.
3. Interview in Jenin, 20 October 1988.
4. Interview in Husan, 13 October 1988.
5. Interview in Gaza City, 17 December 1988.
6. Interview in East Jerusalem, 5 November 1988.
7. For Israeli appeals to the elder generation, see *Jerusalem Post*, 23 December 1987, p. 1; 18 January 1988, p. 1; 12 February 1988, p. 2.
8. *Jerusalem Post*, 11 January 1988, pp. 1–2.
9. *Ibid.*, p. 2.
10. Jerusalem Domestic Service in Hebrew, 13 January 1988, in *FBIS*, 13 January 1988, p. 44.
11. *Jerusalem Post,* 13 January 1988, p. 1. For stone-throwing as the main component of Intifada violence, see *al-Quds* (Jerusalem), 31 August 1988, p. 3.
12. *Jerusalem Post*, 20 January 1988, p. 1.
13. *Yediot Aharonot*, 15 January 1988, pp. 4, 19, in *FBIS*, 19 January 1988, p. 42.

14. *Jerusalem Post,* 20 January 1988, p. 1.
15. *Jerusalem Post,* 15 January 1988, p. 5. See also *ibid.*, 21 January 1988, p. 2.
16. *Jerusalem Post,* 18 December 1987, p. 2.
17. *Jerusalem Post,* 28 December 1987, pp. 1, 4.
18. *Jerusalem Post,* 1 January 1988, p. 6.
19. *Ibid.*
20. *Jerusalem Post,* 20 January 1988, p. 1.
21. *Jerusalem Post,* 18 December 1987, p. 20.
22. Interview in West Jerusalem, 12 December 1988.
23. For this, see Emile Sahliyeh, *In Search of Leadership: West Bank Politics Since 1967* (Washington, D.C.: The Brookings Institution, 1988), pp. 63 ff.
24. Israelis often received bribes for giving Palestinians licences and permits. Interviewees, Palestinian and Israeli, made this point. Meron Benvenisti, *1986 Report: Demographic, Economic, Legal, Social and Political Developments in the West Bank* (Jerusalem: West Bank Data Base Project, 1986), p. 35; Benvenisti, *1987 Report: Demographic, Economic, Legal, Social and Political Developments in the West Bank* (Jerusalem: West Bank Data Base Project 1987), p. 36.
25. For this and what follows, see Sahliyeh, *op. cit.,* pp. 63–85.
26. *Hadashot,* 14 January 1988, p. 16, in *FBIS,* 20 January 1988, pp. 40–1.
27. Benvenisti, *1986 Report,* p. 40.
28. *Jerusalem Post,* 1 January 1988, p. 8.
29. *Jerusalem Post,* 2 February 1988, p. 1.
30. Interview in Beit Sahour, 10 December, 1988.
31. *Jerusalem Post,* 12 February 1988, p. 20.
32. For the press and schools, see Carmel Shalev, 'The Price of Insurgency: Civil Rights in the Occupied Territories', West Bank Data Base Project, Jerusalem, October 1988, pp. 45–60; al-Haq Law in the Service of Man, 'Punishing a Nation: Human Rights Violations during the Palestinian Uprising, December 1987–December 1988', Ramallah, 1988, pp. 198–202, 296–8, 312, 314; *Jerusalem Post,* 4 February 1988, p. 8; interview with Ibrahim Karaeen in East Jerusalem, 23 November 1988.
33. Information in this paragraph derives from Shalev *op. cit.,* pp. 35, 47, 50; al-Haq, *op. cit.,* pp. 194–6; *Jerusalem Post,* 31 January 1988, p. 1; 4 February 1988, p. 8.
34. al-Haq, *op. cit.,* p. 177.
35. Information in this paragraph came from Shalev, *op. cit.,* p. 35; *Jerusalem Post,* 9 February 1988, p. 2; *al-Fajr,* 14 February 1988, p. 14.
36. al-Haq, *op. cit.,* p. 185.
37. Interview in East Jerusalem, 7 October 1988.
38. al-Haq, *op. cit.,* p. 192.
39. *Jerusalem Post,* 18 January 1988, p. 1.
40. *Jerusalem Post,* 17 January 1988, p. 2.
41. *Jerusalem Post,* 20 January 1988, p. 1.

42. *Jerusalem Post,* 19 January 1988, pp. 1, 10.
43. Shalev, *op. cit.,* p. 35.
44. al-Haq, *op. cit.,* pp. 196–7; Shalev, *op. cit.,* p. 36.
45. *Ibid.,* p. 38.
46. al-Haq, *op. cit.,* pp. 277–8.
47. Spokesman at Ittihad al-Nisai hospital, interviewed in Nablus, 1 October 1988.
48. Official at the Arab Orphanage School, interviewed in Tulkarm, 1 October 1988.
49. *Jerusalem Post,* 15 January 1988, p. 5.
50. *Jerusalem Post,* 2 February 1988, p. 10. IDF sources denied Sharita's claims that he was beaten. Jerusalem Domestic Service in Hebrew, 2 February 1988, in *FBIS,* 3 February 1988, p. 24.
51. *Jerusalem Post,* 3 February 1988, p. 1.
52. Interview in Jenin, 1 October 1988.
53. al-Haq, *op. cit.,* p. 21.
54. *al-Fajr,* 14 February 1988, p. 13.
55. *Jerusalem Post,* 22 February 1988, p. 1.
56. al-Haq, *op. cit.,* p. 187.
57. *Jerusalem Post,* 15 February 1988, p. 1; *al-Fajr,* 7 February 1988, p. 2.
58. *Jerusalem Post,* 19 February 1988, p. 7.
59. This practice was criticized by a team of Israeli doctors. *Jerusalem Post,* 9 June 1988, p. 4.
60. Interview at Maqassed hospital, 18 November 1988. The interview at Ittihad al-Nisai took place on 1 October 1988.
61. On the damage and destruction of property, see Shalev, *op. cit.,* p. 33.
62. *Jerusalem Post,* 19 February 1988, p. 7.
63. *Jerusalem Post,* 16 February 1988, p. 4.
64. *Jerusalem Post,* 19 February 1988, p. 7.
65. *Jerusalem Post,* 12 February 1988, p. 1.
66. Shalev, *op. cit.,* p. 3. This estimate is based upon figures for the first ten months of the uprising.
67. *Jerusalem Post,* 22 February 1988, p. 1.
68. *Jerusalem Post,* 12 February 1988, p. 1.
69. *Jerusalem Post,* 12 February 1988, p. 6.
70. Shalev, *op. cit.,* p. 2. Dedi Zucker, member of the Knesset, estimated that one out of every 200 males over the age of 18 had been detained without trial.
71. *Ibid.,* p. 29.
72. *Ibid.,* pp. 31–3; see also al-Haq, *op. cit.,* chapter 6.
73. Dr 'Mahmud', interviewed in East Jerusalem, 10 November 1988.
74. Shalev, *op. cit.,* p. 26; *Jerusalem Post,* 27 May 1988, p. 10.
75. Shalev, *op. cit.,* p. 26. See also *ibid.,* p. 25. An interesting account of the problems faced by arrested Palestinian youths can be found in *Jerusalem Post,* 27 May 1988, p. 8.
76. I am grateful to André Rosenthal, an Israeli lawyer, for providing

me with this information.

77. *Jerusalem Post,* 27 May 1988, p. 9.
78. Shalev, *op. cit.,* p. 31.
79. *Ibid.,* p. 43.
80. al-Haq, *op. cit.,* pp. 27 ff. On the new CS gas, see also Shalev, *op. cit.,* p. 15.
81. See the Israeli doctors' report in *Jerusalem Post,* 9 June 1988, p. 1.
82. Interview at Maqassed Hospital, 18 November 1988.
83. *Jerusalem Post,* 11 January 1988, p. 1.
84. Cited in *al-Fajr,* 17 January 1988, p. 15.
85. *Jerusalem Post,* 12 February 1988, p. 6.
86. Shalev, *op. cit.,* p. 15.
87. *Jerusalem Post,* 9 June 1988, pp. 1, 4.
88. These statistics (and other UNRWA data used in this book) were kindly made available to me by Rolf van Uye of UNRWA.
89. *Jerusalem Post,* 12 February 1988, p. 6.
90. *Jerusalem Post,* 22 January 1988, p. 7.
91. Shalev, *op. cit.,* pp. 12–13; al-Haq, *op. cit.,* p. 20.
92. Shalev, *op. cit.,* pp. 12–13. For examples of beatings and the use of force, see *ibid.,* pp. 13 ff.
93. *Ibid.,* p. 14.
94. Interview in West Jerusalem, 25 November 1988.
95. For this and what follows, see David Shipler, *Arab and Jew: Wounded Spirits in a Promised Land* (New York: Penguin Books, 1987), pp. 195–6, 233, 268, 412–13. On the Jewish image of Arabs as violent, see chapter 5.
96. Shalev, *op. cit.,* pp. 61–2.
97. *Ibid.,* pp. 53–8. On the dual standard of justice prior to the Intifada, see Shipler, *op. cit.,* pp. 91, 121, 133. According to Shalev (p. 59), whose report was issued after the first ten months of the Intifada, the Military Police had opened about 450 investigative files on deaths and other incidents arising from complaints made. Of these, half were closed at the end of the investigation. (This may be measured against the more than 200 cases of excesses in soldiers' behaviour each month, according to an April report.) Charges of manslaughter were brought against Israeli soldiers in only a few cases. According to the Israeli Information Centre for Human Rights in the Occupied Territories, after almost two years of the Intifada, only one of the 102 cases in which Palestinian children were killed by Israeli soldiers had resulted in the jailing of a soldier. In all, four Israeli soldiers had been imprisoned for killing Palestinians during the uprising. (The Jerusalem Media and Communication Centre, *Weekly Report,* 26 November–2 December 1989, p. 2.)
98. *al-Fajr,* 7 February 1988, p. 3. For the commercial strikes, see Salim Tamari, 'The Revolt of the Petite Bourgeoisie: Urban Merchants and the Palestinian Uprising', in Jamal R. Nassar and Roger Heacock, eds, *Intifada: Palestine at the Crossroads* (New

York: Praeger, 1990), pp. 159–73.

99. *Jerusalem Post*, 3 February 1988, p. 1.
100. *Jerusalem Post*, 18 January 1988, p. 2.
101. For this and what follows, see *Jerusalem Post*, 18 December 1987, pp. 1, 20; *al-Fajr*, 27 December 1987, p. 13.
102. For this and the other coercive measures noted, see *Jerusalem Post*, 10 January 1988, p. 1; 22 January 1988, p. 1; 5 February 1988, p. 6; 14 February 1988, p. 1.
103. Interview in Jenin, 20 October 1988.
104. *Jerusalem Post*, 13 January 1988, p. 1.
105. *Jerusalem Post*, 31 January 1988, p. 2; 3 February, p. 1; *al-Fajr*, 7 February 1988, p. 3.
106. This was reported in *al-Fajr*, 7 February 1988, p. 3.
107. *Jerusalem Post*, 18 January 1988, p. 2.
108. *Jerusalem Post*, 18 January 1988, p. 2.
109. *al-Fajr*, 20 March 1988, p. 2.
110. *Ibid.*, p. 3.
111. al-Haq, *op. cit.*, p. 275.
112. *al-Fajr*, 20 March 1988, p. 3.
113. al-Haq, *op. cit.*, p. 276. The incident described occurred in April.
114. *al-Fajr*, 28 February 1988, p. 4.
115. Gail Pressberg, 'The Uprising: Causes and Consequences', *Journal of Palestine Studies* 17, no. 3 (1988), p. 43.
116. *al-Fajr*, 7 February 1988, p. 2.
117. Interview with UNRWA spokesman in Gaza City, 17 December 1988.
118. *Jerusalem Post*, 17 February 1988, p. 9.
119. *Jerusalem Post*, 18 January 1988, p. 2.
120. *Jerusalem Post*, 3 February 1988, p. 10.
121. *Jerusalem Post*, 17 February 1988, p. 2.
122. *Jerusalem Post*, 19 February 1988, p. 5.
123. *al-Fajr*, 22 May 1988, p. 1. In June stores were opening and closing when they wished.
124. *Jerusalem Post*, 18 January 1988, p. 2.
125. Interview in East Jerusalem, 6 September 1988.
126. Jerusalem Domestic Service in English, 25 February 1988 in *FBIS*, 25 February 1988, p. 34.
127. *Jerusalem Post*, 22 January 1988, p. 1.
128. *Jerusalem Post*, 21 January 1988, p. 2.
129. *Jerusalem Post*, 8 February 1988, p. 8. His stated reason was that both Israelis and Palestinians had rejected the idea of a Palestinian–Jordanian confederation, which he supported.
130. *Jerusalem Post*, 15 February 1988, p. 2.
131. The information on the Qabatya incident in this and the following paragraphs derives from the following sources: Shalev, *op. cit.*, p. 36; *al-Fajr*, 28 February 1988, p. 3; Jerusalem Domestic Service in Hebrew, 24 and 25 February 1988 and Jerusalem Domestic Service in English, 25 February 1988 in *FBIS*, 25 February 1988,

pp. 33–4; *Maariv*, 26 February 1988, pp. A1, 2 in *FBIS*, 26 February 1988, p. 38; Jerusalem Television Service in Hebrew, 27 February 1988, and *Maariv*, 28 February 1988, pp. A1, 2 in *FBIS*, 29 February 1988, pp. 42, 45; Jerusalem Domestic Service in Hebrew, 1 March 1988 in *FBIS*, 1 March 1988, p. 36; interview with Dr Abdulfattah in Jenin, 20 October 1988. I am particularly grateful to Dr Abdulfattah and Dr al-Jarbawi for providing information that helped me to understand this incident.

132. For this and what follows, see *Yediot Aharonot*, 1 February 1988, p. 7 in *FBIS*, 2 February 1988, p. 28; *Jerusalem Post*, 1 February 1988, p. 2. Interview with Dr al-Jarbawi in Ramallah, 17 August 1989.

133. *Jerusalem Post*, 11 February 1988, pp. 1, 8.

134. My discussion of Hamas, the Muslim Brotherhood and Islamic Jihad, unless otherwise indicated, came from the following sources: Ali al-Jarbawi, *The Intifada and the Political Leadership in the West Bank and Gaza* [in Arabic] (Beirut: Dar al-Taliya Press, 1989), pp. 106–14, 117–18, 121–3; Jean-François Legrain, 'The Islamic Movement and the Intifada', in Nassar and Heacock eds, *op. cit.*, pp. 175–89.

135. Interview in East Jerusalem, 6 September 1988.

136. For this, see *Jerusalem Post*, 7 February 1988, p. 1; 11 February 1988, p. 8; 14 February 1988, p. 1. For the villagers in the revolt, see Husain Jameel Bargouti, 'Jeep versus Bare Feet: The Villages in the Intifada', in Nassar and Heacock eds, *op. cit.*, pp. 107–23.

137. Interview in Taibeh, 25 September 1988.

138. On settler violence, see Shalev, *op. cit.*, pp. 4–5, 51–3; *Jerusalem Post*, 8 February 1988, p. 2; 12 February 1988, p. 20; al-Haq, *op. cit.*, pp. 123–5.

139. *al-Fajr*, 7, 14, 21 and 28 February 1988, all on page 1.

140. *Jerusalem Post*, 7 February 1988, p. 1.

141. *Jerusalem Post*, 17 February 1988, p. 1.

142. *Jerusalem Post*, 12 February 1988, p. 6.

CHAPTER 5

1. Hanna Siniora, 'An Analysis of the Current Revolt', in *Journal of Palestine Studies*, 17, no. 3 (1988), p. 6.

2. Ziad Abu-Amr, 'The Palestinian Uprising in the West Bank and Gaza Strip', *Arab Studies Quarterly* 10, no. 4 (1988), p. 402.

3. *Al Hamishmar*, 2 May 1988, p. 7 in *FBIS*, 6 May 1988, pp. 32–4.

4. Information in this and the following paragraph is based upon Abu-Amr, *art. cit.*, pp. 390–3; Jerusalem Domestic Service in English, 1 March 1988 in *FBIS*, 1 March 1988, p. 37; Jerusalem Domestic Service in Hebrew, 10 March 1988 in *FBIS*, 11 March 1988, p. 45. *Yediot Aharonot*, 23 March 1988, p. 3 in *FBIS*, 24 March 1988, p. 49; (clandestine) *al-Quds* Palestinian Arab Radio in Arabic, 28 May 1988 in *FBIS*, 1 June 1988, p. 2; Baghdad Voice of the PLO in

Arabic, 29 May 1988 in *FBIS*, 1 June 1988, p. 3.

5. Abu-Amr, *art. cit.*, p. 390.
6. Jerusalem Television Service in Hebrew, 1 March 1988, in *FBIS*, 2 March 1988, p. 39.
7. (clandestine) *al-Quds* Palestinian Arab Radio in Arabic, 28 May 1988; Baghdad Voice of the PLO in Arabic, 29 May 1988, in *FBIS*, 1 June 1988, pp. 2–3.
8. Jerusalem Domestic Service in English, 19 June 1988 in *FBIS*, 20 June 1988, p. 30; Baghdad Voice of the PLO in Arabic, 22 June 1988 in *FBIS*, 23 June 1988, pp. 3–4.
9. Abu-Amr, *art. cit.*, p. 390.
10. I wish to thank Dr Jad Isaac for explaining this point to me.
11. Abu-Amr, *art. cit.*, pp. 392–3.
12. *Manama Wakh* in Arabic, 2 June 1988 in *FBIS*, 2 June 1988, p. 2.
13. Abu-Amr, *art. cit.*, pp. 393–94.
14. For this debate, see *Haaretz*, 14 April 1988, p. 9 in *FBIS*, 15 April 1988, p. 39; *Al Hamishmar*, 26 May 1988, p. 6 in *FBIS*, 27 May 1988, pp. 20–1; *Haaretz*, 15 June 1988, p. 9 in *FBIS*, 16 June 1988, pp. 35–6. The two tendencies in the nationalist camp are discussed by Abu-Amr, *art. cit.*, pp. 401–02.
15. Information on these resignations comes from *Jerusalem Post*, 7 March 1988, p. 1 in *FBIS*, 7 March 1988, p. 38; *Jerusalem Post*, 7 March 1988, p. 2, in *FBIS*, 8 March 1988, p. 40; *Hadashot*, 9 March 1988, p. 7 in *FBIS*, 10 March 1988, p. 41; Jerusalem Domestic Service in Hebrew, 11 March 1988 in *FBIS*, 11 March 1988, p. 45; Jerusalem Domestic Service in Hebrew, 12 March 1988, in *FBIS*, 14 March 1988, p. 43; IDF Radio in Hebrew, 13 March 1988 in *FBIS*, 14 March 1988, p. 44; IDF Radio in Hebrew, 14 March 1988 in *FBIS*, 15 March 1988, p. 41; IDF Radio in Hebrew, 15 March 1988 in *FBIS*, 15 March 1988, p. 42; *Haaretz*, 14 April 1988, p. 9 in *FBIS*, 15 April 1988, p. 39.
16. On pressure upon Israeli-appointed personnel, see Abu-Amr, *art. cit.*, p. 392; Jerusalem Domestic Service in English, 13 April 1988 in *FBIS*, 13 April 1988, p. 30; Jerusalem Domestic Service in Hebrew, 7 April 1988, in *FBIS*, 7 April 1988, p. 29; *Jerusalem Post*, 1 April 1988, pp. 1, 2 in *FBIS*, 1 April 1988, p. 29; *Maariv*, 9 June 1988, p. A7, in *FBIS*, 9 June 1988, pp. 35–6.
17. For this argument by Rabin, see *Haaretz*, 14 April 1988, p. 9 in *FBIS*, 15 April 1988, p. 39.
18. *Al Hamishmar*, 2 May 1988, p. 7, in *FBIS*, 6 May 1988, p. 34.
19. *Hadashot*, 12 February 1988, pp. 35, 37 in *FBIS*, 19 February 1988, p. 30.
20. Jerusalem Domestic Service in English, 31 May 1988, in *FBIS*, 1 June 1988, p. 23. The abandonment of the principle of individual punishment for collective punishment, a writer for *Davar* noted, brought the 'once-passive' residents of the territories into the circle of hostility. *Davar*, 13 March 1988, p. 7, in *FBIS*, 16 March 1988, p. 49.
21. Interview in Ramallah, 1 August 1989.

22. *al-Nahar* (Jerusalem), 31 May 1988, p. 1 in *FBIS*, 2 June 1988, p. 2. The rest of the information contained in this paragraph was drawn from the following sources: Jerusalem Television Service in Hebrew, 17 February 1988 in *FBIS*, 18 February 1988, p. 42; *Haaretz*, 13 March 1988, p. 2, in *FBIS*, 16 March 1988, p. 47; *ibid.*, 18 March 1988, pp. 1, 11 in *FBIS*, 22 March 1988, pp. 38–9.

23. *Haaretz*, 28 April 1988, p. 11, in *FBIS*, 29 April 1988, pp. 37–8.

24. *Jerusalem Post*, 7 March 1988, p. 1, in *FBIS*, 7 March 1988, p. 38.

25. For this and the following information, see IDF Radio in Hebrew, 13 March 1988 in *FBIS*, 14 March 1988, p. 44; Jerusalem Domestic Service in Hebrew, 14 April 1988, in *FBIS*, 15 April 1988, p. 38; *al-Nahar* (Jerusalem), 31 May 1988, p. 1, in *FBIS*, 2 June 1988, p. 2; Jerusalem Television Service in Arabic, 11 July 1988 in *FBIS*, 12 July 1988, p. 25; *al-Fajr* (in Arabic), 16 July 1988, p. 1, in *FBIS*, 20 July 1988, p. 36.

26. The exception was the Hebron area, where a number of Palestinians did not leave their posts or returned to work. Jerusalem Television Service in Hebrew, 14 March 1988 in *FBIS*, 15 March 1988, p. 41; IDF Radio in Hebrew, 4 May 1988, in *FBIS*, 4 May 1988, p. 18.

27. The mayors of Gaza, Nablus and Ramallah resigned or stopped going to work. (*Maariv*, 9 June 1988, p. A7, in *FBIS*, 9 June 1988, p. 35.) Palestinian sources maintain that many more than three mayors left their posts, but that the Israeli government refused to make this information public. For resignations of Israeli-appointed council and committee members, see *Jerusalem Post*, 9 February 1988, p. 10; Baghdad Voice of the PLO in Arabic, 22 June 1988 in *FBIS*, 23 June 1988, p. 4.

28. In February, some residents of East Jerusalem and the Golan Heights destroyed their cards. *Jerusalem Post*, 19 February 1988, p. 4.

29. *Jerusalem Post*, 8 July 1988, p. 2 in *FBIS*, 8 July 1988, p. 30; 'The Beit Sahour saga', unpublished manuscript drawn up in July 1988 by residents of Beit Sahour, p. 13. On the Beit Sahour incident, readers may consult Daoud Kuttab, *Middle East International* 330 (22 July 1988), p. 10.

30. Laurent Corbaz, interviewed in East Jerusalem, 22 November 1988.

31. Jerusalem Domestic Service in Hebrew, 3 April 1989, in *FBIS*, 4 April 1989, p. 28; *Hadashot*, 4 April 1989, p. 7, in *FBIS*, 5 April 1989, p. 27.

32. Jerusalem Domestic Service in English, 13 March 1988 in *FBIS*, 14 March 1988, p. 43.

33. Interviews in Gaza, 17 December 1988.

34. Interview in Ramallah, 1 December 1988.

35. Interview in Ramallah, 24 November 1988.

36. Interview in Jenin, 20 October 1988.

37. Interview with a lawyer in Gaza City, 17 December 1988.

38. Interview in Ramallah, 24 November 1988.

39. Interview in Gaza City, 17 December 1988.

40. Interview in Ramallah, 24 November 1988.
41. Interview with Dr Jad Issac in East Jerusalem, mid-August 1989.
42. Miss Nora Kort, interviewed in East Jerusalem, 9 December 1988.
43. Interview with a lawyer in Gaza City, 17 December 1988.
44. Interview in Ramallah, 1 December 1988.
45. For information on victory gardens, home retail trade and Palestinian industry, I have relied upon interviews and the following printed sources: 'The Beit Sahour Saga'; *Maariv*, 10 May 1988, p. A3, in *FBIS*, 11 May 1988, p. 35; *al-Fajr*, 20 March 1988, p. 8; 22 May 1988, pp. 8–9, 13; 1 May 1989, p. 8.
46. Interview in Jenin, 20 October 1988.
47. Interview in East Jerusalem, 9 December 1988.
48. Interview in Ramallah, 12 October 1988.
49. Interview in East Jerusalem, 9 December 1988.
50. Interview in Ramallah, 1 December 1988.
51. *al-Talia* (Jerusalem), 17 March 1988, p. 1, in *FBIS*, 22 March 1988, p. 38.
52. *Ibid.*
53. Information gained during visit to Husan, 13 October 1988.
54. 'The Beit Sahour Saga', p. 3.
55. Interview in Ramallah, 12 October 1988.
56. 'The Beit Sahour Saga', p. 4.
57. Interview in East Jerusalem, 17 August 1989.
58. Interview in Husan, 10 August 1989.
59. Abu-Amr, *art. cit.*, p. 388.
60. Interview in Ramallah, 12 October 1988.
61. Interview in Jenin, 20 October 1988.
62. Interview in East Jerusalem, 6 September 1988.
63. Abu-Amr, *art. cit.*, pp. 398–9; *Jerusalem Post*, 26 June 1989, p. 10.
64. The UNL leaflets prescribed in minute detail the tasks of these committees in organizing support for Palestinian civil disobedience. See, for example, *al-Quds* Palestinian Arab Radio in Arabic, 28 May 1988 in *FBIS*, 1 June 1988, p. 3.
65. Interview in Taibeh, 25 September 1988.
66. *al-Quds* Palestinian Arab Radio in Arabic, 18 June 1988 in *FBIS*, 20 June 1988, p. 5.
67. Ali al-Jarbawi, 'Palestinian Elites in the Occupied Territories: Stability and Change through the Intifada', in Jamal R. Nassar and Roger Heacock, eds, *Intifada: Palestine at the Crossroads* (New York: Praeger, 1990), p. 298.
68. *Al Hamishmar*, 2 May 1988, p. 7 in *FBIS*, 6 May 1988, p. 32.
69. *Ibid.*; Abu-Amr, *art. cit.*, p. 398.
70. I am grateful to Miss Kort for providing me with this information.
71. *Al Hamishmar*, 2 May 1988, p. 7 in *FBIS*, 6 May 1988, p. 32.
72. See, for example, *Haaretz*, 1 March 1988, pp. 1, 3, in *FBIS*, 1 March 1988, p. 37.
73. This defeat was recognized by some Israeli analysts. *Haaretz*, 9 May 1988, p. B1, in *FBIS*, 10 May 1988, pp. 26–7.

74. *Davar*, 13 March 1988, p. 7, in *FBIS*, 16 March 1988, p. 49.
75. Interview in Beit Sahour, 10 December 1988.
76. Interview in Ramallah, 14 December 1988.
77. Interviews in Tulkarm (10 October 1988), Taibeh (25 September 1988), and with Dr Ashrawi (12 October 1988).
78. Interview in Husan, 13 October 1988.
79. Interview with Dr Jad Issac, Beit Sahour, 10 August 1989.
80. Interview in Gaza City, 17 December 1988.
81. Interview in Ramallah, 1 December 1988.
82. Visit of 1 October 1988.
83. Related by Ms Zuhayra Kamal, 5 October 1988.
84. Interview in Ramallah, 14 December 1988.
85. Interview in Ramallah, 14 December 1988.
86. Interview in East Jerusalem, mid-August 1989.
87. The source of this and what follows is an UNRWA spokesman who has worked in Gaza. Interview in East Jerusalem, 19 August 1989.
88. Interview in Central West Bank, October 1988.
89. See Shalev, 'Price of Insurgency: Civil Rights in the Occupied Territories', West Bank Data Base Project, Jerusalem, October 1988, pp. 37–9.
90. Jerusalem Domestic Service in English, 26 May 1988 in *FBIS*, 26 May 1988, p. 19.
91. Interview in Ramallah, 1 December 1988. In the autumn of 1988 this amount was reduced to 200 Jordanian dinars.
92. Shalev, *op. cit.*, pp. 48–9.
93. The agricultural centre in Beit Sahour was closed down by military order on 5 June. For this, and the rest of the information found in this paragraph, see 'Beit Sahour Saga', p. 7; Nora Kort interview; Shalev, *op. cit.*, pp. 37–8; al-Haq, 'Punishing a Nation: Human Rights Violations during the Palestinian Uprising, December 1987–December 1988', Ramallah, 1988, pp. 283–4; *Yediot Aharonot*, 28 June 1988, p. 2 in *FBIS*, 28 June 1988, p. 37; *Bitter Harvest: Israeli Sanctions Against Palestinian Agriculture During the Uprising, December 1987–March 1989* (Jerusalem: The Jerusalem Media and Communication Centre, 1989), pp. 5–21.
94. Information contained in this paragraph is found in Jerusalem Domestic Service in English, 18 April 1988 in *FBIS*, 21 April 1988, p. 27; *Jerusalem Post*, 17 May 1988, p. 8 in *FBIS*, 18 May 1988, p. 33; *Haaretz*, 28 June 1988, p. 12 in *FBIS*, 29 June 1988. Jerusalem Domestic Service in Hebrew, 22 March 1989 in *FBIS*, 22 March 1989, p. 39; *Jerusalem Post*, 30 March 1989, p. 12 in *FBIS*, 4 April 1989, p. 27; *Yediot Aharonot*, 13 May 1988, pp. 34–6 in *FBIS*, 20 May 1988, pp. 18–19.
95. Interview in East Jerusalem, 6 September 1988.
96. Danny Rubenstein, 'Return to the Green Line', *New Outlook*, August 1988, p. 21.

CHAPTER 6

1. On the Shultz plan, see William Quandt, 'The Uprising: Breaking a Ten-Year Deadlock', paper presented at a conference on the Palestinian uprising and the search for peace, 8 December 1988, and reprinted in *American–Arab Affairs*, no. 27 (Winter 1988–9), p. 20; *Jerusalem Post*, 15 February 1988, p. 8; *Middle East International*, no. 319, 20 February 1989; Kenneth Stein, 'The Palestinian Uprising and the Shultz Initiative', *Middle East Review*, vol. 21, no. 2, Winter 1988–9, pp. 13–14. See also *Jerusalem Post*, 1, 2, 3, 11, 14 February 1988, pp. 1,3; 1–3; 1,10; 1–2; 1, 8, respectively.

2. For this and what follows on the PLO, see Alain Gresh, *The PLO: The Struggle Within* (London: Zed Books, 1988), pp. 167–71.

3. *Middle East International*, no. 313, 21 November 1987, pp. 3–4.

4. On the PLO's gains in the Arab world and the setback to Jordan, see Lamis Andoni, 'Jordan and the PLO', in *Middle East International*, no. 318, 6 February 1988, pp. 12–13; *al-Fajr*, 12 June 1988, pp. 1–2.

5. Quandt, *loc. cit.*, p. 19; Ziad Abu-Amr, 'The Debate Within the Palestinian Camp', *American–Arab Affairs*, no. 26, fall 1988, p. 41.

6. Abu-Amr, *art. cit.*, p. 49.

7. For information on this debate, see *ibid.*, pp. 40–9. My discussion of it is based upon this article.

8. On the Abu Sharif document, see *Jerusalem Post*, 24 June 1988, p. 4; *al-Fajr*, 19 June 1988, pp. 1, 13; *ibid.*, 26 June 1988, p. 16.

9. Interview in East Jerusalem, 17 November 1988.

10. On the draft declaration of independence, see *al-Fajr*, 14 August 1988, pp. 1–2, 5.

11. See the comments of Quandt, *loc. cit.*, p. 19.

12. For the contents of this paragraph, see Abu-Amr, *art. cit.*, pp. 43, 48–9.

13. My analysis of the new Palestinian programme is based upon the Independence Declaration and the political communiqué issued by the PNC, reprinted in *Journal of Palestine Studies*, vol. 18, no. 2 (winter 1989), pp. 213–23. I have also followed the analysis by Quandt, *loc. cit.*, pp. 21–4.

14. Interview in East Jerusalem, 17 August 1989.

15. Quandt, *loc. cit.*, pp. 21–3.

16. Interview in East Jerusalem, 17 August 1989.

17. For this, see *ibid.*, p. 21; and *Jerusalem Post*, 8 December 1988, p. 1. The analysis which follows is based upon the text of Arafat's speech before the UN General Assembly of 13 December 1988, and of his 14 December press conference. Both are reprinted in *Journal of Palestine Studies*, vol. 18, nos. 3 and 4 (1989), pp. 161–71 and 180–1, respectively.

18. Interview in East Jerusalem, 17 November 1988.

19. Interview in East Jerusalem, 17 November 1988.

20. Interview in Ramallah, 6 July 1989.

21. Shortly after the Intifada began, Shamir announced his acceptance

of the Camp David Accords and began talking about Palestinian 'autonomy'. This was not a serious peace proposal. Shamir's interpretation of autonomy was even more restricted than that found in the Camp David Accords, rejected by the Palestinians and opposed by Shamir himself until the Intifada.

22. Meron Benvenisti, 'Impact of the Uprising on Prospects for Peace', paper presented at a conference on the Palestinian uprising and the search for peace, 8 December 1988, and reprinted in *American–Arab Affairs*, no. 27 (winter 1988–9), p. 11.

23. Meron Benvenisti, *1986 Report. Demographic, Economic, Legal, Social and Political Developments in the West Bank* (Jerusalem: West Bank Data Base Project, 1986), pp. 82–3.

24. Mordechai Bar-On, 'Israeli Reactions to the Palestinian Uprising', *Journal of Palestine Studies*, vol. 17 (1987–8), p. 53.

25. Meron Benvenisti, *The West Bank Handbook* (Jerusalem: The Jerusalem Post, 1986), p. 5.

26. *Maariv*, 1 January 1988, pp. A1, 2, in *FBIS*, 4 January 1988, pp. 30–1.

27. Interview with Dr Shye in West Jerusalem, 30 August 1988.

28. Interview in West Jerusalem, 12 December 1988.

29. On the changing electorate between 1981 and 1988, see *Jerusalem Post*, 9 and 23 December 1988, p. 7 (both issues).

30. 'National Unity Government', in Susan Rolef, ed., *Political Dictionary of the State of Israel* (New York: Macmillan Publishing Company, 1987), p. 228.

31. Interview in West Jerusalem, 25 November 1988.

32. The details on Shamir and the Likud found in this and the subsequent paragraph were taken from *Political Dictionary of the State of Israel*, pp. 108, 143–4, 158–9, 162, 201–2, 261, 271–2.

33. For this, see Benvenisti, *1986 Report*, pp. 25–36, 46–62.

34. Interview in West Jerusalem, 25 November 1988.

35. Interview in West Jerusalem, 12 December 1988.

36. On the resurgence of the left wing in Israel, see Edy Kaufman, 'The Intifadah and the Peace Camp in Israel: A Critical Introspective', *Journal of Palestine Studies*, 17, no. 4 (summer 1988), pp. 66–80; and Bar-On, *art. cit.*, pp. 54–8.

37. Carmel Shalev, 'The Price of Insurgency: Civil Rights in the Occupied Territories', West Bank Data Base Project, October 1988, pp. 14–15.

38. These results were cited by Eric Silver at a talk given in West Jerusalem in November 1988.

39. Cited in *al-Fajr*, 14 August 1988, p. 4. The poll was conducted by researchers from the Hebrew University and from the Israeli Institute of Applied Social Research and Communications Research.

40. Bar-On, *art. cit.*, pp. 52–3.

41. Interview in West Jerusalem, 25 November 1988.

42. Interview in West Jerusalem, 9 September 1988.

43. Interview in West Jerusalem, 25 November 1988.

44. Bar-On, *art. cit.*, p. 59.

45. Interview in West Jerusalem, 25 November 1988.
46. Interview in East Jerusalem, 23 November 1988.
47. Interview in West Jerusalem, 25 November 1988.
48. Interview in West Jerusalem, 9 September 1988.
49. Interview in West Jerusalem, 25 November 1988.
50. *Jerusalem Post*, 23 December 1988, p. 1.
51. *Ibid.*, p. 7. My analysis of the Israeli elections is based upon *Jerusalem Post*, 9 December 1988, p. 7; *ibid.*, 15 December 1988, p. 4; *ibid.*, 21 December 1988, p. 4; Azmy Bishara, 'Israel Faces the Uprising: A Preliminary Assessment', *Middle East Report*, no. 157 (March–April), pp. 6–14; Don Peretz and Sammy Smooha, 'Israel's Twelfth Knesset Election: An All-Loser Game', *Middle East Journal*, 43, no. 3 (summer 1989), pp. 388–405.
52. On Rabin's 'plan' and these meetings, see *al-Fajr*, 6 February 1989, pp. 1, 15; and 20 February, pp. 1, 15.
53. *Maariv*, 5 April 1989, p. A14 in *FBIS*, 6 April 1989, pp. 24–5.
54. *New York Times*, 8 February 1989, pp. 1, 4.
55. *New York Times*, 6 March 1988, p. 4.
56. For the Shamir plan, see *Jerusalem Post*, 15 May 1989, p. 2 in *FBIS*, 15 May 1989, pp. 28–30.
57. *New York Times*, 7 April 1989, pp. 1, 9A.
58. *Ibid.* See also *New York Times*, 24 and 28 April 1988, pp. A3 and A11, respectively.
59. Jerusalem Television Service in Hebrew, 7 April 1989 in *FBIS*, 10 April 1989, pp. 17–18.
60. *Yediot Aharonot*, 11 April 1989, pp. 1, 12, in *FBIS*, 11 April 1989, p. 18.
61. *Haaretz*, 20 March 1989, p. 1 in *FBIS*, 21 March 1989, p. 29; *Jerusalem Post*, 21 March 1989, pp. 1, 12 in *FBIS*, 21 March 1989, p. 29.
62. *Haaretz*, 4 April 1989, p. 13 in *FBIS*, 6 April 1989, pp. 23–4.
63. *Jerusalem Post*, 21 July 1989, p. 6.

CHAPTER 7

1. Interview in Beit Sahour, 10 August 1989.
2. Interview in Ramallah, 17 August 1989.
3. Interview in East Jerusalem, 16 November 1988.
4. Information was provided by Dr Abu-Amr.
5. *Jerusalem Post*, 28 December 1988, p. 12.
6. Interview in Ramallah, 13 December 1988.
7. *Jerusalem Post*, 7 April 1989, p. 1. My characterization of these meetings is based upon information found in *FBIS*, January–April 1989.
8. *Al Hamishmar*, 10 March 1989, p. 2 in *FBIS*, 10 March 1989, p. 29.
9. *Al Hamishmar*, 27 March 1989, p. 1 in *FBIS*, 27 March 1989, p. 21.

10. Baghdad Voice of PLO in Arabic, 1 January 1989, in *FBIS*, 3 January 1989, p. 9.
11. Sanaa Voice of Palestine in Arabic, 27 February 1989, in *FBIS*, 28 February, pp. 4–5.
12. Baghdad Voice of PLO in Arabic, 15 March 1989, in *FBIS*, 16 March 1989, p. 6.
13. See, for example, Radio Monte Carlo in Arabic, 16 February 1989, in *FBIS*, 17 February, 1989, p. 18.
14. *Haaretz*, 23 February 1989, p. 14 in *FBIS*, 1 March 1989, p. 41; Jerusalem Television Service in Hebrew, 16 March 1989, in *FBIS*, 17 March 1989, pp. 20–1. Shamir's admission was made in a statement to the Knesset on 14 March 1990; *The Times-Picayune* (New Orleans), 15 March 1990, p. A–22.
15. IDF Radio in Hebrew, 4 April 1989, in *FBIS*, 6 April 1989, p. 27.
16. Dr al-Jarbawi, interviewed in Ramallah, 8 August 1989.
17. Sanaa Voice of Palestine in Arabic, 31 March 1989 in *FBIS*, 3 April 1989, p. 6.
18. *Al Hamishmar*, 17 April 1989, p. 3 in *FBIS*, 18 April 1989, p. 31.
19. Interview in Ramallah, 8 August 1989.
20. On Israeli efforts to promote the political brokers, see *Jerusalem Post*, 3 February 1989, p. 1, 7, 20.
21. This and what directly follows is drawn from Ali al-Jarbawi, 'The Palestinian Elites in the Occupied Territories: Stability and Change through the Intifada', in Jamal R. Nassar and Roger Heacock, eds, *Intifada: Palestine at the Crossroads* (New York: Praeger, 1990), pp. 298–9.
22. Interview in Husan, 10 August 1989.
23. Interview in Ramallah, 8 August 1989.
24. PLO leaders, for example, approved the meeting between Shamir and four prominent public personalities. *Al Hamishmar*, 27 March 1988, p. 1 in *FBIS*, 27 March 1989, p. 21. See also *ibid.*, 26 March 1989, p. 3 in *FBIS*, 27 March 1989, p. 21.
25. Interview in Ramallah, 1 August 1989.
26. Kuwait *Al Ray al-Amm* in Arabic, 26 February 1989, p. 25 in *FBIS*, 2 March 1989, p. 7.
27. Radio Monte Carlo in Arabic, 16 February 1989, in *FBIS*, 17 February 1989, p. 18; *ibid.*, 28 March 1989, in *FBIS*, 29 March 1989, p. 6.
28. *Jerusalem Post*, 7 April 1989, p. 1; *ibid.*, 27 April 1989, p. 12.
29. *Jerusalem Post*, 24 March 1989, p. 1; *Al Hamishmar*, 26 March 1989, p. 3 in *FBIS*, 27 March 1989, p. 22.
30. Jerusalem Domestic Service in Hebrew, 26 April 1989, in *FBIS*, 27 April 1989, p. 22.
31. This analysis and the argument which follows is taken from Ali al-Jarbawi and F. Robert Hunter, 'Shamir's Election Plan: An Analysis', *Middle East International*, no. 358 (8 September 1989), pp. 15–16.
32. On the brokers as a bridge between Israel and the PLO, see

Jerusalem Post, 3 February 1989, p. 7.

33. For this, see *Jerusalem Post*, 6 July 1989, pp. 1, 12.
34. *Jerusalem Post*, 21 July 1989, pp. 1–2.
35. *Jerusalem Post*, 3 August 1989, p. 12.
36. Interview in Beit Sahour, 10 August 1989.
37. This analysis derives from Dr al-Jarbawi.
38. *Jerusalem Post*, 17 July 1989, p. 8.
39. *Jerusalem Post*, 19 July 1989, p. 12.
40. *Jerusalem Post*, 26 July 1989, p. 12.
41. *Jerusalem Post*, 20 and 28 July 1989, pp. 12 and 16, respectively.
42. *Jerusalem Post*, 1 August 1989, p. 2.
43. *Jerusalem Post*, 2 August 1989, p. 12.
44. Interview in Ramallah, 8 August 1989.
45. *Jerusalem Post*, 3 August 1989, p. 12.
46. Information on the meeting was provided by Dr al-Jarbawi. See also *Jerusalem Post*, 9 August 1989, p. 1.
47. Interview in Ramallah, 14 August 1989.
48. Interview in Jerusalem, 15 August 1989.
49. Unless otherwise indicated, the information in this paragraph comes from the following sources: *Jerusalem Post*, 28 December 1989, p. 1; *ibid.*, 17 February and 27 July 1989, pp. 4, 12 respectively; *Bitter Harvest: Israeli Sanctions Against Palestinian Agriculture During the Uprising* (Jerusalem: The Jerusalem Media and Communication Centre, May 1989), pp. 10–12; *al-Fajr*, 20 February and 11 September 1989, pp. 3, 3, respectively; *ibid.*, 21 August 1989, pp. 3, 12.
50. Interview with UNRWA spokesperson in East Jerusalem, 13 August 1989.
51. The figure covers the period from the beginning of the uprising through March 1989: *Bitter Harvest*, pp. 14–15. This report contains a reference to a statement made by the Hebrew-language daily, *Haaretz* that 23,440 trees had been uprooted by the IDF during the first year of the uprising. The IDF denied that figure, claiming that only 1,000–2,000 trees had been uprooted.
52. Except where otherwise indicated, this paragraph is based upon the following sources: *Jerusalem Post*, 10 February 1989, pp. 1, 16; *ibid.*, 17 February and 27 July 1989, pp. 4, 12 respectively; *al-Fajr*, 28 August, 11 September 1989, pp. 6, 3, respectively; Sanaa Voice of Palestine in Arabic, 27 February and 31 March 1989, in *FBIS*, 28 February and 3 April 1989, pp. 5, 8, respectively.
53. Interview with UNRWA spokesman in East Jerusalem, 13 August 1989.
54. *al-Fajr*, 28 August 1989, p. 6.
55. *Jerusalem Post*, 17 February 1989, p. 4.
56. On 10 July 1989 Yasser Abu-Ghosh, seventeen years old, was shot to death by Israeli security men in Ramallah. al-Haq took statements from at least 30 eyewitnesses to this incident. al-Haq Law in the Service of Man, 'Summary Execution in Ramallah',

Press Release, 22 July 1989.

57. At the beginning of the Intifada, soldiers were to open fire only when their lives were in danger: *Jerusalem Post*, 5 July 1989, p. 1.

58. *Jerusalem Post*, 17 March 1989, p. 1. In March (*Jerusalem Post*, 3 March 1989, p. 20) IDF troops destroyed the homes of the families of five members of underground groups; and in June (*Jerusalem Post*, 21 June 1989, p. 12) they demolished the house of a Qalqilya resident suspected of setting fire to an Israeli car. According to the Israeli Information Centre for Human Rights, 334 houses had been demolished or sealed since the beginning of the Intifada, many as a result of the lack of construction permits. This, of course, was another form of pressure upon the Palestinians: *al-Fajr*, 9 October 1989, p. 6.

59. *Jerusalem Post*, 13 August 1989, p. 8.

60. *Maariv*, 3 May 1989, p. A12 in *FBIS*, 8 May 1989, p. 30.

61. Interview in East Jerusalem, 13 August 1989.

62. These casualty figures were provided by UNRWA.

63. *Jerusalem Post*, 15 June and 1 August 1989, pp. 12, 1, respectively.

64. *al-Fajr*, 9 October 1989, p. 3.

65. *Jerusalem Post*, 26 June and 20 August 1989, pp. 10, 1, respectively.

66. *Jerusalem Post*, 26 May 1989, p. 9.

67. Interview at Hebrew University, Jerusalem, 11 July 1989.

68. On these arrests, see *Jerusalem Post*, 5 and 17 July, 1989, pp. 1, 12 and 8, respectively.

69. Interview in East Jerusalem, 13 August 1989.

70. Interview in Ramallah, 8 August 1988.

71. *al-Fajr*, 22 May 1989, p. 1.

72. *Davar*, 19 May 1989, p. 13 in *FBIS*, 19 May 1989, pp. 29–30.

73. On this, see *Jerusalem Post*, 19 June, 30 July and 2 August 1989, pp. 1, 8, 12 respectively.

74. Interview in East Jerusalem, 13 August 1989.

75. *Davar*, 19 May 1989, p. 13 in *FBIS*, 19 May 1989, p. 29.

76. Interview in Ramallah, 8 August 1989.

77. *Jerusalem Post*, 11 August 1989, p. 16.

78. Interview with 'Ahmad', Husan, 10 August 1989.

79. Interview in Ramallah, 17 August 1989.

80. *Jerusalem Post*, 17 February 1989, p. 1.

81. Interview with UNRWA spokesperson in East Jerusalem, 13 August 1989.

82. On the shooting down of kites, see *Jerusalem Post*, 6 July 1989, p. 12. Plastic chairs bearing the colours of the Palestinian flag were confiscated (*Jerusalem Post*, 24 July 1989, p. 8), and one Palestinian was beaten because he had a 'V' sign and a Palestinian flag tatooed on his arm (*Jerusalem Post*, 1 August 1989, p. 2). Meanwhile, the annexation process continued. According to Israel's Central Bureau of Statistics, some 6,000 people settled in the West Bank and Gaza Strip in 1988. (*Jerusalem Post*, 8 August

1989, p. 12).

83. Interview in Ramallah, 17 August 1989.
84. *Jerusalem Post*, 4 and 15 August 1989, pp. 16, 1, respectively.
85. *Jerusalem Post*, 7 July 1989, p. 1.
86. *Jerusalem Post*, 9 July 1989, p. 1.
87. *Jerusalem Post*, 16 July 1989, p. 2.
88. Information contained in this paragraph is based upon *Jerusalem Post*, 20 January, and 29 and 30 June 1989, pp. 20, 12, 10, respectively.
89. Interview in Husan, 10 August 1989.
90. Baghdad Voice of the PLO in Arabic, 7 January 1989, in *FBIS*, 9 January 1989, p. 10.
91. See, for example, *Jerusalem Post*, 30 June 1989, p. 10.
92. *Jerusalem Post*, 18 July 1989, p. 2.
93. Palestinians who were interviewed told the author that they could not trust anyone and had to be very careful in whom they confided. This had always been true to a certain extent, but had become even more so by the autumn of 1988.
94. Sanaa Voice of Palestine in Arabic, 27 February 1989, in *FBIS*, 28 February 1989, p. 4.
95. The explanation I have offered for the increased killing of collaborators is based upon interviews with former Palestinian political prisoners, popular committee members in villages, social workers, UNRWA officials and leading Palestinian intellectuals.
96. Interview in East Jerusalem, 17 August 1989.
97. For an interesting analysis of the fate of Palestinian middlemen, see *Haaretz*, 5 May 1989, p. B3 in *FBIS*, 10 May 1989, pp. 27–9.
98. *Jerusalem Post*, 27 April 1989, p. 1.
99. Courtesy of Dr Ifrah Zilberman.
100. Interview in Ramallah, 1 August 1989.
101. al-Jarbari, *art. cit.*, p. 303.
102. Interviews with 'Ahmad', Husan, 13 October 1988 and 10 August 1989.
103. Interview in Ramallah, 1 August 1989.
104. This figure comes from the Israeli Information Centre for Human Rights in the Occupied Territories: *Jerusalem Post*, 9 August 1989, p. 12.
105. This information was provided by Dr Zilberman.
106. Ali al-Jarbawi, *The Intifada and the Political Leadership in the West Bank and Gaza* [in Arabic] (Beirut: Dar al-Taliya Press, 1989), p. 128.
107. Interview in Ramallah, 1 August 1989.
108. See, for example, (clandestine) *al-Quds* Palestinian Arab Radio in Arabic, 21 March 1989, in *FBIS*, 23 March, 1989, pp. 4–5.
109. See, for example, *Jerusalem Post*, 12 July 1989, p. 7.
110. Interview in Ramallah, 17 August 1989.
111. Interview in Ramallah, 17 August 1989.
112. Interview in East Jerusalem, 24 July 1989.

113. This and what follows was acquired in interviews with Palestinians. I am particularly grateful to Ms Kort for her help.
114. Interview with UNRWA spokesman in East Jerusalem, 13 August 1989.
115. Information provided by Ms Kort.
116. Interview in East Jerusalem, 17 August 1989.
117. Interview with 'Yunis' in East Jerusalem, 17 August 1989.
118. Interview in East Jerusalem, 13 August 1989.
119. Interviews with Dr Zilberman in Jerusalem on 11 July and 15 August 1989.
120. *Haaretz*, 5 May 1989, p. B3 in *FBIS*, 10 May 1989, p. 29.
121. Interview in East Jerusalem, 18 August 1989.
122. Interview in East Jerusalem, 24 July 1989.
123. Interview in Husan, 10 August 1989.
124. Interview in central West Bank village, August 1989.
125. Interview in East Jerusalem, 18 August 1989.
126. Interview in Ramallah, 1 August 1989.
127. For this and what follows, see *Jerusalem Post*, 30 December 1989, p. 9.
128. Dr Zilberman, interviewed 15 August 1989.
129. Interview in East Jerusalem, 18 August 1989.
130. Interview in Ramallah, 17 August 1989.
131. I am grateful to Dr al-Jarbawi for this information.
132. For a brief discussion of Leaflet 44, see *Jerusalem Post*, 17 August 1989, pp. 1, 12. Earlier in the summer, the UNL had called in a leaflet for greater unity among the factions: *Jerusalem Post*, 12 July 1989, p. 7.
133. This figure and those which follow, unless otherwise indicated, are taken from the Associated Press and from an article by Max Frankel in the *Washington Post*. *The Times-Picayune*, 8 December 1988, p. A–23 and *ibid.*, 9 December 1989, p. A–28. For the UNRWA estimate of Palestinians wounded, see *Haaretz*, 6 December 1989, p. 2 in *FBIS*, 13 December 1989, p. 34.
134. This comparison is made on the basis of estimates of Palestinian and US populations at the start of these two conflicts. In 1962, when there were 11,000 American soldiers in Vietnam, the US population was 186,000,504. According to Meron Benvenisti and Shlomo Khayat (*West Bank and Gaza Atlas* [Jerusalem: West Bank Data Base Project, 1988], pp. 28, 112) the Palestinian population in the occupied territories on the eve of the Intifada stood at 1,701,435. On the basis of the 1962 population estimate, American combat losses in Vietnam were 31 per 100,000.
135. *Jerusalem Post*, 17 February 1989, p. 4.

EPILOGUE

1. Interview in Ramallah, 1 December 1988.
2. Interview in Ramallah, 17 August 1989.
3. Interview in Ramallah, 17 August 1989.

Bibliography

I. PRIMARY SOURCES

(a) Formal Interviews*

Date	Place	Person(s)
30 August 1988	West Jerusalem	Dr Shye [Israel Institute of Applied Social Research]
6 September 1988	East Jerusalem	Mahdi Abd al-Hadi
6 September 1988	East Jerusalem	Azmi Bishara
7 September 1988	Jerusalem – Old City	'Yunis'
8 September 1988	West Jerusalem	Moshe Negbi
9 September 1988	East Jerusalem	Yehuda Litani
14 September 1988	West Jerusalem	Danny Rubenstein
25 September 1988	Taibeh	'Antoun' and others
1 October 1988	Nablus, Jenin, Tulkarm	Kamal Abdulfattah, 'Ali' and others
5 October 1988	East Jerusalem	Zuhayra Kamal
5 October 1988	East Jerusalem	Palestinian journalist (anonymous)
7 October 1988	East Jerusalem	UNRWA officials
8 October 1988	Central West Bank Village	'Muhammad'
11 October 1988	Ramallah	Marty Rosenbluth Fateh Azzem
12 October 1988	Ramallah	Hanan Ashrawi
13 October 1988	Husan	'Ahmad' and others
16 October 1988	Court at Lod, Israel	André Rosenthal
20 October 1988	Jenin	Kamal Abdulfattah and others
21 October 1988	East Jerusalem	Nadia Habash and others
23 October 1988	West Jerusalem	Meron Benvenisti
5 November 1988	East Jerusalem	Azmi Bishara

* These exclude the many unscheduled or unplanned talks and meetings I had with people, some of whom requested anonymity.

Date	*Place*	*Person(s)*
6 November 1988	West Jerusalem	André Rosenthal
8 November 1988	Ramallah	Ali al-Jarbawi
10 November 1988	East Jerusalem	Dr 'Mahmud' and 'Aziz'
14 November 1988	Hebrew University Mt. Scopus	Joshua Schoffman
16 November 1988	East Jerusalem	Dr 'Mahmud', 'Aziz' and others
17 November 1988	East Jerusalem	Sari Nuseibeh
18 November 1988	East Jerusalem	Spokespersons, Maqassed Hospital
22 November 1988	East Jerusalem	Spokesman, International Committee of the Red Cross
23 November 1988	East Jerusalem	Mahdi Abd al-Hadi
23 November 1988	East Jerusalem	Ibrahim Karaeen
23 November 1988	East Jerusalem	Chris George, Save the Children
24 November 1988	Ramallah	Ali al-Jarbawi
25 November 1988	West Jerusalem	Tom Segev
26–27 November 1988	Gaza Strip	UNRWA officials, Palestinian refugees, former political prisoners, Gazan lawyers, journalists and other professionals
1 December 1988	Ramallah	Ali al-Jarbawi and others
9 December 1988	East Jerusalem	Nora Kort
10 December 1988	Beit Sahour	Jad Issac and others
12 December 1988	West Jerusalem	Danny Rubenstein
13 December 1988	Ramallah	Ali al-Jarbawi
14 December 1988	Ramallah	Ziad Abu-Amr
17 December 1988	Gaza Strip	As above
26 June 1989	Hebrew University, Mt. Scopus	Naomi Chazan
6 July 1989	Ramallah	Ali al-Jarbawi
11 July 1989	Hebrew University, Mt. Scopus	Yifrah Silberman
24 July 1989	East Jerusalem	Nora Kort
26 July 1989	East Jerusalem	Maher Abukhater
1 August 1989	Ramallah	Ali al-Jarbawi
8 August 1989	Ramallah	Ali al-Jarbawi
10 August 1989	Husan	'Ahmad' and others
10 August 1989	Beit Sahour	Jad Issac and others
13 August 1989	East Jerusalem	UNRWA officials

Date	Place	Person(s)
14 August 1989	Ramallah	Ali al-Jarbawi
15 August 1989	Hebrew University, Mt. Scopus	Yifrah Silberman
17 August 1989	East Jerusalem	'Yunis' and 'Antoun'
17 August 1989	East Jerusalem	Nora Kort
17 August 1989	Ramallah	Ali al-Jarbawi
17 August 1989	Ramallah	Ziad Abu-Amr
19 August 1989	East Jerusalem	UNRWA spokesman

(b) Reports, Papers, Documents, Statistics

Amnesty International. 'Report 1988: Israel and the Occupied Territories', London, 1988. *Journal of Palestine Studies* 18 (1989): 173–206. Four reports.

'The Beit Sahour Saga'. Unpublished manuscript on Beit Sahour's role in Intifada. By unnamed residents of this town. July (?) 1988.

Bishara, Azmi. 'Stages and Development of Islamic Fundamentalism'. Unpublished paper presented to workshop on 'Islamic Fundamentalism', 10 April 1989, sponsored by Harry S. Truman Research Institute and Leonard Davis Institute, Hebrew University, Mt. Scopus, Jerusalem, Israel.

'Facts about the Palestinian Press under Occupation (Closures, Arrests, Administrative Detention, Town Arrest and Other Measures)'. July 1988. Provided by Ibrahim Karaeen, Palestinian Journalist, East Jerusalem.

al-Haq Law in the Service of Man. *Punishing a Nation: Human Rights Violations during the Palestinian Uprising, December 1987–December 1988.* Ramallah, West Bank 1988.

al-Haq Law in the Service of Man. 'Summary Execution in Ramallah', Press Release. 22 July 1989.

'Israel's Peace Initiative – Document'. *Jerusalem Post* 15 May 1989: 2.

The Jerusalem Media and Communication Centre. *Bitter Harvest: Israeli Sanctions Against Palestinian Agriculture During the Uprising, December 1987–March 1989.* Jerusalem: The Jerusalem Media and Communication Centre, May 1989.

The Jerusalem Media and Communication Centre. *Weekly Report.* Jerusalem: The Jerusalem Media and Communication Centre.

Nixon, Anne. 'The Status of Palestinian Children During the Uprising in the Occupied Territories'. Report, in three volumes, issued by Save the Children Fund, Sweden, 1990.

Palestine National Council, 'Palestinian Declaration of Independence' and 'Political Communiqué', Algiers, 15 November 1988. *Journal of Palestine Studies* 18 (1989): 213–22.

'The Palestinians' Fourteen Demands'. *Journal of Palestine Studies* 17 (1988): 63–5.

Shalev, Carmel. 'The Price of Insurgency: Civil Rights in the Occupied Territories'. Report issued October 1988 by West Bank Data Base Project, Jerusalem, Israel.

Tzemach, Mina, and Tzin, Ruth. 'Attitudes of Adolescents with Regard to Democratic Values: Findings of a Survey of Attitudes Conducted among Adolescents by the Dahaf Research Institute at the Request of the Van Leer Jerusalem Foundation'. Unpublished report. Jerusalem: The Van Leer Jerusalem Foundation, September 1984.

United Nations Relief Works Agency. 'Casualties: Children under 16 (9 December 1987–30 August 1988)'.

'Casualties in Gaza as of 1 December 1988'.

'Casualties in the Gaza Strip, 9 December 1987–13 February 1989'.

'Casualties in the Gaza Strip, 9 December 1987–8 December 1988'.

'Casualties in the Occupied Territories as of June 30, 1988'.

'Curfews in Gaza and the West Bank, 9 December 1987–19 November 1988'.

'Curfews imposed in the Gaza Strip, December 1987–June 1989'.

'Curfews through 7 October 1988'

'Gaza Daily Casualty figures, 1 April–30 June 1989'.

Table A. 'Casualties in the Gaza Strip, 1–30 April 1989'.

Table B. 'Casualties in the Gaza Strip, 9 December 1987–30 April 1989'.

Van Leer Jerusalem Institute. 'Endot Politiyot ve-Chevratiyot be-kerev Benei Noar'. [Political and Sociological Positions of Youth] Results of opinion polls. Survey conducted by the invitation of the Van Leer Jerusalem Institute, September 1987.

'Yasser Arafat, speech before the forty-third session of the United Nations General Assembly on the Palestine question', Geneva, 13 December 1988. *Journal of Palestine Studies* 18 (1989): 161–71.

'Yasser Arafat, text of press conference statement', Geneva, 14 December 1988. *Journal of Palestine Studies* 18 (1989): 180–1.

(c) Official Publications and Edited Documents

International Committee of the Red Cross. *The Geneva Convention of August 12, 1949*. Geneva: International Committee of the Red Cross, n.d.

II. SECONDARY SOURCES

(a) Books, Monographs, Booklets, Pamphlets, Edited Works, Parts of

Series

Abd al-Sitar, Qasim. *al-Tajriba al-Itiqaliya fi al-Mutaqalat al-Sihyuniya* [The Arrest Experience in Zionist Detention Camps]. Beirut: Dar al-umma li-Nashr, 1986.

Abed-Rabbo, Samir and Satie, Doris, eds, *The Palestinian Uprising*, FACTS Information Committee, Jerusalem. Belmont, Massachusetts: Association of Arab–American University Graduates, 1990.

Abu-Amr, Ziad. *al-Haraka al-Islamiya fi al-Diffa al-Gharbiya wa Qita Ghazza: Ikhwan al-Muslimin wa al-Jihad al-Islami* [The Islamic Movement in the West Bank and Gaza: The Muslim Brotherhood and the Islamic Jihad]. Akka and Beirut: Dar al-Aswar Press and Dar al-Taliya, 1989.

Abu-Amr, Ziad. *The Intifada: Causes and Factors of Continuity.* Jerusalem: Palestinian Academic Society for the Study of International Affairs, 1989.

Abu-Amr, Ziad. *Usul al-Haraka al-Siyasiya fi Qita Ghazza,1948–1967* [The Origins of the Political Movement in Gaza, 1948–1967]. Akka, Israel: Dar al-Aswar Press,1987.

Abu-Lughod, Ibrahim. *The Transformation of Palestine: Essays on the Origin and Development of the Arab–Israeli Conflict.* Evanston: Northwestern University Press, 1971.

Aruri, Naseer, *The Intifada.* Brattleboro: Amana Books, 1989.

Bahiri, Simcha. *Industrialization in the West Bank and Gaza.* Jerusalem: West Bank Data Base Project, 1987.

Benvenisti, Meron. *1986 Report: Demographic, Economic, Legal, Social and Political Developments in the West Bank.* Jerusalem: West Bank Data Base Project, 1986.

Benvenisti, Meron. *1987 Report: Demographic, Economic, Legal, Social and Political Developments in the West Bank.* Jerusalem: West Bank Data Base Project, 1987.

Benvenisti, Meron and Khayat, Shlomo. *The West Bank and Gaza Atlas.* Jerusalem: West Bank Data Base Project, 1988.

Benvenisti, Meron. *The West Bank Handbook: A Political Lexicon.* Jerusalem: The Jerusalem Post, 1986.

Bennis, Phyllis and Cassidy, Neal. *The Palestinian Intifada: From Stones to Statehood.* London: Zed Press, 1989.

Brand, Laurie A. *Palestinians in the Arab World: Institution Building and the Search for State.* New York: Columbia University Press, 1988.

Cobban, Helena. *The Palestinian Liberation Organization: People, Power, and Politics.* New York: Columbia University Press, 1984.

Fuller, Graham E. *The West Bank of Israel: Point of No Return?* Santa Monica: The Rand Corporation, 1989.

Golan, Galia. *The Soviet Union and National Liberation Movements in the Third World.* Boston: Allen and Unwin, 1988.

Gresh, Alain. *The PLO: The Struggle Within.* London: Zed Books, 1988.

Grossman, David. *The Yellow Wind.* New York: Farrar, Straus and Giroux, 1988.

al-Jarbawi, Ali. *al-Intifada wa al-Qiyadat al-Siyasiya fi al-Diffa al-Gharbiya wa Qita Ghazza* [The Intifada and the Political Leadership in the West Bank and Gaza]. Beirut: Dar al-Taliya Press, 1989.

Kahan David. *Agriculture and Water Resources in the West Bank and Gaza, 1967–1987.* Jerusalem: West Bank Data Base Project, 1987.

Lesch, Ann Mosley. *Political Perceptions of the Palestinians on the West Bank and the Gaza Strip.* Washington, D.C.: The Middle East Institute, 1980.

Lesch, Ann Mosley and Tessler, Mark. *Israel, Egypt and the Palestinians: From Camp David to Intifada*. Bloomington: Indiana University Press, 1989.

Lockman, Zachary and Beinin, Joel, eds. *Intifada: The Palestinian Uprising against Israeli Occupation*. Boston, Mass.: South End Press and MERIP, 1989, and London: I.B.Tauris, 1990.

McDavid, Mary and Krogh, Peter. *Palestinians under Occupation: Prospects for the Future*. Washington, D.C.: Center for Contemporary Arab Studies–Georgetown University, 1989.

McDowall, David. *Palestine and Israel: The Uprising and Beyond*. London: I.B. Tauris and Co., 1989.

Mattar, Philip. *The Mufti of Jerusalem. al-Hajj Amin al-Husayni and the Palestinian National Movement*. New York: Columbia University Press, 1988.

Nakhleh, Emile A. *The West Bank and Gaza: Toward the Making of a Palestinian State*. Washington, D.C.: American Enterprise Institute, 1979.

Nassar, Jamal R. and Heacock, Roger, eds. *Intifada: Palestine at the Crossroads*. New York: Praeger, 1990.

Peretz, Don. *Intifada: The Palestinian Uprising*. Boulder, Colo.: Westview Press, 1990.

Quandt, William, Jabber, Fuad and Lesch, Ann Mosely. *The Politics of Palestinian Nationalism*. Berkeley: University of California Press, 1973.

Rolef, Susan, ed. *Political Dictionary of the State of Israel*. New York: Macmillan Publishing Company, 1987.

Roy, Sara. *The Gaza Strip: A Demographic, Economic, Social, and Legal Survey*. Jerusalem: West Bank Data Base Project, 1986.

Sahliyeh, Emile. *In Search of Leadership: West Bank Politics Since 1967*. Washington, D.C.: The Brookings Institution, 1988.

Schiff, Zeev and Yaari, Ehud. *The Palestinian Uprising – Israel's Third Front*. Ed. and trans. by Ina Friedman. New York: Simon and Schuster, 1990.

Scholch, Alexander, ed. *Palestinians over the Green Line: Studies on Relations between Palestinians on Both Sides of the 1949 Armistice Line since 1967*. London: Ithaca Press, 1983.

Segal, Jerome M. *Creating the Palestinian State: A Strategy for Peace*. Chicago: Lawrence Hill, 1989.

Segev, Tom. *1949: The First Israelis*. New York and London: The Free Press and Macmillan Publishers, 1986.

Shehadeh, Raja. *Occupier's Law: Israel and the West Bank*. Revised edn. Washington, D.C.: Institute for Palestine Studies, 1988.

Shinar, Dov and Rubenstein, Danny. *Palestinian Press in the West Bank: The Political Dimension*. Jerusalem: West Bank Data Base Project, 1987.

Shipler, David K. *Arab and Jew: Wounded Spirits in a Promised Land*. New York: Penguin Books, 1987.

Stein, Kenneth. *The Intifadah and the 1936–1939 Uprising: A Comparison of Palestinian Arab Communities*. Occasional Paper Series, Vol. 1, no.

1. Atlanta: The Carter Center of Emory University, 1990.

Sullivan, Antony Trail. *Palestinian Universities under Occupation*. Cairo Papers in Social Science, Vol. 11, monograph 2. Cairo: American University of Cairo Press, 1988.

White, Patrick. *Let Us Be Free: A Narrative before and during the Intifada*. Leaders, Politics, and Social Change in the Middle East, Vol. VII. Princeton: Kingston Press, 1989.

(b) Articles

Abdulfattah, Kamal. 'The Geographical Distribution of the Palestinians on Both Sides of the 1949 Armistice Line'. Alexander Scholch, ed., *Palestinians over the Green Line*. London: Ithaca Press, 1983.

Abu-Amr, Ziad. 'Notes on Palestinian Political Leadership'. *Middle East Report* 154 (September–October 1988): 23–5.

Abu-Amr, Ziad. 'The Debate Within the Palestinian Camp'. *American–Arab Affairs* 26 (1988): 40–9.

Abu-Amr, Ziad. 'The Palestinian Uprising in the West Bank and Gaza Strip'. *Arab Studies Quarterly* 10 (1988): 384–405.

Abu-Amr, Ziad and al-Jarbawi, Ali. 'The Struggle for West Bank Leadership'. *Middle East International* 304 (1987): 16–18.

Andoni, Lamis, 'Jordan and the PLO'. *Middle East International* 318 (1988): 12–13.

Bargouti, Husain Jameel. 'Jeep versus Bare Feet: The Villages in the Intifada'. Jamal R. Nassar and Roger Heacock, eds, *Intifada: Palestine at the Crossroads*. New York: Praeger, 1990.

Bar-On, Mordechai. 'Israeli Reactions to the Palestinian Uprising'. *Journal of Palestine Studies* 17 (1987–1988): 46–65.

Benvenisti, Meron. 'Impact of Uprising on Prospects for Peace'. *American–Arab Affairs* 27 (Winter 1988–1989): 10–13.

Bishara, Azmi. 'Israel Faces the Uprising: A Preliminary Assessment'. *Middle East Report* 157 (March–April 1989): 6–14.

Bishara, Azmi. 'To Channel This Energy'. *New Outlook* (August 1988): 18–20.

Black, Ian. 'The Uprising against Israel'. Reprinted from *Manchester Guardian Weekly*. *Journal of Palestine Studies* 17 (1988): 159–61.

Chazan, Naomi. 'Israel and South Africa: Some Preliminary Reflections'. *New Outlook* (June 1988): 8–11.

Cobban, Helena. 'The PLO and the Intifada'. *Middle East Journal* 44 (Spring 1990): 207–33.

Cossali, Paul. 'Gaza's Union Elections'. *Middle East International* 308 (1987): 14–15.

Dakkak, Ibrahim. 'Back to Square One: A Study in the Re-emergence of the Palestinian Identity in the West Bank 1967–1980'. Alexander Scholch, ed., *Palestinians over the Green Line*. London: Ithaca Press, 1983.

Hertzberg, Arthur. 'The Illusion of Jewish Authority'. *New York Review of Books* 35 (1988): 6–12.

Islam, Shada. 'Germans Take the Lead'. *Middle East International* 318 (1988): 8–9.

Islam, Shada. 'Weighing their Words'. *Middle East International* 319 (1988): 10.

Issac, Jad. 'A Socio-economic Study of Administrative Detainees at Ansar III'. *Journal of Palestine Studies* 18 (1989): 102–09.

al-Jarbawi, Ali. 'al-Siraa bayn 'Jumhuriya Filistin al-Ula' wa 'Jumhuriya Israil al-Thaniya'' [The Struggle between the First Palestinian Republic and the Second Israeli Republic]. *Shuun Arabiya* [Arab Affairs] 55 (1988): 29–53.

al-Jarbawi, Ali and Hunter, F. Robert. 'Shamir's Election Plan: An Analysis'. *Middle East International* 358 (1989): 15–16.

al-Jarbawi, Ali. 'Palestinian Elites in the Occupied Territories: Stability and Change through the Intifada'. Jamal R. Nassar and Roger Heacock, eds, *Intifada: Palestine at the Crossroads*. New York: Praeger, 1990.

Kagian, Jules. 'The United Nations: The Four Resolutions'. *Middle East International* 317 (1988): 8–10.

Kaufman, Edy. 'The Intifadah and the Peace Camp in Israel: A Critical Introspective'. *Journal of Palestine Studies* 17 (1988): 66–80.

Khalidi, Walid. 'Toward Peace in the Holy Land'. *Foreign Affairs* 66 (1988): 771–89.

Kuttab, Daoud. 'A Profile of the Stone Throwers'. *Journal of Palestine Studies* 17 (1988): 14–23.

Kuttab, Daoud. 'Fundamentalists on the March'. *Middle East International* 311 (1987): 8–10.

Kuttab, Daoud. 'The Palestinians' Unified Command'. *Middle East International* 318 (1988): 10–12.

Kuttab, Daoud. 'The Uprising'. *Middle East International* 320 (1988): 8–9.

Kuttab, Jonathan. 'The Children's Revolt'. *Journal of Palestine Studies* 17 (1988): 26–35.

Legrain, Jean-François. 'The Islamic Movement and the Intifada'. Jamal R. Nassar and Roger Heacock, eds, *Intifada: Palestine at the Crossroads*, New York: Praeger, 1990.

Lesch, Ann Mosley. 'The Palestine Arab Nationalist Movement Under the Mandate'. William Quandt, Fuad Jabber and Ann Mosley Lesch, eds, *The Politics of Palestinian Nationalism*. Berkeley: University of California Press, 1973.

Makhul, Makram Khuri. 'This Is Not a Revolt – This Is a War'. Reprinted from *HaIr. Journal of Palestine Studies* 17 (1988): 91–9.

Mishal, Shaul, '"Paper War" – Words Behind Stones: The Intifada Leaflets'. *The Jerusalem Quarterly* 51 (Summer 1989): 71–94.

Peretz, Don and Smooha, Sammy. 'Israel's Twelfth Knesset Election: An All-Loser Game'. *Middle East Journal* 43 (Summer 1989): 388–405.

Pressberg, Gail. 'The Uprising: Causes and Consequences'. *Journal of*

Palestine Studies 17 (1988): 38–50.

Quandt, William. 'The Uprising: Breaking a Ten-Year Deadlock'. *American–Arab Affairs* 27 (Winter 1988–1989): 18–28.

Rubenstein, Danny, 'The Political and Social Impact of the Intifada on Palestinian Arab Society'. *The Jerusalem Quarterly* 52 (Autumn 1989): 3–17.

Rubenstein, Danny. 'Return to the Green Line'. *New Outlook* (August 1988): 21.

Siniora, Hanna. 'An Analysis of the Current Revolt'. *Journal of Palestine Studies* 17 (1988): 3–13.

Stein, Kenneth. 'The Palestinian Uprising and the Shultz Initiative'. *Middle East Review* 21 (Winter 1988–1989): 13–20.

Steinberg, Matti. 'The PLO and Palestinian Islamic Fundamentalism'. *The Jerusalem Quarterly* 52 (Autumn 1989): 37–54.

Tamari, Salim. 'The Revolt of the Petite Bourgeoisie: Urban Merchants and the Palestinian Uprising'. Jamal R. Nassar and Roger Heacock, eds, *Intifada: Palestine at the Crossroads*. New York: Praeger, 1990.

(c) Newspapers (Israeli publications unless otherwise indicated)

Davar
al-Fajr (Jerusalem Palestinian weekly, in English)
al-Fajr (Jerusalem, Arabic-language daily)
Haaretz
Hadashot
Al Hamishmar
Jerusalem Post
Maariv
al-Nahar (Jerusalem Palestinian newspaper)
New York Times (New York)
al-Quds (Jerusalem Palestinian newspaper)
al-Ray al-Amm (Kuwait)
al-Talia (Jerusalem Palestinian newspaper)
The Times-Picayune (New Orleans)
Xinhua (Beijing)
Yediot Aharonot

(d) Radio and Television

Baghdad Voice of the PLO in Arabic
IDF Radio in Hebrew
Jerusalem Domestic Service in English
Jerusalem Domestic service in Hebrew
Jerusalem Television Service in Arabic
Jerusalem Television Service in Hebrew
Manama Wakh in Arabic
al-Quds Palestinian Arab Radio in Arabic
Radio Monte Carlo in Arabic
Sanaa Voice of Palestine in Arabic

Index

277